STUDIES IN IMPERIALISM

Established in the belief that imperialism as a cultural phenomenon had as significant an effect on the dominant as on the subordinate societies, Studies in Imperialism seeks to develop the new socio-cultural approach which has emerged through cross-disciplinary work on popular culture, media studies, art history, the study of education and religion, sports history and children's literature. The cultural emphasis embraces studies of migration and race, while the older political, and constitutional, economic and military concerns will never be far away. It will incorporate comparative work on European and American empire-building, with the chronological focus primarily, though not exclusively, on the nineteenth and twentieth centuries, when these cultural exchanges were most powerfully at work.

STUDIES IN
IMPERIALISM

general editor John M. MacKenzie

Ephemeral vistas

THE *EXPOSITIONS UNIVERSELLES*, GREAT EXHIBITIONS AND WORLD'S FAIRS, 1851–1939

Paul Greenhalgh

**MANCHESTER
UNIVERSITY PRESS**

Distributed exclusively in the USA and Canada
by ST. MARTIN'S PRESS, New York

Published by Manchester University Press
Oxford Road, Manchester M13 9NR, UK

Distributed exclusively in the USA and Canada
by St. Martin's Press
175 Fifth Avenue, Room 400, New York, NY 10010, USA

British Library cataloguing in publication data

Greenhalgh, Paul
　Ephemeral vistas: a history of the Expositions Universelles, great exhibitions and
　world's fairs, 1851–1939. – (Studies in imperialism).
　1. Exhibitions – History
　I. Title　　II. Series
　607'.34　　T395

Library of Congress cataloging in publication data applied for

ISBN 0 7190 2300 9 *paperback*

Reprinted 1994

Photoset in Linotron Trump Mediaeval by
Northern Phototypesetting Co. Ltd., Bolton
Printed in Great Britain
by Bell and Bain Ltd., Glasgow

CONTENTS

ILLUSTRATIONS

1 Interior view of the Crystal Palace, Great Exhibition 1851, architect Joseph Paxton. From the Official and Descriptive Catalogue of the Great Exhibition

2 View of the Exposition building and Grounds, Paris 1867. From the Art Journal Illustrated Catalogue of the Universal Exhibition.

3 [facing] Interior view of the Main Building, Philadelphia Centennial 1876. From Frank Leslie's Illustrated Historical Register of the Centennial Fair. Courtesy Paddington Press.

4 Palais de Trocadéro, Paris Exposition Universelle 1878. Contemporary album of engraved views, courtesy Victoria and Albert Museum.

5 [facing, upper] Interior of the Palace of Fine Art, American Sections, Paris Exposition Universelle 1889, from the American Reports of the Universal Exposition, Washington 1890.

6 [lower] The Galeries des Machines, rear view during construction, Paris Exposition Universelle 1889, architects Dutert and Cotamin, from the American Reports of the Universal Exposition, Washington 1890.

7 General view of the Chicago Columbian Exposition, showing the Administration Building, 1893. Courtesy of Bounty Books, New York.

8 [facing, upper] Interior view of the Women's Building, Chicago Columbian, showing the North tympanum and a view of Mary Cassatt's mural 'Modern Woman', architect Hayden, interior designer Rideout, Courtesy Bounty Books.

9 [lower] Dahomeyan Villagers Parading on the Midway Plaisance, Chicago Columbian Exposition, 1893, from a contemporary souvenir album.

10 Neo-baroque lamp-posts and balustrade of the Pont Alexandre III, with the Grand Palais in the background, Paris Exposition Universelle 1900, from a recent photograph taken by the author.

11 [facing, upper] View of the Rue des Nations from the Pont Alexandre III, Paris Exposition Universelle 1900, featuring, from left to right, Belgium, Norway, Spain, Monaco and Sweden. Taken from a contemporary souvenir album.

12 [lower] Art nouveau style Metropolitain Railway Station Entrance, Paris Exposition Universelle 1900, architect Hector Guimard. Photograph taken recently by the author.

13 The Senegalese Village, Franco–British Exhibition, 1908. Contemporary postcard.

[vii]

The illustrations are placed between pp. 82 and 83

GENERAL EDITOR'S FOREWORD

Imperialism was more than a set of economic, political, and military phenomena. It was a habit of mind, a dominant idea in the era of European world supremacy which had widespread intellectual, cultural, and technical ramifications. The 'Studies in Imperialism' series is designed to explore, primarily but not exclusively, these relatively neglected areas. Volumes are planned on the scientific aspects of imperialism, on education, disease, the theatre, literature, art, design, and many more. But in redressing the balance in favour of these multi-disciplinary and cross-cultural studies, it is not intended that the economic, political, and military dimensions should be ignored. The series will contain books in these fields too and will seek to examine colonial and imperial developments in a variety of periods and in diverse geographical contexts. It is hoped that individually and collectively these works will illumine one of the most potent characteristics of modern world history.

Paul Greenhalgh's book illustrates the breadth and depth of the imperial idea extremely well. The international exhibitions examined here were a product of the European and American sense of being involved in a mighty global enterprise. In concentrating on the progression from raw materials to manufactured goods (via technical processes and the application of design values) the exhibitions reflected the economic geography of imperial specialisation. In displaying the marriage of scientific advance to manufacture, trade, and transport, they were affected by and in turn influenced the contemporary traditions of spectacular theatre, architectural eclecticism, and showmanship arising from a fascination with human and natural historical taxonomies. They offered a racial commentary on the alleged superiority of European civilisation, produced spectacular displays associated with conquest and frontiersmanship, and stimulated the appearance of commemorative ephemera, bric-à-brac, and music. As well as touching on every aspect of the industrial and imperial system, they provide insights into domestic developments in art and design, the status and self-assertion of women, the expression of national character, and the articulation of both private and governmental agencies in planning and funding. They were at the same time global and local, reducing complex sets of economic, scientific, and cultural interactions to one vast display.

As Paul Greenhalgh shows, they were both magnificent and disappointing, progressive and reactionary, sometimes fostering misunderstanding and aggression rather than conciliation. They became entrammelled in an overblown grandiloquence, a riotous eclecticism that led the public to regard them as little more than gigantic funfairs. Disentangling intention and effect is always problematical and this is particularly true of the exhibitions. Their treatment of Asian and African peoples neatly illustrates the point. People from Asia and Africa were used for racial display bordering on the peep-show. Yet the influence of Asian music (principally through Indonesian gamelan players) reached European composers through exhibition performances, while displays of African art, treated as no more than 'ethnic' curios, had a profound effect on post-impressionism. The exhibitions sucked the world into patterns of dependence, dominance and subjection on one great site, but they also permitted unexpected contacts to take place and mutual influences to flourish.

John M. MacKenzie

ACKNOWLEDGEMENTS

There are a lot of people to thank. First and foremost, the students of Cardiff College of Art and Design have been a constant inspiration to me. Likewise my colleagues in the School of History and Theory of Art and Design: Patricia Cusack, Martin Gaughan, Jenny Godfrey, Howard Harris, Helen Long and, perhaps most of all, Noel Upfold. The staff at the Open University in Cardiff and the students of the Arts Foundation course there. My proof readers proved resilient and vital: David Gould, Belinda Greenhalgh, Jackie and Mike McCandless, Judith Harper and Stephen Young. Stuart Meeling, Rose Newman, Julian Sheppard and Laurence Simon gave great assistance with the illustrations. The book could not have been written without the unending support of John Beynon, tutor-librarian of Cardiff College of Art and Design. Also the library staff of the Royal Society of Arts, The Victoria and Albert Museum and the British Library, Colindale. The patience and support of Ray Offord and his staff at Manchester University Press was welcome. Here follows a list of those who in one way or another helped to forge the various positions the book takes; I apologise in advance to those I forget, I am sure the list could go on: Tim Benton, Michael Casson, James Castle, Michael Crowther, Ray Crozier, Geoff Davies, Diane Duffield, André Garo, David Gould, Bill Greenhalgh, Julian Holder, Michael Hose, Donald Knight, Bernard Mader, John MacKenzie, Alan Reece, Beryl Robinson, Peter Sharpe, Penny Sparke, Peter Starkey, Chris Stevens, Stephen Young.

FOR BELINDA AND JACK-HECTOR,
WITHOUT WHOM THIS COULD NOT
HAVE HAPPENED

INTRODUCTION

'A World's Fair – the idea was fresh and fascinating; for here, after the appearance of so many marvellous mechanical devices, was the device of bringing them all together. Here, after such unparalleled progress in increasing production, in extending communications, in freer and free trade, was the occasion of inventory and stock-taking; best of all, here was the greatest opportunity that the working world had ever seen of combining business with pleasure, of having the very best of market-days and holidays in one. For what is better for a man than that he should enjoy the good of all his labour?'

Patrick Geddes, 'The Closing Exhibition – Paris 1900',
The Contemporary Review November 1900.

Imagine an area the size of a small city centre, bristling with dozens of vast buildings set in beautiful gardens; fill the buildings with every conceivable type of commodity and activity known, in the largest possible quantities; surround them with miraculous pieces of engineering technology, with tribes of primitive peoples, reconstructions of ancient and exotic streets, restaurants, theatres, sports stadiums and band-stands. Spare no expense. Invite all nations on earth to take part by sending objects for display and by erecting buildings of their own. After six months, raze this city to the ground and leave nothing behind, save one or two permanent land-marks.

The international exhibitions held around the world between 1851 and 1939 were occurrences such as this, spectacular gestures which briefly held the attention of the world before disappearing into an abrupt oblivion, victims of their planned temporality. Millions of visitors strolled through the sites, were taught, indoctrinated and mesmerised by them. Urban centres were re-planned to accommodate them, national economies damaged, fortunes made and wars postponed. They were the largest gatherings of people – war or peace – of all time. On both a high and a popular level they ranked amongst the most important events held in the nineteenth and twentieth centuries; they remain unsurpassed in their scale, opulence and confidence.

During the ninety year period under discussion hundreds of international exhibitions were staged all over the world, in Africa, Asia, Australasia and South America as well as Europe and North America. This text could not hope to examine in any meaningful way the whole tradition, nor does it attempt to. Rather, it is a study of how the events emerged, how they gained legitimacy as a medium of national expression and how they maintained it through one of the most traumatic stretches in world history. It concentrates almost exclusively on exhibitions held in Britain, France and the United States of America, as these nations were responsible for defining the shape and scope of events everywhere. Known in Britain as Great Exhibitions, in France as Expositions Universelles and in America as World's Fairs, under the guidance of the three the genre became a self-perpetuating phenomenon, the extraordinary cultural spawn of industry and empire. The British inaugurated the tradition in 1851, the French embellished its form and became the acknowledged masters of it, the Americans pushed its size and expense to a final extreme. Having shaped the exhibitions, the three stabilised and institutionalised their baroque excesses, sanctioning and lauding costs which edged onto economic and moral absurdity.

Even within the three main nations the sheer numbers of exhibitions prevents an empirical completeness; hopefully the study is close enough to this to inspire confidence in its conclusions. Some thirty events are dealt with in detail and around forty further ones, of a national as well as international character, are treated with varying degrees of brevity. Where necessary, exhibitions of importance other than those held in America, Britain and France come into the discussion. Amongst these are included ones held in Amsterdam, Antwerp, Barcelona, Dublin, Moscow, Vienna and Turin. After two chapters of an introductory and general nature, the text is constructed thematically rather than chronologically or nationally, each chapter concentrating on a single topic. This appeared the best way to emphasise correlations and divergences in exhibiting policies and it also allowed for the highlighting of aspects previously left in shadow. I hope this proves to be an aid to clarity rather than confusion for the reader.

CHAPTER ONE

Origins and conceptual development

International Exhibitions did not spring into existence with all the features this book is dedicated to discussing. Rather, they evolved slowly as a cultural phenomenon for almost a century before the first event identifiable as an international exhibition actually took place, in 1851. Through this preliminary period, in tandem with the unfolding of the industrial revolution, institutions formed in France and Britain with the specific aim of promoting the principle of display. In the first instance this was to be a device for the enhancement of trade, for the promotion of new technology, for the education of the ignorant middle classes and for the elaboration of a political stance. Backed firmly by government, early establishers of the art of exhibiting attempted to formulate a system of presentation in the absence of any adequate precedents, to invent a way of showing manufactured objects so as to render them meaningful beyond themselves.

The French were the first to establish an ongoing national policy for the holding of large displays of industrial and craft produce, when the need to stimulate trade and industry in the post-revolutionary period became acute. The idea of an exhibition as an economic expedient appeared a logical one to French statesmen, whose predecessors had founded Fine Art training and display centres as far back as the reign of Louis XIV.[1] These earlier institutions had had political and economic motives behind their creation. The aim was simple enough in the first exhibition, held in 1797, and that was to sell produce. The Directory sanctioned it in the hope that a good showing would not only dispose of stockpiled goods but also show the French public that their industry was still intact and capable of competing internationally. Two men are customarily credited with the idea, the Marquis d'Avèze and François de Neufchâteau. In early 1797 d'Avèze, one of the few aristocrats to survive the Terror intact and with power, decided to have a public display of goods in the forecourt of the Louvre. At the time he was one of the major controllers of the three great national (formerly Royal) factories, Sèvres, Les Gobelins and Les Savonneries. The exhibition principally consisted of the wares of the three, namely ceramic, tapestries and carpets, and was intended to help dispose of produce which had proven difficult to sell in the aftermath of 1789. At that time also, the English were blockading French ports as the Napoleonic Wars grew toward their most active phase, making the export of goods extremely difficult. The event lasted four days, proving to be a success on two levels; it sold produce, but more than this, it attracted crowds. People were willing, even keen it seems, to amble through stalls and stands of quality goods, even if purchase was not an intention. At this point François de Neufchâteau, minister for the Interior, stepped in with a plan to expand the concept.

With the help of d'Avèze, Neufchâteau planned a second exhibition, to be held in 1798, this time in specially constructed temporary facilities on the Champs de Mars, the still unspoiled edge of Paris where Napoleon was to celebrate his victories. The prestige of the site, despite its novelty, the money allocated to the preparation of the buildings and the association of the event itself with issues of national importance, marked out the 1798 exhibition as being different from any previous cultural event of its type. The aims of the exhibition were expanded well beyond those of the first one. Selling was still a central aim but an instructive element entered into the rationale, directed principally at the manufacturers of France. They were encouraged to try harder, to take note of self-presentation as an issue and to introduce a more abrasive competitive edge into their marketing techniques. The developing age of capital, led by the ever advancing English, was beginning to exert its first real influence on French craft trades. The exhibition was a national event, but the concerns which motivated it were, economically speaking, international. The fear of English industries amongst French manufacturers and politicians was becoming acute even in those early days of the industrial revolution, as cheap English goods revealed their ability to penetrate the French market and dismantle home industry. Textiles and ceramics in particular by 1795 were English dominated areas of produce. The growth of the factory system in Lancashire created a surplus which sold cheaply in Europe, alarming indigenous producers everywhere. Dependence upon England for anything was undesirable, but for something as fundamental as cloth it was unthinkable. More wounding than the textile industry, not least in terms of pride, were the activities of Josiah Wedgwood in Staffordshire. By the time of his death in 1795, he had created a ceramic empire that was in the process of bringing the great Royal Factories of Europe, Sèvres included, to their knees. The superior quality of the material, the elegance of the fashionable classical style and the strikingly low cost of Wedgwood ware proved irresistible everywhere. A progressive Liberal passionately in support of the Revolution, Wedgwood was not slow to take advantage of the love of classicism in France which was growing with revolutionary activity; he had written as early as 1786 to the Duc de Choiseul, minister of finance, to complain of import duties and to extol the virtues of free trade. He remarked in this correspondence, not without irony, on the desirability of allowing his produce lower tarifs, 'knowing the taste they have in France for everything which comes from England.'[2] The young Republic was justifiably wary of the guile of such entrepreneurs, the national exhibitions being early evidence of the struggle against them.

Fear of damage to French industry from abroad was only one aspect of the economic outlook of Neufchâteau however, as he himself stated:

> The French have surprised Europe with the rapidity of their military exploits, and must advance with the same ardour on the paths of commerce and of peace . . . This is not merely an episode in the struggle against English industry, but also the first stone in a mighty edifice which time alone can complete and which will be adorned each year by the joint efforts of industry and commerce.[3]

The exhibition was decidedly Utopian in its projection of French life after the Revolution, a firm attempt to suggest that what the English had done to their industries was not impossible in France. It aimed, as many of its international successors would, to breed popular confidence via example. What France had achieved already and would go on to achieve was the key note, intended to stir the buying public into economic patriotism and to give manufacturers courage to expand their horizons. Altogether there were 110 exhibitors, a collection of firms and individual entrepreneurs who were allocated amounts of space in the 'Temple of Industry', the centre-piece of the site. Around the Temple the other structures formed an arcaded square boasting sixty large arches. This was designed by the painter J. J. L. David, France's premier artist and fervent supporter of the Revolution. In fact the most memorable aspects of the event in contemporary eyes were not the exhibits themselves but the splendour of the setting around them. A plethora of activity filled the Champs de Mars; there were military parades, splendid balls, firework displays and dozens of unofficial sideshows and stalls on the edge of the site. The strange combinations of carnival and ceremony, of circus and museum, of popularism and elitism which typified the Expositions Universelles therefore emerged in embryonic form at the very opening of the tradition. Several features of the administration equally anticipated the later events. One of these was a specially compiled catalogue, containing the names and addresses of participating firms. The potential of this publication as an effective free advertiser was quickly realised by manufacturers, making them keen supporters of succeeding events. The decision to hold exhibitions on a regular basis was an even more significant move. In isolation, any exhibition has limited importance, but when a policy is formed providing for the staging of events at regular intervals, the opportunity for development and growth appears. Between 1797 and 1849 ten national exhibitions were held, each one increasing in size and scope from its predecessor, establishing a firm notion of continuum. The importance of these for Government at the time was evident; they were no mere trade fairs or festive celebrations, they were outward manifestations of a nation attempting to flex economic, national, military and cultural muscles.

The exhibitions of 1801 and 1802 were held in the Louvre courtyard and attracted 220 and 540 manufacturing firms and craft workshops respectively as exhibitors. 1802 also saw the founding of the Société d'Encouragement, largely under the guidance of Chaptal, Neufchâteau's successor.[4] The Société established a jury for the assessment of exhibits and awarded medals as prizes at events after 1802. The exhibition of 1806 moved over to the Esplanade des Invalides and lasted twenty-four days with a total of 1,422 exhibitors. Apparently Napoleon himself fixed the date of this show in February, so that it could function as a celebration of the Peace of Presbourg in December 1805.[5] The exhibitions of 1819, 1823 and 1827 were staged inside the Louvre and moved from thirty-five, to fifty, to sixty-two days in length over the three events. The 1827 display had 1,695 exhibitors. In 1834 buildings off the Place de la Concorde were used for the first (and only) time, before the principle of erecting temporary structures was finally returned to. In 1839, 1844 and 1849 temporary buildings were constructed on the Champs Elysées and the timescale for exhibitions was expanded from two months for the first two to six for the last one. The latter was to be the commonly accepted length of international exhibitions in the future. The 1849 event was also closer to the grand size of these; 4,532 exhibitors were present at the Champs Elysées,[6] arousing a great deal of foreign interest even though the enterprise was strictly national in scope. The Parisian successes encouraged other French cities to stage their own events, the most impressive of which were held in Nantes (1827), Lille (1835), Bordeaux (1835 and 1845), Toulouse (1836) and Dijon (1836).[7] National exhibitions had become a recognised and regular feature of the cultural calendar, participation in them being, by 1849, a most desirable thing, causing other European nations to envy the French initiative. The somewhat eccentric ploy by the Marquis d'Avèze in 1797 had had consequences that no-one could have forseen, least of all the unenthusiastic manufacturers who were initially cajoled into participation.

By 1839 the French national exhibitions had acquired an atmosphere of cultural pageantry exceeded only by the international exhibitions they were the forerunners of. It would be a mistake however to see these as the only precedents. From a remarkably early date in fact, exhibitions of art and industry of some size had been held in England, albeit in a far more modest way. These were organized by an association founded by William Shipley in 1754 called 'The Society for the Encouragement of Arts, Manufactures and Commerce'. The association was more commonly known as the 'Society of Arts', and after 1847 as the 'Royal Society of Arts'.[8] Shipley was a drawing-master working in Northampton at the time he had the idea of forming the Society, publishing a pamphlet in 1753 suggesting 'proposals for raising by subscription a fund to be distributed in premiums for the promoting of improvements in the liberal arts and sciences, manufactures, etc.'[9] A meeting was held in 1754 at a coffee house in Covent Garden at which the Society was founded and Lords Folkstone and Romney named as its first and second presidents. It was the first in England of its type, the only other associations in existence which could be seen as even vaguely similar were the Royal Society, wholly concentrated upon science or 'natural philosophy', and the Society of Antiquaries. It soon attracted a wide spectrum of members, including noted artists, architects, business entrepreneurs and enlightened aristocrats. Shipley's aim was to give rewards to worthwhile ventures in the liberal arts where they could be shown to have beneficial effects upon commerce and industry. For example, one of the first awards was offered for the discovery of cobalt and the growth of madder. These were dyes vital to the textile industry, still in its preindustrial days, and thus proved of immediate practical use. Later a collection was built of mechanical devices, including some of the most important inventions in the early industrial revolution. Stansfield's saw-mill, Kay's Flying shuttle and Hargreaves Jenny were all in the Society's holdings. Design for industry was also a central concern, Shipley determining 'to bestow premiums on a certain number of boys or girls under the age of sixteen who shall produce the best piece of drawing . . . it being the opinion of all present that the Art of Drawing is absolutely necessary in many employments, trades and manufactures.'[10] In 1760, the Society expanded its own brief and decided to make a display of the arts, crafts and inventions it considered worthy. Kenneth Luckhurst has rightly labelled this the 'first fully organised public exhibition of art in this country.'[11]

The Society of Arts exhibitions were small and unambitious compared with the later French ones, but they had the intellectual advantage of being borne not out of economic desperation but out of curious dilettantism. Paintings, sculptures, architectural models, pumps, ploughshares and weaving looms were displayed together under the communal heading of 'inventions', for the edification of the membership and the enlightenment of farmers, manufacturers and businessmen. Experimentation was encouraged, as was the ideal of making the various branches of intellectual endeavour work in harmony. Founded as it was before the age of specialisation and the division of labour, the Society was not afflicted with the compartmentalization which was to undermine the effectiveness of later institutions. Indeed, the diversity of its exhibiting policy was one of the best features it bestowed on the international exhibitions it heralded. At the core of it of course was a dour English insistence on making all things work toward a useful end, i.e. art was to enhance industry and hence improve trade, yet even so the Society has to be seen as one of the more positive institutions of the English Enlightenment. As the eighteenth century drew to a close, its exhibitions became popular events amongst the middle classes, and kept art as an idea constantly in focus as an important ingredient in civilized life. In 1769, the Royal Academy was founded, largely through the efforts of the Society of Arts.

Into Victoria's reign the scope of English exhibitions was widened by the Mechanics Institutes. Inspired by the example of the Royal Society but concerned mainly with the leisure and education of the working classes, the Mechanics Institutes began to stage large displays of art and industry after 1837. The first was held in that year in Manchester, setting the pace for what was to be essentially a northern English phenomenon. The Manchester Guardian publicised it, describing its contents as 'Models of Machinery, Philosophical Instruments, Works in Fine and Useful Arts, Objects in Natural History and Specimens of British Manufacturers, etc., etc.'[12] It was an enormous success and was followed in the immediately succeeding years by literally dozens of similar ventures, held usually on the premises of the Mechanics Institutes themselves. Sunderland, Newcastle, Salford, Leeds, Sheffield, Stoke, Derby, Birmingham, Preston, Macclesfield, Wigan, Halifax, Huddersfield, Nottingham, Wakefield, Stockport, Stroud, Leicester, Liverpool, Bradford, Ripon and Oldham were among the many towns and cities which staged events, often erecting extra facilities to house them.[13] The flavour of all Mechanics Institutes exhibitions was philanthropic rather than economic, the aim being principally to stimulate working class consciousness and to generally advance industrial culture. The obvious links to Trade Unionism tended to politicise the events, but to no extensive degree, as this almost certainly would have led to conflict with central government. The achievements of these exhibitions taken as a whole were to render the urban-industrial environment less despicable in the eyes of the educated classes, and to provoke debate on the nature of working class culture. There can be no doubt that the social and moral philosophy they presented had an effect on the coming generation of international events. Whilst the latter were ultimately to be of dubious benefit to the working classes, they did not ignore them in the way most earlier cultural manifestations had done.

Between the two of them, the French and British national exhibitions showed an impressively complete range of produce from all areas of their respective cultures, housing the exhibits in increasingly lavish surroundings. Up to 1849 however, there was little in the way of a commonly understood rationale as to what an exhibition in itself should constitute, a vision of what the exhibition as a medium should hold within its scope. The Society of Arts exhibitions in particular tended to be 'catch-all' in principle, in that the parameters were only set by what was of economic, scientific, artistic, and curiosity value at the time the show was arranged. The idiosyncracy of the national exhibitions in both countries, excepting the last French one in 1849, prevented them from having a widespread or lasting effect. Left at that point of development the tradition of arts and industries exhibitions would hardly have been a memorable one. Several stages of conceptual and physical growth had to take place before the events could exercise a genuine cultural insertiveness, the critical one being the move to internationality.

There were a number of exhibitions similar to the French and British ones in other European countries from the turn of the century, the French model being the one generally followed. The most important were in Munich (1818), Ghent (1820), Stockholm (1823), Tournai (1824), Haarlem (1825), Dublin (1826), Madrid (1827), New York (1828), Moscow (1829), St.Petersburg (1829) and Brussels (1830).[14] This latter show included Netherlandish countries, and so could make claims to being international in character, as could the most dramatic and impressive of those held outside of France, the Berlin 'All German Exhibition' of 1844. The most interesting aspect of the 'All German' though was not the co-operation of independent German States, but the tacit recognition that an exhibition could exert influence in an international political arena as well as in a local cultural and economic one. Such an exhibition clearly had an eye on the foreign visitor and was intended as a showcase for German national identity. Similarly, the French national exhibition which followed it five years later took care to cater for the foreigner, concentrating on the image of France as a European power, fully in the knowledge that the rest of Europe was looking on. But so far, no exhibition had risked opening an event to the produce of a wholly separate foreign power for the purpose of generating a discourse between nations. This was partly due to the fear most European nations still had of economic competition, a fear exacerbated by the voracious capacity of English industries to flood a market with cheap mass-produced goods. Even though free trade as an economic ideal was increasingly popular by the mid-century, few wished to see their home industries destroyed by foreign produce. The French, after all, had begun having exhibitions in the first place in order to stimulate production and consumption at home. The English for their part had not, up to 1847 (when the Society of Arts acquired its Royal Charter) seen the need for exhibitions to become international. At that point in time the emphasis in their events had not been directly on selling but on technological advance, it being widely considered that in this area the English had little to learn from anyone else, industrially speaking at least, and so would not benefit from foreign participation. By 1850 however, when the largest exhibition ever held in Britain was going through its initial planning phase, it was decided, for the first time anywhere, to invite all nations of the world to participate. The raison d'être of English exhibitions had thus gone through an abrupt change. Whilst in London English industry was still considered to lead the world, it was also recognised that competition was growing and that the only way to defeat it was to out-sell it. To invite all nations of the world to take part in 'the friendly competition' of an international exhibtion was to create a potential for market expansion abroad. One of the main motives behind the international character of the Great Exhibition of 1851 therefore was economic; Britain wanted more market, and was confident when the foreigner came he would buy British goods.

In retrospect it seems logical that the nation with the most advanced industry and with a free trade policy would be the first to open its doors to foreign exhibitors to inaugurate the tradition of international exhibitions. Interestingly enough however, the idea of making exhibitions international evolved not in Britain but in France, some time before 1851. French government, despite its usual inclination toward protectionism, genuinely felt its manufacturers might benefit from seeing foreign produce up close. As early as 1834, a Monsieur Boucher de Perthes, President of the Societé Royale d'Emulation, recommended the French exhibitons become international:

> Let us not quarrel with competition. That alone will enlighten us, and point out the path of our industry. It is competition that makes the good workman, because it is competition that indicates to each one his proper task. Exhibitions, which have so beneficial an influence upon industry are but an embodiment of this rivalry. It is here that the producer brings the fruit of his labour side by side with that of his neighbour − takes the measure of his efforts, estimates the merits of his productions . . . exhibitions are better than prohibitions, which tend to separate men and isolate them. Why then are exhibitions still restrained within narrow limits? Why should we be afraid to open our halls to manufacturers whom we call foreign; to the Belgians, to the English, to the Swiss, to the

Germans? How noble would be a European exhibition, and what a mine of instruction it would be for all. Do you imagine that the country in which it should take place would be the loser by it? . . . No gentlemen, France would not suffer any more than the foreigner; exhibitions are always beneficial, and beneficial to all.'[15]

Boucher de Perthe's idea was simple enough. No-one would really lose from the presence of foreign exhibitors at exhibitions, and the French stood to gain from the experience in various ways. He hints also that beyond immediate material needs, more wholesome and brotherly aspects would emerge. His idea failed to become a reality for several reasons. French manufacturers did not believe him, and through the offices of local councils objected violently. Also, in the absence of any indication from the French government that tarifs on imported goods would be reduced, foreign producers were less than enthusiastic about the idea. Competition could hardly be fair, it was reasoned, when the opposition was heavily handicapped. For a second time, in 1849, the French government, through the offices of the Minister of Agriculture and Commerce, attempted to gain support for the principle of an international exhibition. The issue was raised in a circular sent out to manufacturers and townhalls:

At a time when my colleagues in office and myself are busily engaged in doing all we can to give the exhibition, which opens on June 1st. next, a character of public utility, it has occurred to me that it would be interesting to the country in general to be made acquainted with the degree of advancement towards perfection attained by our neighbours in those manufactures in which we so often come into competition with in foreign markets . . . you will therefore, give your opinion on the abstract principle of exhibiting the productions of other countries; and to enumerate to me officially the articles you consider would be the most conducive to our interests when displayed in the ensuing exhibition.'[16]

The circular was replied to aggressively by interested parties all over France still unconvinced of the free trade principle behind internationalism. The idea was dropped and the 1849 exhibition remained national. It was left to Englishman Henry Cole, main organiser of the Great Exhibition of 1851 in London, to take up the unrealised French idea and advance exhibitions into the international arena. Apparently the idea was given to him in Paris whilst he was visiting the 1849 exhibition. He decided to put it to the President of the Royal Society of Arts, Prince Albert, on his return to England. He recorded his discussion with the Prince:

I asked the Prince if he had considered if the exhibition should be a national or an international exhibition. The French had discussed if their own exhibition should be international, and preferred that it be national only. The Prince reflected for a minute, and then said, 'It must embrace foreign productions', to use his words, and added emphatically, 'International certainly.'[17]

Thus, the tentative attempts of French government to enlighen their public by bringing in foreign nations was seized upon by the English for their most ambitious scheme to date. Through the participation of the most industrially advanced nations of the world and their empires, the 'Great Exhibition of the Industry of all Nations' became the largest exhibition so far held anywhere, with a scope in terms of produce which rendered all previous exhibitions redundant. Of the nations invited to take part through the diplomatic channels, thirty-four accepted. These were Austria, Belgium, Brazil, Bremen, Chile, China, Denmark, Egypt, France, Germany (the States of the Zollervein), Greece, Hamburg, Hanover, Holland, Lubeck, Mexico, Mecklenburg–Strelitz, New Granada, Oldenburg, Persia, Peru, Portugal, Rome, Russia, Sardinia, Schleswig-Holstein, Society Islands, Spain, Sweden, Switzerland, Tunis, Turkey, Tuscany and the United States of America. Future events would add to this number, but on average between twenty and thirty nations normally participated in first class events. If the various empires are added into the statistics – for Britain alone this would mean around thirty nations – the global scope of the events is apparent.[18] The Great International Exhibition as a concept had arrived; it was quickly to be taken up by nations all over the world.

The sheer size of the Great Exhibition of 1851 was its most impressive feature. A single vast building covering almost nineteen acres, and enclosing thirty-three million cubic feet, was erected to house most of the exhibition, which was sited centrally in London at Hyde Park.[19] The Crystal Palace, as it was christened, became a symbol which earned comment and emulation around the world; in itself it was responsible for attracting a large proportion of the six and a half million visitors. Many of the exhibits inside it were self-consciously showy, providing a source for spectacular entertainment for the crowds and beginning a trend whereby the international exhibition would aim to present produce in the most overblown proportions possible. The highest, biggest, newest and costliest of artefacts and structures became the commonplaces of all events, often in vulgar exercises tantamount to criminal waste. The Great Exhibition also created the four exhibiting categories later to become standard, Manufactures, Machinery, Raw Materials and Fine Arts, and provided the model for space allocation. Half the floor area was given over to Britain and her empire and half to participating countries and empires, Britain occupying the western side of the building and foreign exhibitors the east. The mix of exhibits was extraordinary, ranging from classical sculpture to giant lumps of coal, from a Nubian Court to wrought iron fire-places, from steam engines to Indian miniatures, from rubber plants to stained-glass windows. The artefacts in this lavishly orchestrated jamboree had only one thing in common, the awesome power of the technologies that had taken them there. Everything was explicable directly or indirectly in terms of technology; the prefabricated building housing the exhibition, the steam engines, the manufactured products, the colossal objects transported to the site by machinery, the imperial produce won with commercial and military technology. The Great Exhibition, like virtually all its successors around the world, fetishised the machine, choosing exclusively to see in it a glorious past and the chance of a blemishless future.

The only inadequate areas of the Great Exhibition were the fine art sections. These were concentrated mainly into exotic 'courts', with major emphases on architectural fittings, decorative art and sculpture.[20] Elsewhere in the building, in keeping with the general rule, the visual arts had to demonstrate an element of scientific, technological or industrial advance to gain admittance. There were no official painting areas; the sections devoted to various print media were there for their technical innovation. Architectural exhibits were few and mainly associated with developments in building strategies and materials. Sculpture was adequately presented, but it was seen as a medium for harmonising the building through the decoration of courts and vistas, rather than as a self contained category. Thus the vital rôle the fine arts were to play in most future exhibitions did not emerge in 1851, many of the earlier national exhibitions having had far more complete representations in this area. The organizers of the Great Industrial Exhibition in Dublin in 1853 recognised this inadequacy and went some way toward correcting the imbalance. Whilst accepting the primacy of the industrial or 'utilitarian' arts, a case was made for including the fine arts;

> In truth it is difficult, when once we have emerged from the rudest and most elementary stage of society, to deny that the fine arts themselves are utilitarian. The desires of the eye for that which is beautiful in form and colour, if not essential to mere existence, assuredly are so to the enjoyment of life; and hence sculpture and painting, in the abstract, may, it is presumed, be fitly exhibited without transgressing the strict limits which should be assigned to an Industrial Exhibition . . . under this conviction the committee have admitted works which are not utilitarian, in the ordinary sense of the word.'[21]

It was left to the French however to determine a clear and central rôle for the fine arts, when their first international exhibition was arranged for 1855. In many ways the Paris Exposition Universelle of 1855 can be seen as a direct reply to the Great Exhibition, various areas seemingly being developed in response to successes and failures of the 1851 event. Particularly clear in retrospect was the French determination to confirm the notion of Paris as the pre-eminent artistic centre, this being achieved principally through the presentation of a vast art section at the Exposition. The event was also intended in a wider sense to stamp France as the supremely artistic nation, a label believed to have far more than merely cultural significance. Concern for the fine arts at the Exposition was such that a decree was sent out signed by Napoleon the Third himself to guarantee their standing amongst other exhibits,

> We have decided and do thereby decree as follows, Article one: An universal exhibition of the fine arts will be held at Paris at the same time as the universal exhibition of industry. The place at which this exhibition will be held will be designated hereafter. Article two: The annual exhibition of the fine arts of 1854 is postponed to 1855, and will be united with the universal exhibition. Article three: Our minister of state is charged with the execution of the present decree, given at the Palace of Saint Cloud, this 22nd. June 1853.'[22]

An accompanying letter sent to all potential exhibitors in all countries further explained the rôle Napoleon and his government had given the fine arts in the French national profile:

> Considering that the improvement of manufactures is closely connected with that of fine arts; that however, all the exhibitions of industrial products which have been hitherto held, have admitted the works of artists in only very insufficient proportion; that it belongs to France, whose manufactures owe so much to the Fine Arts, to assign to them in the coming Universal Exhibition, the place which they merit.'[23]

The desire to see the fine arts as part of the French ethos led to a massive inclusion of it not only in 1855, but in all subsequent Paris Expositions Universelles. More than this, it guaranteed the fine arts would enjoy a heavy inclusion in all major international exhibitions around the world after 1855. The French had added the final ingredient to the newly established tradition.

Within months of the closing of the Great Exhibition other nations began planning their own along similar lines. In 1853 the aforementioned Great International Exhibition took place in Dublin and one was held in New York in the same year. Both followed the lines of the Great Exhibition closely, especially with regard to the building, Crystal Palaces being erected in like fashion and in consultation with the original architect, Joseph Paxton.[24] By the time the Exposition Universelle opened in Paris in 1855, a spirit of rivalry had inevitably surfaced, the competition to have the most impressive event becoming the critical factor. Into the 1880's an atmosphere of meglomania came to surround the exhibitions, as nations struggled to better immediately preceding foreign shows. Initially a British–French story, the rivalry grew to its most reckless pitch between France and America, where extraordinary and spectacular excesses were perpetrated in the name of art, science and education. The Great Exhibition set the first standard by which organizers measured themselves, providing the statistics that had to be equalled or surpassed if an event was to function as an international centre-piece; but by 1867 it was to Paris all looked in order to gauge their success. From then until the eve of the Second World War, France stayed in the ascendent. American Fairs were often more monumental than any European equivalents, but it was Paris which bestowed the elements of flamboyance and lavishness on the tradition, dispensing with practicality and reserve in an attempt to sum up and transform the world. It was the French who broke with the notion of a single huge exposition building in favour of a site with numerous pavilions, including those erected by foreign participants. This, predictably enough, triggered a secondary tier of rivalry; not only did it become necessary to have vast exhibitions of ones own but one had to build the grandest pavilions on foreign sites. Between 1855 and 1914 an event involving more than twenty nations was held somewhere in the world on an average of every two years. After 1914 exhibitions were fewer but vaster than their predecessors. At the grand climax of the tradition, the Paris Exposition Universelle of 1937 erected buildings with a total interior space of two hundred and fifty acres, whilst the New York World's Fair two years later sprawled over a 1,200 acre site.

By that time an international agreement had been signed to try and regulate and control these extraordinary events. Meeting in Paris in 1928, delegates from ninety-two nations signed a 'Convention Relating to International Exhibitions' designed to prevent anyone abusing the genre to political or commercial ends. Evidence existed to suggest some nations had deliberately boycotted exhibitions in the hope of spoiling them, or, still worse, that some had spontaneously organized an event to detract from another elsewhere. The huge cost of exhibitions could prove ruinous if competing nations deliberately detracted from attendances and publicity. The Convention first of all took it upon itself to define what was meant by an international exhibition, then it drew up a forty point directive stipulating their frequency and form:

> The expression 'official or officially recognised international exhibitions'
> shall be deemed to include every display . . . to which foreign countries are
> invited through the diplomatic channel, which is not generally held
> periodically, of which the principal object is to demonstrate the progress
> of different countries in one or several branches of production, and in

which, as regards admission, no distinction in principle is made between buyers and visitors . . . The duration of any international shall not exceed six months.'[25]

Exhibitions of three weeks or less were not included in the Convention, or specialist exhibitions of fine art or science. If an exhibition required foreign participants to build pavilions, then the host country was not permitted to hold such an event more than once every fifteen years; if foreign participants did not have to provide their own building, the host nation could stage an event once a decade. There was to be no exhibition anywhere with separate national pavilions more than once every six years; there was to be no exhibition without separate national pavilions more than once every two years. It was hoped these points would spread exhibitions evenly through the decennial calendar and prevent them from deteriorating into arenas for commercial or political propaganda. It was inevitable that the scale of the events would lead to attempts to harness them such as this, but sadly for the organizers of the Convention their efforts failed. Within a decade numerous nations flouted the agreement, as it was not binding by international law. Ultimately it was not the Convention that halted the continuing growth of international exhibitions but the Second World War.

At the same time the international exhibitions as physical phenomena came to maturity, a conceptual apparatus for the justification and explanation of them also appeared. A plethora of discussion congealed into a cohesive discourse concerning the merits of exhibitions and their benefits to humankind, this having a considerable effect on other disciplines in succeeding decades. Before vast sums could be lifted from public funds and charities for the construction of these epic cultural edifices, convincing criteria for their existence had to be provided. Whatever the real motives behind any particular show – some of these have already been described – the professed reasons had to be carefully constructed and profoundly ideal. Each event tended to have a celebratory circumstance peculiar to itself sanctioning its lavishness, followed by a secondary tier of more general motives. The Philadelphia Centennial (1876) celebrated a century of American independence, the 1889 Paris Universelle marked the centenary of the Revolution, the Chicago Columbian (1893) commemorated the landing of Columbus in the New World, the 1900 Paris show heralded the new century, the St Louis Fair (1904) celebrated the Louisiana Purchase, the Franco–British (London 1908) the Entente Cordiale and so on. Beyond these laudable excuses, standard moral justifications were made use of between 1851 and 1940 which remained constants through the period despite marked shifts in the societies they catered for. The most prominent perennials were: Peace amongst nations, Education (especially of the masses), Trade, and Progress.

Queen Victoria set the pattern for the first of these in her opening speech at the Crystal Palace: 'It is my anxious desire to promote among nations the cultivation of all those arts which are fostered by peace, and which in their turn contribute to maintain the peace of the world.'[26] 'Helix', a critic writing on the prospective Great Exhibition in 1850, listed what he considered its aims to be. Despite a certain eccentricity, they are not untypical:

> The grand objects of the Exhibition, as we regard them, may thus be summed up: 1. To promote brotherhood amongst mankind. 2. To make all cognisant of what we can do for others. 3. To diminish human drudgery by mechanism. 4. To promote art of the higher kind. 5. To show how clothing may best be made by machines without handicraftry. 6. New preparations for human food.'[27]

As with most others, peaceful concerns are at the top of his list. Brotherly love and understanding between nations was the single most laboured aspect of exhibition diatribe, the sentiment usually being ridiculed by displays of military technology, imperial conquest and abject racism on the sites themselves. Elsewhere in his article Helix revealed an extraordinary range of values, constructing for example in the same passage a defence of military conquest and a moral case for vegetarianism. His vision of the world in 1850 and the rôle of the Great Exhibition in it embodied values that in a later age would seem contradictory, not least his joint love of imperialism and universal peace. The London Exhibition of 1862 continued the theme of love amongst the peoples of the world, often using it to drag other issues into the public arena. Particularly interesting in this light are some of the odes and volumes of poetry produced specially for the exhibition. One, published by Hatchard and Company, managed as part of its plea for peace to praise the industrial age, attack socialism and make symbolic references to the army and empire, all in the space of eleven short lines:

> Hissing engines – puffing, fuming –
> Palm-like from the hoarding risen
> All at once a Palace looming . . .
> More dream'd of universal love,
> And vow'd the Golden Age was come,
> Ignoring eagles for the dove,
> Prefering bagpipes to the drum.
> No 'Red Republic' ruled the town,
> No gaunt-eyed famine thinned our ranks,
> No plague-stroke cut the people down,
> Round father Thames' crowded banks.[28]

Rhetoric on the theme of peace was much the same in other countries, though French and American angles on brotherly love usually stressed the freedom republicanism afforded and the opportunities all men had in the post-revolutionary world. One sentiment however was an apolitical constant, that whenever different peoples came together to show off the achievements of their respective cultures, this would result in a reduction of differences and the growth of fellowship. Sadly, instances when such understanding could be witnessed were extremely sparse in relation to the numerous occasions when exhibitions openly generated bitterness and hatred. The very raison d'etre of many exhibitions was envy, not love of other nations, or a manic desire to out-do them. The Exposition Universelle of 1900 was enflamed and expanded by the thought that the hated Germans might try to hold an exhibition in the same year, whilst inter-State rivalry in America provoked shockingly violent debates across the American continent. The tendency of white peoples to consciously denigrate other races likewise made fellowship an unlikely resultant of the events. For many exhibitors and politicians, the point of the international aspect was to emphasize national and racial difference, not similarity.

Peace between nations had another undercurrent during the nineteenth century, especially for the British; it helped maintain the status quo. A peaceful world in 1851 meant one thing alone to the British, that the empire was safe. In this one regard at least, the plea for peace was sincerely felt and remained so as long as imperial-economic interests were observed. Less cynically, exhibitions up to 1914 were one of the favourite meeting places of religious organizations around the world, conventions being held where the idea of peace meant more than political rhetoric or economic advantage. Often these conventions would be on a huge scale, for example the two held at the Chicago Columbian Exhibition of 1893, the 'Congress of World Religions' and the 'World's Congress of Representative Women', which both boasted thousands of delegates.[29] Within the ideological limits of the time, religious discourse at international exhibitions did attempt to resolve differences among peoples and foster a more wholesome rapport. Alongside the handful of idealists involved on central committees, the religious lobby represented a genuine plea for peace amongst men, that may have had some small positive effect. On the whole however, it is difficult to see the 'peace-mongering' of exhibition speech-makers as anything other than empty banter.

Unlike Peace, Education was more than a pleasant theme for shrewd politicians. Education was the fetish of exhibitions, especially the kind which sought to edify the masses. Beginning in embryonic form before 1851 as a feature of both the Society of Arts displays in London and the exhibitions organized by the Mechanics Institutes in the north of England, the educational principle at work was simple enough: if you exposed ideas to an ignorant audience in a language they could understand, you would have influence over them. These early exhibitions had various aims; they sought to improve the taste of the middle classes, to inform manufacturers about mechanical improvements and to morally educate the working classes. The French national exhibitions were also concerned with technical and aesthetic education, although here it was far from a rigorously considered element. By 1851 in Britain though, the educational resolve had firmly established itself, the curious visitor to the Great Exhibition being able to expect lessons in geography, physics, chemistry and art in the form of produce arranged and labelled with the instruction aspect in mind. Commentators in 1851 expressed particular surprise at the seriousness with which the artisan classes took the educational intention of the exhibition: 'The fact is, the Great Exhibition is to them more of a school than a show . . . what was a matter of tedium, and became ultimately a mere lounge for gentlefolks, is used as a place of instruction by the people'.[30] The 1862 exhibition in London continued the policy of educational orchestration of display areas, often with a religious theme. One writer noted that the exhibits '..show, from about the commencement of the second half of the nineteenth century, the progress civilization is making over the globe; and every educational phase in which this appears – religious, social and mental – declares the dependence of the creature upon the creator.'[31] At the 1874 exhibition at South Kensington, education was the professed rationale behind the whole event. The Official Guide made this clear by informing the visitor that 'It must always be remembered that the main object of this series of exhibitions is not the bringing together of great masses of works, and the attraction of holiday-making crowds, but the instruction of the public in art, science and manufacture, by collections of selected specimens.'[32] Such motives remained close to organizer's hearts through to the outbreak of the First World War, although by then entertainment facilities were given far greater consideration than those aimed specifically at education. The White City Exhibitions (London 1908–14) attempted to fuse the two elements, in order to give popular interest to one and respectability to the other. The Duke of Argyll, honorary president of the Imperial International (held on the site in 1909) expressed this duality in his opening speech, stressing 'amusement without excess and knowledge without fatigue' as the main aims of the exhibition.[33] This was not the stalwart voice of Victorian paternal morality but of the Edwardian profit-margin. The British had discovered education did not pay, but that entertainment did.

Having had an ambivalent attitude toward education at the national exhibitions, the French steadily developed it at the first four Expositions Universelles, to the point where the last of these was seen by many as a museum of global explanation. Frederic Le Play, the brilliant organizer of the 1867 show was more responsible than anyone else for this aspect, his influence remaining through to 1889. Le Play belonged to a small group of committed Saint-Simonians which included fellow organizers Michel Chevalier and Jules Simon, making his (and hence the exhibition's) view of world history at once social and paternal. More than anything else the 1867 Exposition was intellectually rooted in communal ideas of family and work, the building itself being constructed so that these themes, especially work, would unfold as the visitor walked around. It was he and his confreres who developed the notion of the Encyclopaedia in relation to exhibitions in an attempt to present a vision of total knowledge. The crowds were to be educated not by selective instruction but by the presentation of every aspect of existence in one spectacular edifice. Individual sections of the Exposition revealed this intention. For example, advance information to potential exhibitors in the 'History of Labour' display outlined its aims as follows: 'This exhibition will be held in a special gallery situated between the fine art gallery and the Central Garden. Works produced in different countries, from the most remote ages to the close of the eighteenth century will be received, including objects of rudimentary character made before the discovery of metals.'[34] The attempt to reveal work in its every aspect, in every nation, throughout time, provided the model for various 'total displays' in following expositions, in which a complete view of a topic would be presented. The most impressive of these was 'The History of Human Habitation' at the 1889 Exposition, conceived of and designed by Charles Garnier, architect of the Paris Opera. The exhibit was in the form of a street of thirty-nine houses, stretching from the Champ de Mars to the Trocadéro, each one representing a culture and a stage in world housing from prehistoric times to the present. The first houses were the Troglodyes, the Age of the Reindeer and the Irish Elk, the Stone Age, Polished Stone, Lake Dwellers, Bronze Age, and Iron Age. From these there unfolded an impressive list of world cultures, including Egypt, Assyria, Phoenician, Hebrew, Pelagian, Etruscan, Hindu, Persian, Germanic Races, Gauls, Greek, Roman Italian, Huns, Gallo-Roman, Scandinavia, Charlemagne, Mediaeval, Renaissance, Byzantine, Slav, Russian, Arab, Turkish, Sweden, Japan, China, Lapland, Eskimo, African Savage, Redskins and Aztec.[35]. The houses were slightly smaller than full size, but were constructed in authentic materials and meticulously detailed inside and out. Le Play had thus established an attitude to education at French exhibitions which had outlasted him, an attitude having as its theoretical mainstay a daunting moral mission, to teach everything to everybody: 'The very poorest student in the poorest school, the most incapable, the most ignorant, the least gifted, is, after all a man and since he is a man, he has the capacity to recognise the truth, to understand and to live by it.'[36]

Following this extraordinary lead, the organizers of the American World's Fairs accepted the challenge of total education, and were largely responsible for the development of tableaux display techniques which sought to inform the bystander regardless of the knowledge he took to the exhibition with him. By 1880 exhibitions everywhere would have lengthy explanations on bill-boards accompanying most exhibits, and individuals would be on hand to explain displays to the visitor. By this date also academic conferences were staged as a normal part of exhibition practice, an aspect probably conceived of by Le Play in 1867. At the Chicago Columbian in 1893 the organizers successfully opened the site as a conference venue to academic, business and leisure groups. Into the twentieth century, conferences were among the least noticeable but most influential of elements at exhibitions. The Paris show of 1900 included conferences on fisheries, libraries, publishing, dentistry, education systems, hypnotism, philately, photography, public health, memismatics, ornithology and medicine. The medicine conference was the largest at six thousand delgates.[37]

The educational element at exhibitions can be seen to shift as the mass appeal of the events increased and as education became increasingly prioritised in society. A pattern is discernable whereby exhibition educationalists gradually moved their attention to areas of the population previously considered outside the educational realm. The early national exhibitions in Britain and France (excepting those of the Mechanic's Institutes) had targeted the middle and upper middle classes as their subjects. This focus was discernable at the Great Exhibition, but already a more disinterested concern for the 'provision of knowledge' lower down the class structure had evolved. By 1867, and increasingly so until the end of the century, it was the lower middle and artisan classes who were the desired audience for educational exhibits. By 1900, the 'masses' proper were referred to as being the true beneficaries of learning, their intellectual development apparently being vital for the survival of Western civilization. The growth of working class consciousness in society – universal suffrage being the most overt resultant – had clearly fired exhibition organizers into action on the education front, for both good and bad reasons. After the First World War youth increasingly became the focus of educational displays and pavilions, especially in America, with adult education sliding as a priority. Young people were to be the citizens of tomorrow it was reasoned, and so should be as informed as possible today. Looking at the period as a whole it can be asserted that educationalists, consciously or otherwise, had continually shifted their emphases to those groups who had most recently come into the reckoning as socio-political forces.

The projection of education as a rationale for exhibitions was therefore not empty gesture, as considerable time and expense was used up on it. Unlike the theme of peace, education was a cause which could be forwarded without harm to the established status quo, in the short-term at least. However, it also had a darker side that proved to be of use to various power groups within society. This was in its ability to misinform. Misinformation presented as education is one aspect of propaganda, a subject which will be dealt with in various later chapters; suffice it to say here that the honest efforts of educational idealists were frequently negated by the vulgar propaganda of government.

More than Peace or Education, the theme of Trade was at the theoretical core of exhibitions, perhaps because it was at the heart of European and American society. Trade had created Western power; the exhibitions were no more than an expression of that power. For the purposes of exhibitions, the idea of trade was transformed from the relatively simple exchange of goods for profit, to a concept having metaphysical dimensions. It was recognised by the literature surrounding the Great Exhibition, and at subsequent events, that all kinds of exhibiting had a rationale in trade, in sale by display. More than this, the literature explained the hegemony of the Europeans and their descendents in terms of their ability to control and manipulate trading systems. On its more mystical side, trade could unite peoples, solve the ills of the world and generate happiness. An eulogy on the Great Exhibition explained this:

> The band of commerce was designed,
> To associate all the branches of mankind;
> And, if a boundless plenty be the robe,
> Trade is the golden girdle of the globe.[38]

Trade, it was readily acknowledged, was the capitalist's tool, his method of creating and controlling markets; for many writers on the Great Exhibition it was also a kind of 'Everyman's reply' to the new political force opposing capital, socialism. 'Helix', in his introduction to the Great Exhibition, tied trade in with religion, imperialism and capitalism in order to explain the 'naturalness' of world order in 1851. The earth, he tells us, has areas of different climate, geography and peoples through divine inspiration,

> . . . for the purpose of exchanging their various productions; thence grew up commerce, i.e. mutual buying and selling, with competition or mutual self-seeking following in its train, and much eschewed by surface-seeking

socialists, whose vision cannot penetrate to the beyond, and who therefore entertain a decided conviction that buying and selling may be abolished over the whole world simultaneously, at any fine morning at exactly a quarter hour before six . . . As the wind carries winged seeds over the earth, so commerce carries arts, and civilization, and humanity as a consequence.'[39]

For Helix, there was nothing wrong in seeing the Great Exhibition as a shop, nor apparently in belonging to a nation of shop-keepers, for it was they who ultimately civilized the world. For him, the meaning of the Great Exhibition was clear: 'Magnificent was the conception of this gathering together of the commercial travellers of the universal world, side by side with their employers and customers, and with a showroom for their goods that ought to be such as the world has never before beheld.'[40] For the Victorian mind the real beauty of trade as a source both of civilization in a wide sense and the exhibitions in an immediate one, was that it allowed the mystical and exotic to freely mingle with the practical and material. Trade was timeless, a uniting force meandering through all the lands of the earth; it also paid handsomely in hard cash if conducted shrewdly. Additionally, it was a convenient way of justifying or even disguising imperial exploitation, 'trading' being a far less unpleasant terminology than 'conquering' or 'controlling'.

Of the themes discussed so far, Education and Trade could be seen to be present physically on exhibition sites, whereas Peace was little more than a rhetorical exercise. The final theme to be examined in this chapter, Progress, fell strangely between the rhetorical and the actual. The word itself appeared in more exhibition mottos and subtitles than any other in the century following the Great Exhibition. For most organizers, the point of an exhibition was to indicate civilization was advancing in some known direction. Especially for the host nation, the exhibition would invariably be a celebration of the past as a preparation for a better future. Therein lay the interest for government, for industry and the arts, that 'things will get better'. There was a positivist dialectic present in the rationale of every exhibition – some British ones excepted – which dictated the certain glory of the future. Progress was the darling of the political left and right through the period; for Marxists and capitalists alike, the world had to be seen as being in some kind of advancing flux, with a stable – and inevitable – future of plenty on the horizon. It was in everyone's interest therefore to keep the world moving, or at least appear to be moving, away from the grim actuality of contemporary life. The problem of course, was that few of the power groups could agree on the direction Utopia lay in, or on who should run it once the world had arrived there.

The most frequently suggested vehicle for achieving the goal of progress was technology. Technology would transform the world, bring plenty, peace, unity, all in the forseeable future. Such beliefs were stated in twentieth century exhibitions more often than their earlier counterparts, but from the Great Exhibition onwards the machine was consistently presented as the Messiah which would lead the human race to the Promised Land. Courtesy of new technology, the idea of progress determined the stylistic outlook of many exhibitions after the First World War, as designers attempted to show their audience how the world would be at some vaguely determined point in the future. The Chicago 'Century of Progress' exhibition of 1933 was typical in its summing up of technologies to date and in its dramatic suggestions for the future. The New York's World Fair of 1939 appeared as a veritable 'Futuropolis', its insistence on the benefits of technical progress were so intense, whilst the more elite 1937 Paris Universelle put its faith in the mystical ability of abstract artforms,in conjunction with technology, to solve the world's ills. Western obsession with the ability of the machine to control and improve the world had deep pyschological roots, reaching back to the very beginning of the industrial revolution. The machine had given the West world power, a certain degree of safety from the natural elements and, importantly, comfort. Life without the machine was inconceivable and so the future had to be invented in terms of it. Progress, when it was associated with technology, could be gauged, a quantifiable quality confirming the steady improvement of existence. Moral, cultural and social progress were likewise assumed to be measurable qualities, in an age when everything of worth was considered ultimately to be material and rational. Universal advance of civilization via the achievement of science was both a canon and an assumption at exhibitions. Thus it was reasoned, the bigger and more technologically determined exhibitions were, the more progress was being made. Few of them suggested the world was not making progress, and none hinted at a possible decline, even though as many of them opened the socio-economic situation certainly indicated this.

International exhibitions grew and matured in a way which in retrospect seems at once tentative but inevitable. The conditions allowing them to come into existence fell haphazardly into place, but once there they grew with startling rapidity. Between the two of them, the Great Exhibition of 1851 and the Exposition Universelle of 1855 established a form that was to go on to unbelievable heights of embellishment. As cultural manifestations, they revealed an expansive West in its most flamboyant and bombastic state; baroque, overblown expressions of societies that felt they ruled the material world absolutely. So far, only the bare bones of these events have been examined, the following chapters will hopefully reveal the nature of the flesh which hung upon them.

Notes

1 See Nikolaus Pevsner, *Academies of Art Past and Present*. Da Capo Press, New York 1973. Colbert organised the Salon under the directive of Louis XlV in 1667. It remained spasmodic until 1737 when it was finally stabilised and made into a permanent feature of the court calendar.
2 Quoted from R. Reilly and G. Savage *Wedgwood – The Portrait Medallions*, London 1973.
3 See J.Wines *Quelle Exposition Universelle?*, Connaissance des Arts July–August 1983 p.p. 35–43. This often-used quote appears in slightly different form in different texts (see for example Luckhurst, note 6.)
4 See Charles Robin, *Histoire Illustrée de l'Exposition Universelle, par Categories d'Industries avec Notes sur les Exposants*, Paris 1955.
5 See Paul Dupays,*Vie Prestigieuse des Expositions Historiques*. Paris 1939, pub. Didier.
6 Figures taken from Kenneth Luckhurst, *The Story of Exhibitions* London 1951.
7 See Dupays, note 5.
8 Sir Henry Truman, *The Official History of the Royal Society of Arts*, London; see also G.K. Menzies *The Story of the Royal Society of Arts*. London 1934.
9 Ibid.
10 Ibid.
11 See note 6.
12 By far the best material on these can be found in Toshio Kusamitsu, *Great Exhibitions before 1851'*, History Workshop Journal Number 9, Spring 1980.
13 Ibid.
14 There is an amount of dispute as to when the Dublin exhibition took place. 1825, 1826 and 1829 have been forwarded by sources published as early as 1876. What is clear is that exhibitions were held on a triennial basis by the Royal Dublin Society from the mid 1820's, with the largest occurring in 1850. After this it was decided that the one scheduled for 1853 should be international in scope. A large national exhibition was also held in Cork in 1852. See The Official Catalogue of the Great Industrial Exhibition, Dublin 1853 and A.C.Davies, *The First Irish International Exhibition*. Irish Economic and Social History, Vol.2 1975, p.p. 46–59. A substantial number of Fairs and Exhibitions were held after 1800, the ones listed here were amongst the most significant. The datings came from Richard D. Mandell, *Paris 1900: The Great World's Fair*. Univ. of Toronto Press 1967, and Paul Dupays, see note 5.
15 Taken from The International Exhibition of 1862 Illustrated Catalogue of the Industrial Department. London, 1862, H.M.S.O.
16 Anonymous article *Official Catalogue of the Great Exhibition*, Edinburgh Review Vol. 94, No. 192 October 1851.
17 C.H. Gibbs-Smith. *The Great Exhibition of 1851*. London 1981, H.M.S.O.
18 The list was taken from *The Great Exhibition 1851 Official Descriptive and Illustrated Catalogue*, Part 1 (of 4), London 1851.
19 See Chapter 6.
20 See Chapter 8.
21 *The Official Catalogue of the Great Industrial Exhibition, Dublin 1853*, Dublin 1853.
22 *Reports on the Paris Universal Exhibition*, 3 Volumes, presented to both Houses of Parliament, 1856. The decrees are contained in appendices, translated and with notes by Henry Cole.
23 Ibid.
24 George F. Chadwick, *The Works of Sir Joseph Paxton, 1803–1865*. London 1965, Architectural Press. See also Chapter six.
25 *Convention Relating to International Exhibitions*, Paris 1928.
26 *The Crystal Palace Exhibition, Illustrated Catalogue 1851*. The Art Journal Special Issue. Reprinted by Dover Publications, New York 1970.

27 Helix, *The Industrial Exhibition of 1851*. Westminster and Foreign Quarterly Review, April 1850.
28 *The World's Palace, Old and New : An Ode*. London 1862, Hatchard and Company.
29 See Chapter 7.
30 Henry Mayhew, *The Shilling People*, quoted from Humphrey Jennings (Ed.), *Pandæmonium*, London 1985, Andre Deutsch.
31 Anonymous, *Educational Advantages of the International Exhibition*. Sixpenny Magazine August 1862.
32 *London International Exhibition 1874. Official Guide (Illustrated)*
    Published by J.M.Johnson and Sons, London 1874.
33 *Daily Mail* May 15th.
34 *Reports on the Paris Universal Exhibition, Volume One*, 3 Vols. in total, London 1867.
35 There are countless references to the *History of Human Habitation* exhibit, the most available primary source is *Paris and its Exhibition*. Pall Mall Gazette Extra, Friday July 26th. 1889.
36 Quoted from Mandell, see note 14.
37 Ibid.
38 Quoted from Aaron Scharf, *The Crystal Palace and the Great Exhibition*, from *Art and Industry*, Open University Foundation Course Units 33 and 34, A100, Open University Press 1971.
39 See note 27.
40 Ibid.

CHAPTER TWO

Funding, politics and society

Exhibitions cost an enormous amount to stage. It would be inconceivable that events of the relative scale of those held at South Kensington, Chicago, St. Louis or Paris could happen now. No-one could afford them and more importantly, no-one has adequate reason to bother; the rôles they fulfilled are now taken care of by various separate media. The vast sums expended on exhibitions up to 1939 are a testament to the power they were seen to hold for those involved in their organization. They were a principal means whereby government and private bodies presented their vision of the world to the masses; because of this, the funding behind them invariably involved political machination of one kind or another. Those who paid for the exhibitions normally had motives which went undiscussed in the official literature.

The exhibitions up to 1914 were saturated with Liberal ideology. The peculiar mixture of free trade, material progress, philanthropy, imperialism and capital that animated the more dramatic decades of the nineteenth century could be found everywhere on exhibition sites. These were the arenas where the grand entrepreneurs could justify, define and congratulate themselves; where imperial free trade could strut, temporarily in the absence of the profound contradictions it embodied. Thoroughly in the spirit of the first industrial age, the exhibitions illustrated the relation between money and power, and revelled in the belief that the uncontrolled expression of that power was the quintessence of freedom. Philanthropy, one of the humane spin-offs from the governing system, found its place on exhibition sites functioning as a conscience to the age, although even here morality was inextricably linked to economic efficiency and expansion. Ideologically and technologically, the exhibitions could not have happened in any other age, the politico-economic situation being crucial to their growth and the form they took.[1] Once the conditions were finally and irretrievably altered, after the Second World War, they ceased to occur in the way they had done before.

There were basically four types of source from which the money to initiate the events emerged; government, private sponsorship (including individuals, charities and companies), lotteries and exhibition companies founded specifically for the purpose of organization and funding. Some exhibitions made use of all four methods at the same time and almost all of them had at least two. It was normal to have conflict between the different funding bodies, this usually hinging on the awkward truth that some were not particularly concerned about the size of the profit margin whilst others very definitely were. The exhibits and site architecture were usually compromised by variant interests at funding level. Looked at collectively however, those who paid for the exhibitions did have common concerns, three of which over-rode all others: to maximise attendance; to publicise a socio-political position; to profit those who had proferred funds in the first instance. Organizers throughout the period regarded the most successful exhibitions as those which accomplished all three in the highest degree. The organizational models used everywhere were ones evolved separately in America, Britain and France, these coming to influence each other until they shared numerous aspects by 1900. Clear differences did remain however through to the Second World War, necessitating separate examinations of the three. The logical place to begin is with the Great Exhibition of 1851.

In organizational terms, the Great Exhibition provided the model for all Victorian exhibitions. A Royal Commission was established to control the whole enterprise, with Prince Albert as its Honorary President. The Commission was largely a result of lobbying by the Royal Society of Arts and particularly of pressure brought to bear by Henry Cole. The latter played a central rôle and can rightly be thought of as the founding father of British international exhibitions.[2] The Commission created committees to publicise its cause, making maximum use of the enthusiastic Prince to legitimise their quest. A body of willing sponsors was gathered to guarantee the initial funding, at which point the event became real enough to require the permission of Parliament to proceed. After receiving governmental approval, a site was provisionally rented and foreign governments were invited to participate through the various ambassadors. At home manufacturers in all industries were informed, regulations were issued and, once replies were received from potential exhibitors, calculations were made as to how much space would be needed to house everything. After this a competition was launched to find a design for the building. By then the path should have been smooth, as it was to be for most future shows, but unfortunately for the Prince and his team of workers, conservative opinion in Parliament turned against the notion of the exhibition and a series of debates ensued as to its worth. These were resolved after numerous compromises, not the least of which was to leave three elm trees standing inside the building itself.[3]

The total expenditure on the exhibition was £335,742. Therefore a considerable sum had to be taken in entrance fees if sponsors were to be recompensed in any way and a profit made. Initially, Henry Cole had convinced a Mr. Fuller to advance £10,000 as prize money, while Mr. Fuller himself had persuaded the firm Messrs. Munday to provide the total basic funding in return for a proportion of the eventual gate-money. However, after touring the country to win support for the venture Cole realised that it would be possible to have hundreds of small sponsors. Deciding that this was preferable to a single private specu-lation, he bought Munday out within the terms of the agreement, compensating him £5,120. Sponsorship for the exhibition was then spread amongst thousands of contributors, almost on a share basis, giving the exhibition a public base even though government had itself contributed virtually nothing.[4] Over four hundred local committees were formed around Britain to gather the funds and organize local exhibitors. The sums contributed varied considerably, for example Ashburton sent £7 to the General Fund, Bolton £630, Exeter £90, Glas-gow £2,400, Maidstone £74-4s-6d, Manchester £4000, Oxford £150, Salisbury £70-19s, Staffordshire Potteries £247 and York £100. Ulti-mately the exhibition cleared £522,179 making a net profit of £186,437, providing all who participated with returns and leaving a sizable residue in the coffers of the Commission. As with most held in Britain after it, the exhibition had used the organs of government to legitimise its activities and to help with organization, but the money had come from the private sector.

The Great Exhibition was a result of an extraordinary set of circum-stances. From a world perspective, it chose to be international in order to celebrate to the fullest extent Britain's imperial and industrial lead. The free trade ethos demanded an international audience, as did British manufacturers eager to get foreign orders. From a national perspective, the exhibition was designed to show the indigenous population the extent of British power. This was not intended for celebratory purposes alone. Prince Albert, one of the central figures in the executive struc-ture, was only too aware that his adopted nation was not united in its vision of the British way of life. Chartism and Trade Unionism had shown that the working populations of the north were not prepared to be continuously exploited and impoverished. Moreover, the year plans for the exhibition were begun, 1848, was marked by revolutionary activity all over Europe, revealing the instability of regimes previously assumed to be eternal. The Great Exhibition can thus be viewed as a giant counter-revolutionary measure; indeed, from its earliest days it was conceived of as an event to foster fear as well as pride in the minds of the British public, an immense show of strength designed to intimidate potential insurrectionists. The magazine Art Union said as much in 1849: 'The loyalizing effect of such an exhibition is not the least of its moral recommendations. Every man who visited it would see in its treasures the result of social order and reverence for the majesty of the law.'[5] Early objectors to the idea of the exhibition equally understood its intended rôles as intimidator and social distractor, their opposition usually coming not out of disagreement with these aims, but simply out of the belief that it would not work. Rather than subduing and loyalising the population, they thought it would simply serve as a focal point for undesirables of every description. Some of these would undoubtedly be revolutionaries from both home and abroad, others mere vagabonds and rogues: 'All the bad characters at present scattered over the country will be attracted to Hyde Park . . . that being the case, I would advise persons residing near the Park to keep a sharp look-out after their silver forks and spoons and servant maids'.[6] When the exhibition actually opened, the predicted hoards of thieves and revolutionaries did not arrive, as Lord Macaulay, a supporter of the exhibition throughout, noted with a hint of relief: 'I was struck by the number of foreigners in the streets. All however, were respectable and decent people. I saw none of the men of action with whom the Socialists are threatening us . . . There is just as much chance of a revolution in England as of the falling of the moon'.[7] The awesome power on display at the Crystal Palace, even if it failed to convince revolutionaries of the futility of their task, certainly served to reassure their adversaries that all was far from lost.

The admission fees to the exhibition showed the eagerness of the organizers to attract the artisan classes; they also revealed the rigidity of English class structure. The most expensive tickets were for the season, at three guineas for men and two for women. Other prices varied depending on month and day, going from £1-00, to five shillings, two shillings and sixpence to one shilling. The shilling tickets functioned from Monday to Thursday after May 26th., twenty-six days after the opening. A Popular Guide cost two pence and the abridged catalogue a shilling. Thus by contemporary standards, admission was by no means cheap, the shilling fee being fixed so as to guarantee that the lower reaches of the working class would be absent. The audience for the Great Exhibition began at the lowest end with the more prosperous artisan and trades-people, these being treated by contemporary commentators as though they were a reflection of the condition of the whole of the labouring classes.[8] Although the entrance fees give no real indication of the number of this class present, it is a striking feature that out of 6,039,195 visitors, 4,439,419 were so-called 'shilling people'.

Even more striking was the mixture of incredulity and distain with which middle class commentators viewed their working class companions:

> Vulgar, ignorant, country people: many dirty women with their infants were sitting on the seats giving suck with their breasts uncovered, beneath the lovely female figures of the sculptor. Oh! How I wish I had the power to petrify the living, and animate the marble: perhaps a time will come when this fantasy will be realised and the human breed be succeeded by finer forms and lovelier features, than the world now dreams of.[9]

> For many days before the 'shilling people' were admitted to the building, the great topic of conversation was the probable behaviour of the people. Would they come sober? will they destroy things? will they want to cut their initials, or scratch their names on the panes of the glass light-houses?[10]

If the main purpose of the exhibition with regard to these people was to educate them into acceptable modes of behaviour, it was a task many members of the middle and upper classes accepted with distinct reluctance. Philanthropy, regardless of its underlying motives, was far from an infectious condition in Victorian England.

The substantial profit the Great Exhibition made was used to organize display activities on land purchased at South Kensington. This would be the centre for British international exhibitions until the turn of the century, by which time a splendid array of permanent museums had been built on the site. The success of the Great Exhibition meant the problems faced in the setting up of exhibitions after 1851 were not of a fundamental kind, such as the generating of interest and funds, but of a legalistic, bureaucratic and political nature. The second event held, the South Kensington Exhibition of 1862, blossomed out of a plethora of paperwork rather than the flames of a vitriolic Parliamentary debate. Over two hundred and fifty official documents were drawn up during the course of the organization and over eighty-four thousand items of correspondence posted.[11]

The finding of sponsors for the 1862 event was no problem after the success of 1851. Within weeks of issuing their statement the Commission was financially secure and had received nine thousand eight hundred applications for space, some eight thousand in the industrial sectors; the element of risk was no longer a feature of British exhibitions. The organization began with the Royal Commissioners of 1851 in conjunction with the Royal Society of Arts requesting permission from the Queen to dispose of the profits from the Crystal Palace. Victoria responded by issuing them with a Charter allowing for dispersal of the funds. In March 1861, the commissioners and Royal Society met and drew up a statement to publicise their intention of holding an exhibition

at South Kensington from May 1st. 1862, with the possibility of further
ones at ten year intervals:

> It (the Queen's Charter) gives us the power to dispose of the surplus in the
> furtherance of any plans that may be devised by us, to invest it in such
> manner as we may think fit . . . it also gives us power to purchase and hold
> lands in any part of Her Majesty's dominions, and dispose of them in all
> respects as we may think fit.[12]

A ten point plan was issued concerning the exhibition specifically.
Effectively this became the official charter specifying the type of
building; it also allowed the Commission to include or exclude
whichever exhibits it wished. The points, or variations of them, were
taken up and used by future exhibition organizers around the world as
basic legal stipulations for exhibitors. Specific items included: painting
sections to be housed in brick facilities; no rents to be charged for space;
no machinery made before 1850 to be exhibited; foreign exhibitors to be
allowed subject to the approval of the commissioners; no fundamental
veto to be issued on any exhibitor; every kind of produce to be admissi-
ble except those subject to deterioration through time, such as foodstuffs, live animals, plants, detonating and other dangerous substances;
alcohol and inflammable liquids to be allowed on the site only with a
license from the commissioners; all produce to be fitted into four main
categories: Mineral and vegetable substances, Machinery and tools,
Manufactures made by industrial and craft processes, Fine arts.[13]

After 1862 the principle of exhibitions at decennial intervals was officially adopted. However, by the time the planning for the 1871 exhibition began, policy shifted to the idea that future exhibitions should be
held annually in the same, semi-permanent facilities. Thus exhibitions
were projected for 1872, 1873 and 1874, each one having the essential
features of an international exhibition, albeit with a reduced scope.
Tied into the rapidity of the series was the notion of specialisation. Each
event, apart from having the usual range of categories, would pick three
or more additional areas to specialise in. These would be themes such as
shipping, civil engineering, the building trade, lace-making, or any
other clearly identifiable discipline. In short, the exhibitions were losing their interest in the state of popular political consciousness and
were becoming increasingly concerned with the rate at which European
and American industry were catching Britain up. The South Kensington
exhibitions of the 1870's were far less celebratory and ebullient, far
more studious and unpretentious. Despite the position Britain still
occupied in the world, the fact that industry and empire were perceivably no longer exclusive properties of the English visibly worried a culture grown used to being in the ascendant. These exhibitions also

revealed the haughty refusal of the organizers to move the same way as French and American events with regard to popular entertainment. South Kensington, it was affirmed, was to be a centre for the enhancement of science and trade, of research into the exploitation of empire and a place where the population could receive education and culture. Entertainment was a side issue and something not catered for in the general sense of the term. Indeed, care was taken to avoid allowing the cultural status of the exhibitions to deteriorate; in the minds of the organizers, the worst possible fate for the whole enterprise was that it might be taken for a fair. When applications for exhibiting space arrived in 1862, by far the most common ground for refusal involved the status of the objects. Rejected, for example, were the preserved remains of Julia Pastrana, half woman half baboon, the oldest loaf in the world and a man-powered flying machine. This was not particularly because of the dubious scientific validity of the objects (far more incredible items of Victorian genius were accepted) but because of their association with fairground side-shows. However, as foreign exhibitions had already begun to demonstrate, the key to material success lay in a blend of popular and high culture; the fact that the British ignored this lesson until the new century meant events up to then became increasingly unsuccessful.

The last significant international exhibitions held at South Kensington were based around particular commodities. Between 1883 and 1886 four were held, on Fisheries, Health, Inventions and Colonial and Indian produce, all of these having the feel of giant conferences or trade fairs except for the last, the exotic content of which made it more widely popular.[14] The intention behind these exhibitions was to examine the state of commerce and industry, profits from entrance fees taking second place to wider issues of national economy. Only the Colonial and Indian had an air of pageant about it, celebrating the one area Britain clearly led the world in. Not for the last time, empire was a focus for lavish indulgence. Coming at the beginning of the era of imperial propaganda, the Colonial and Indian served numerous political purposes for a British government increasingly aware of its fallibility.

In France, the first three Expositions Universelles were paid for exclusively out of public monies, namely the government and the Paris city council. As such they were virtually unique events within the tradition as a whole. The initial outlay was to be recouped, in theory at least, from entrance fees. Government participation at this level meant the selection of the site was considerably less of an issue than it was in London, the Champs de Mars being given over to the purpose, succeeding expositions gradually creeping along the banks of the Seine as far down as the Esplanade des Invalides and the Tuileries. From 1889 the Parc de Vincennes was used as an additional site. An Imperial Commission fulfilled most administrative rôles, juries controlled the produce on display and the various organs of the city council took care of the massive practical problem of accomodating the numbers converging on the capital. Because the third exposition, of 1878, made a heavy loss, the funding system for events after it was changed. In 1889, of the 41,500,000 francs basic outlay, the State paid seventeen, the city council eight and the rest was guaranteed by banks. The latter recouped their investment by selling books of admission tickets, nicknamed 'bons'. As a sales incentive, these also served as lottery tickets for draws projected as far forward as 1964.[15] The sale of lottery tickets had been common in French provincial Salons for some time, with paintings as prizes; it is to be assumed that this was where the idea came from. The use of lotteries to encourage sale of tickets remained very much a French ploy, although in Britain lottery competitions were occasionally organized in the early twentieth century with visits to the exhibition as prizes. In 1889 rent was charged for space given over to private pavilions, providing another source of income. The colonies were asked to contribute, Tunisia and Algeria giving the most at a half and a third of a million francs respectively. Thus the State was alleviated from what would have been considered a risky speculation without losing overall control. In the event these various measures allowed the Exposition to pay back the initial investment. The expositions held in the twentieth century followed the funding pattern of 1889.

By 1900, the advantages and disadvantages of close governmental participation became a subject of debate in France, especially among private manufacturing concerns. Here it was increasingly felt that State controls over the French exhibits, and the growing advantage foreign manufacturers took of the massive exposition audience, was working against French business. Much foreign produce for example was not subject to jury selection, whereas French sections were jury controlled. In essence though, the discontent of French firms came from an undying mistrust of free trade principles. In British and American exhibitions, where the majority of funding came from private enterprise, it would be fair to suggest that individual manufacturers tended to have a greater control over the display of their own goods. However, commentators in London throughout the twentieth century complained bitterly that because private enterprise controlled the exhibits, national displays invariably lacked a governing plan, were unorchestrated, piecemeal and confused. Thus, they suggested, sales were lost because the overall appearance was weak.[16] Nonetheless, French firms disliked the apparent lack of freedom they had in relation to their foreign competitors. They were also irritated by the less exhaustive interest the State showed toward many foreign exhibitions where orders might have been won. From this discontent came two developments in French expositions and in their contingents in overseas events. At home the government did not relax its hold on areas designated official, consequently there was a proliferation of private pavilions built by manufacturers who felt they could show off their produce better. Menier (chocolate) and Möet and Chandon (champagne) were amongst the first firms to create their own facilities. Abroad, French business interests collaborated to guarantee a fitting presence. In 1884, the 'Comité Française des Expositions à l'Etranger' was formed by a group of businessmen from Nice, headed by a Roger Sandoz. The Comité attempted to rectify what they saw as a lack of concern with commerce in relation to State interests. Between 1900 and 1925, when there was no major exposition in Paris, the Comité assumed a considerable importance, fronting French interests in all foreign exhibitions of any size. By the time of the Franco–British Exhibition (London 1908) it had been partly taken over by the government and was the envy of the rest of the world for the efficient way it molded French manufactures into cohesive displays.[17]

State policy dominated the first five Expositions Universelles. The first two were marked by Napoleon III's determination to adopt Liberal and free trade policies and by his desire to generally streamline France into a progressive industrial state. England was the example perpetually on the Emperor's mind as he attempted to urbanise French rural mentality; the 1855 Exposition was a direct response to the Great Exhibition, a progress report of a nation attempting to expand as rapidly as possible. By 1867 it was clear the social and economic fabric of France was dangerously thin, the bombast of the Second Empire's public face superficial and meaningless. Raymond Isay: '. . . un régime fondé sur l'ambiguité, sur le compromis, sur l'equivogue – tout le malaise politique, sociale et economique, toute le crise industrielle et morale que dissimule une brilliante façade et dont la guerre et la commune ne tarderont pas a marquer le pathetique aboutissement'.[18] If the second exposition glowed brilliantly in ignorance of what was shortly to happen, in 1878 the third struggled to raise its head above the disasters of the previous decade. 1867 saw one of the most hopeful exhibitions ever staged, a strange mixture of imperial-economic ambition and of Saint-Simonian paternalism, it projected a notion of society as a beautifully tuned machine capable of resolving conflicts and harnessing the world to its own ends. The 1878 Exposition had no such idealism, much rather it was an attempt on the part of government to show the foreigner and its own population that recovery from the war and the commune were complete. Even though vast sums were spent on a lavish new building, the Palais de Trocadéro, too few believed in the myth of total recovery; attendance was insufficient to cover costs and the Exposition was a financial disaster.

The Exposition of 1889 celebrated the centenary of the Revolution, and as such virtually every European monarch declined to attend. Queen Victoria went as far as to recall her ambassador, Lord Lytton, so that no representative of the British government was in Paris on the day of the opening. Only Belgium sent representation. More interestingly perhaps, the French aristocracy was equally unready to celebrate an event which marked their own political eclipse. In his study of the period, Raymond Rudorff noted

> For the enemies of the French Republic – and there were still many – the exhibition was simply a gigantic piece of political propaganda and to a certain extent they were right . . . They were the people who closed their shutters on the 14th. of July, who stayed away from the exposition, who refused to put out tricolour flags for the centenary celebrations and who remained aloof while the rest of Paris enjoyed itself in the open.[19]

The stigma 1889 carried for many of France's most monied people caused political problems during the organization which threatened to disrupt the event itself. In like manner, splits within French society almost brought about the collapse of the 1900 show during the organizational phase. In 1900 however Dreyfus was the central issue, not republicanism. Even on the eve of the opening, Alfred Picard, Commissioner-general to the Exposition, was threatened with mass withdrawals, not only from domestic exhibitors but also from foreign ones:

> Boycott here, boycott there, boycott everywhere! This repetition of the same word, somewhat obsessive, a catchword, is the perfectly natural consequence of the importance which a very topical question has assumed in the press. Certain foreign journalists, unhappy with the outcome of the Dreyfus affair, which they have made their concern, with a zeal as intemperate as it is indiscreet, have begun a campaign to have their fellow countrymen unite to punish France.[20]

The British, as opportunist as ever, used the affair to annoy the French because of their sympathy for the Boers in the South African War. Layered over both the 1889 and the 1900 shows was an altogether separate political issue which excited the foreign press and possibly reduced the number of visitors; this was anarchist activity in the city. Whilst no exposition ever suffered from the blight of anarchist bombs, and the total number of incidents over a ten year period was negligible, the anarchists had captured the popular imagination, much to the irritation of exposition organizers. It is impossible now to know whether the size of the audience was affected.

Attendances at the Paris expositions were astronomical by the standards of the time. Moving from a modest four million in 1855 to eleven in 1867 and sixteen in 1878, the 1889 and 1900 shows polled a staggering thirty-two and forty-eight million peoples respectively.[21] The fact that the population of France in 1900 was around thirty-five millions indicates two things; the Parisian events attracted far more foreign visitors than any other exhibitions, and there was a wider selection of the indigenous population present. Both these things were worked towards from 1867 onwards, especially the presence of the masses. Napoleon III should take credit more than anyone in this regard, as it was his policy in 1867 to open the turnstiles to as many people as possible at the base of the French class structure. His wariness of the urban masses led him to court the workers in an attempt to win their approval by consent rather than coercion. In 1864 he had allowed them the rights of association and strike action, in 1867 he encouraged the organizers in their choice of 'work' as a major theme at the Exposition. The placing of Saint-Simonians in executive positions was a calculated move to woo those left of centre. Some extraordinary concessions were given to encourage attendance; free travel was available to the peasantry from numerous provinces and free lodging was provided for sixty-seven thousand people on the site. This resulted in a flood of people into the capital who were without previous travelling experience and who would never have conceived of a visit to Paris. Whilst this show was exceptional for the generosity of its concessions, following ones did cater for the poor far more effectively than those of any other nation. Correspondingly, the expositions of 1889 and 1900 were infectiously popular; reports tell how families saved for years toward an exposition, selling furniture and anything else removable from the house to provide money for spending in Paris. Such eagerness to flood to the capital to see the glory of the French empire undoubtedly thrilled a government constantly aware of periodic outbursts of regional separatism.[22]

By 1889 the funding systems in both Britain and France had stabilised and become nationally standard. In America by 1893 an established order was also in operation. This was more complex than those of Europe however, due to the awkwardness of the relationship between State and Federal authorities, and to the more rigorous attitude the Americans had toward private enterprise. Most of the major Fairs made simultaneous use of disparate funding sources, including sponsorship small amounts of Federal money, city and State council monies and monies generated by specially created companies. All of these were orchestrated into a single pool by the company and the executive of the central organizing committee. In the earlier Fairs, cash advances were also accepted from participating governments, probably in view of the fact that America could not ask for funds from colonies in the way European nations did. The exhibition tradition began in America with the New York World's Fair of 1853, but this has to be regarded somewhat as a one-off private speculative venture, organized principally to profit from the stir caused by the Crystal Palace exhibition in London two years before. Despite its novelty – in a country without museums or academies of any kind – the venture was a financial failure. The real opening of the American Fair tradition came in 1876 with the Philadelphia Centennial Exposition. It was here that a proper organizational base for American World's Fairs was worked out. Funding came from individual sponsors within the States, the Federal government and foreign participants. An Act was passed establishing a 'Centennial Board of Finance' to supervise the fund raising. The Board determined initially how much it would need and how it would collect it:

> The conclusion reached fixed upon the sum of $10,000,000 as adequate for all the purposes of the exhibition. In accordance with this estimate, and with a view to giving every citizen of every state an opportunity to become interested in and connected with this great national exhibition, a quota was now established of a ratio of subscription for the several states, and every effort was made, through the public press, special circulars, and selected agents, to bring about such an interest as would lead to a popular subscription sufficiently large to absorb the capital stock . . .[23]

In essence then, the bulk of the money came from States selling shares to its citizens. The established quota told each State how much it was to raise; for example New York was asked for (and actually paid) $1,136,660, Pennsylvania $913,410, Ohio $691,230, Illinois $658,710, Louisiana $188,520, Idaho $3,890, Nebraska $31,000, Missouri $446,410.[24] Of the foreign participants, Britain (including Australia and Canada) added $250,000, Japan $600,000, France (including Algeria) $120,000, Germany $171,000, Austria $75,000, Spain $150,000.[25] By the time the funds were surrendered up, the organizers believed they had gathered more than they needed.[26]

At the Chicago Columbian Fair seventeen years later, the nature of the private enterprise system had changed, from the inclusion of thousands of small investors to a handful of rich sponsors. Amongst those contributing, Marshall-Field, George Pullmann, Cyrus McCormick, Gustavus Swift and Philip Armour showed up prominently. The finances of the Columbian varied from the Centennial not only in this however, but also in its establishing of a company to handle matters pertaining to money. In so doing it moved the exhibition tradition emphatically into a commercial arena. More than any event before it, it espoused the ideology of the profit margin. The Chicago Company, though constantly teetering on the edge of insolvency even up to 1893, conducted itself with a business-like zeal which had never been part of the European pattern up to that time. For example, a promotions depart-ment was established for publicity, printing up newsletters and format-ted articles which could be slotted straight into newspapers around the world without additional editing.[27] Every communication system available was utilised to present the Fair, and once opened, every pos-sible device was used to keep the site full. Needless to say, commercial concerns prevented government from controlling the event in the way Prince Albert dictated the atmosphere of the Great Exhibition or Napoleon III controlled the first Exposition Universelle. In fact the Chicago Company and the Federal body watching over the Fair, the National Commission, were far from seeing eye to eye on numerous issues. The Columbian, as with many of the World's Fairs after it, whilst being riddled with social, political and ideological discourses, was nevertheless a multi-based and hence more confused affair than its European forerunners.

After 1893, most Fairs established a company to deal with State and Federal officials, to purchase the site and to establish committees for the selection of exhibits. The company would be founded on sponsorship money but would then proceed to generate funds through diverse cam-paign tactics. For example, the proliferation of exhibition ephemera, such as popular books and guides, exhibition trinkets, postcards, textiles and ceramics, whilst beginning in 1851, was brought to a new pitch in America. The material was produced by private firms with permission from the exhibition company. Perhaps the most emulated model was the Louisiana Purchase Exposition Company, created to administer the St. Louis Fair of 1904. The company took on every aspect of its job with an efficiency which probably saved the whole enterprise from financial insolvency. The State authorities had made the event into a high risk venture from the onset by committing themselves to a larger site than had ever been used before for an international exhi-bition. Ultimately the Fair made a loss, this being as small as it was mainly because of the shrewdness and tenacity of the company direc-tors. Exhibition companies reached a definitive and final form in New York in 1939, where 'New York World's Fair Incorporated' operated more independently of government than any before it. A sub-company was founded to deal with the printing side of the operation, 'Expositions Publications', leaving the mother company to develop what was the second largest site ever, the uninviting 'Corona Dumps' on the edge of the city.

The lack of direct control a government could bring to bear or American Fairs was a result of the funding and administrative systems employed. American sources tend to see this as the advantage of the system. Private enterprise however occasionally created problems that perhaps only central government could have resolved, the most difficult one being inter-State rivalry in the staging of Fairs. After the success of the Philadelphia Centennial in 1876, America's growing cities began to countenance the idea of having similar events themselves. By 1890, when the celebration of the five hundredth anniversary of the discovery of America offered itself as the perfect reason for a Fair, the rivalry between States for the right to hold it became intense. Every city with pretensions to any level of sophistication focused on the year 1892 as being the one to show themselves off in. The cost and scale of international exhibitions however meant there could only be one, and whichever city it was in, it would require support from many other States and foreign nations if it was to stand alongside European equivalents. As early as 1876 the city fathers in Washington conceived of the idea of an exhibition to celebrate the landing of Columbus. By the early 1880's New York, Cincinnati, St. Louis and Cumberland Gap also showed interest. It was Chicago however, via its political and social clubs, that made the first decisive moves, beginning a campaign on a nationwide basis for the right to hold the Columbian. By 1889, when Paris was enjoying the largest exposition to date, the race was crystallizing into a struggle between Chicago and New York, the press in both cities reaching a frenzied level of insult. The Chicago Tribune: 'New York is not an American city – in its history, in its relations to the nation, in its attitudes toward the government during the War of the Revolution and Rebellion, or in its social characteristics.'[28] Furthermore it was claimed 'Chicago slaughters and packs its hogs, New York puts them on committees.'[29] When it was finally apparent the issue could not be resolved the matter was made the subject of a debate and vote in Congress. On the first ballot, Chicago polled 115, New York 70, St. Louis 61, Washington 58 and Cumberland Gap 1.[30] After a second round of tactical voting, Chicago triumphed with three votes more than it needed for an overall majority. This was a victory for the growing lobby in America wishing to see cultural development encouraged and recognised away from the east coast. A decade after the Chicago Columbian, St. Louis would confirm the coming of age of the West by holding the largest ever Fair.

The company system used in American Fairs was never utilised in anything but a cosmetic way in Europe, apart from in one notable case, at the Franco–British exhibition of 1908. Here, entrepreneur Imre Kiralfy formed the 'International and Commercial Company Ltd'.[31] He based his exhibitions completely on the American model, going as far as to christen his site the 'White City' in emulation of the Chicago

Columbian. The White City was re-used almost on a yearly basis through to 1914, ultimately proving to be the most consistently profitable exhibition concern throughout the tradition.[32] The money to create the site came from a wider spread of sources than any before it, including the City of London Council, the colonies, private sponsors, the French government, the exhibition company and site rents. Once the exhibition was open additional sources increased the revenue; advertising, gate-money, sale of a vast range of ephemera, company controlled restaurants and amusements. The Daily Mail and Daily Mirror newspapers worked in close harmony with the site organizers, guaranteeing the exhibitions a national audience on a regular basis.[33] Both Houses of Parliament, the Offices of the Lord Mayor of London and various political clubs gave support and administrative help. Thus the White City exhibitions developed to a fine pitch the combination of governmental participation and commercial sponsorship that typified British exhibitions. In the true spirit of liberal/imperial enterprise, government provided the ideological lead and the citizenry provided the funds. Never before in Europe had so many aspects of an exhibition been so carefully orchestrated to the cause of money-making. Kiralfy had learned the lesson of the American Fairs well, combining this knowledge with his European experience to create the definitive exhibition site.

Attendance was the critical factor for all the international exhibitions. Gate money was the economic basis of every event, the staple means whereby investments could be recouped. The financial side of exhibitions could be suspect unless a certain attendance could be achieved, the Vienna and Paris shows of 1873 and 1878, for example, making heavy losses when this did not materialise. The former almost bankrupted the city. Governmental support hinged on the fact that millions of people would see the exhibits on display. Without the promise of a large audience, no government would participate since, crudely speaking, propaganda was their concern and this was meaningless in the absence of a reasonable selection of the population. The exhibitions of 1851 and 1862 in London and of 1855 in Paris attracted millions mainly because of their novelty. The scale of technological advance was enough to mystify and enthrall the crowds. Into the 1870's however, when exhibitions were becoming a norm throughout Europe, technology alone could no longer be relied upon to fill a site. In order to prevent disaster through non-attendance at these later events, organizers gave attention to popular entertainment. This grew as a dimension of exhibitions markedly during the 1880's until it came to be the dominant socio-economic factor on the site. In 1851 the only real elements identifiable specifically as mass entertainment, apart from refreshment facilities, were concerts given by orchestras and brass bands. By 1890 the situation had dramatically changed.

After the embracing of the idea of entertainment, the cultural mixture available on exhibition sites became their single most extraordinary feature. From the exclusive heights of the fine arts, opera, haute couture, Royalty and the aristocracy, to the cheap and plentiful end of production, fairground stalls, joy-rides, trinket sellers, sport, bandstands, music hall and an infinity of buskers. Within the space of a few hundred metres one might engage in a debate between rationalists and historicists in architecture, view a collection of impressionist paintings, watch Olympian athletes compete, ride on a Ferris Wheel, drink coffee in a Turkish bar, examine a life-size elephant constructed entirely from walnuts, watch the Imperial Guard drill, attend a conference on chiropody, buy a suit, listen to a two hundred piece orchestra play Berlioz, go into an erotic dance show or purchase a steam engine. So-called high and popular cultures mixed freely in an environment where all rules appeared to have been temporarily suspended. The embracing of popular forms of culture by exhibition organizers enabled them to predict attendances optimistically and as a bi-product it allowed the rigidity of established class structure to thaw a little at the edges. By 1900 the entertainment side of the exhibitions had gained so much ground that education, commerce and propaganda had to be disguised as pleasurable activities, otherwise the masses they were targetted at would simply breeze by.

The first to realise the importance of entertainment as a crowd-puller were the French, who incorporated an amusement park and fairground into the plans of the Exposition Universelle of 1867. The idea was quickly understood and seized upon by the Americans at the Philadelphia Centennial, where traditional fairground stalls were dotted around the site. The Exposition Universelle of 1889 and the Chicago Columbian finally integrated entertainment fully into the conceptual fabric of the exhibition tradition, notably in the absence and disapproval of the English. This was done not simply by legitimising the fairground activity which normally existed on the edges of all exhibition sites, but by transforming hitherto 'serious' displays into vehicles for entertainment. Thus the Eiffel Tower was not only a symbol of the technological achievement of an age, it was also a pleasurable distraction. Displays of colonial peoples were not only of interest to anthropologists but were, once a backdrop was provided, something for everyone to gaze at. Here entertainment directly served as imperial/racial propaganda.[34] Refreshment areas became exotic restaurants and bars from far-off lands, serviced by equally exotic peoples. Facilities housing exhibits became fantastic edifices, on sites that came to appear as unreal, dream-like cities.

In Chicago the great entertainment entrepreneur P. T. Barnum was consulted with regard to the overall effect of the site and its facilities. The essence of his advice was to go for scale and opulence: 'Make it bigger and better than any that have preceded it. Make it the greatest show on earth – greater than my own Great Moral Show if you can.' [35] Whether it was Barnum himself who bestowed the atmosphere of the circus on American events or some other factor, it was constantly an ingredient from 1893. He later produced shows with Imre Kiralfy in America before the latter became the impresario of British exhibitions, his influence thereby drifting indirectly over the Atlantic. In Chicago a whole area was unashamedly cordoned off and given over to leisure. This, the Midway Plaisance, contained various tribes of primitive people in their dwellings, troupes of actors and musicians, exotic bars, restaurants and a myriad of side-shows. The Chicagoans also applied engineering technology to joy-rides in a way no-one before had contemplated, giving the electrically-lit Midway a spectacular appearance at night; its success made it an essential part of all World's Fairs after it. Larger and larger areas of sites were given over to entertainment through the twentieth century, reaching a grand climax in the 1930's when exhibition guides were filled with publicity for sponsors and listings of the various rides available. The 'Century of Progress' exposition held in Chicago in 1933 called its pleasure area 'the Midway' in recognition of its illustrious forerunner. The Texas Centennial of 1936 in Dallas and the Golden Gate Exposition of 1939 in San Francisco presented profiles via their respective official literatures that seemed like uncomfortable mixtures of the Metropolitan Museum of New York and Disney Land. Perhaps such analogies are not too inaccurate.

New York provided the definitive Fair in terms of entertainment. Over a hundred shows or rides were mentioned in the Official Guide, including 'Admiral Byrd's Penguin Land', 'Ariel Joyride', 'Amazons in No-man's Land', 'Arctic Girl's Tomb of Ice', 'Auto Dodgem', 'Frank Buck's Jungleland', 'Living Magazine Covers', 'Skyride', 'Snapper', 'Laff Land', 'World's Fair Hall of Music' and 'Strange as it Seems'.[36] Interestingly, some displays listed as entertainment might have claimed higher status, or at least those who participated in them were normally associated with things of higher status. Amongst these were the 'Artistic Village', described as 'a gigantic palette adorned with the proverbial daubs of paint and paint brush tops . . . in open booths that face each other a group of artists from many lands practice their art'[37]; or the 'Crystal Palace of 1939', 'a tour through the American World's Fairs 1853–1939'[38]; or 'Bel Geddes Mirror Show', 'known the world over as an industrial designer of distinctly serious intent, Norman Bel Geddes here takes a vacation and turns his talents to the brighter side of life'[39]; and most interestingly, 'Salvador Dali's Living Pictures'. Surrealism's most commercial and cynical showman, Dali created a spectacle that probably confused would-be surrealists as much if not more than the average visitor: 'Surrealism is the most modern form of French Art and is derived from a study of the secrets hidden in the subconscious mind. In a series of living pictures, executed in three dimensions, famed and lively Salvador Dali explains some of these secrets'.[40] A tank thirty feet long and filled with water contained erotically clad female divers ('living liquid ladies') swimming languidly amongst sculpted versions of some of Dali's best known works.

Europe replied quickly to the initiatives taken by America in the entertainment area. The Paris Exposition Universelle of 1900 duplicated several of the features of the Columbian, including the famous Ferris Wheel and an electrically powered moving pavement. The Eiffel Tower remained and alongside it a huge 'Celestial Globe' thrilled the crowds. A myriad of side-shows, cafés and restaurants littered the site. In London, the White City Exhibitions introduced entertainments based on those the commissioner-general, Imre Kiralfy, had seen at Chicago and St. Louis. This was the first time large scale leisure facilities had been used in a British exhibition, marking out the White City as the first site to pay close attention to foreign events with regard to content and organization. The exhibitions staged there had far more in common with American and Parisian shows than they had with earlier British ones. Commentators at the Imperial International, held there in 1909, recognised the discernible shift from philanthropic involvement with education to mass entertainment, attributing this shift to the shrewdness of the commissioner-general: 'The instructive part of the exhibition appears to be in rather an embryo condition, but Mr. Kiralfy knows his public. And his public prefer Biplanes, and Water-whirls, and Witching-waves, and Wiggle-woggles, and Flip-flaps to all the instruction in the world.'[41] By 1912 and the staging of the Latin–British Exhibition, the site boasted an impressive list of features, including the 'Flip-Flap', 'Roly-poly', 'Screamers', 'The House of Troubles', 'Glacier glide', 'Mountain Railway', 'Great Bostock Jungle', 'Witching waves', 'Wiggle-woggle', 'Boomerang', 'Whirlpool', 'Daylight Cinema', 'Scenic Railway', 'Skating Palace', 'Spiral Chute', 'Bowlo', 'Caves of Laughter', 'Mouse trap' and 'Electric launches'.[42] Apart from these, numerous native villages were open for the pleasure of the public. British exhibitions had indeed changed since the days of Henry Cole and Prince Albert.

Probably the most important long term aspect of exhibition leisure activity came in the form of the revival of the Olympic Games. The first modern Olympiad was staged in Athens in 1896, not in conjunction with an exhibition, but the three following ones, all held on exhibition sites, established the pattern still in use today. The 1900 Olympiad in Paris was a somewhat half-hearted affair, winners having to pay for their own medals. The third at St. Louis was markedly better, boasting good facilities, a satisfactory range of events and a reasonable number of international competitors. The fourth Olympiad marked the rise of the modern tradition proper. Held in London at the Franco–British Exhibition, a superb stadium was built for the occasion – later known as the 'White City' – and the number of events increased further still.[43] The internationality of the competing body achieved an impressive spread courtesy of the British and French empires. The stadium was full throughout the Games, guaranteeing the organizers over one hundred thousand fee-paying customers. There can be no doubt that those who visited the Fine and Decorative Art Palaces during those hot July days had their pleasure subsidised by the crowds in the stadium cheering on the athletes, the latter blissfully ignorant of the high culture they were indirectly paying for.

The amount of popular culture available on exhibition sites by 1900 begs the question as to where the inspiration for the form it took came from in the first place. In fact the leisure side of the exhibitions had an impressively long pedigree. Sport, fairground stalls and rides, musical and comic troupes, sellers of food and ephemera all derived originally from the annual market-fairs held around Europe for centuries. Popular entertainment was therefore one of the few genuine links the exhibitions had with pre-industrial festivals and markets, this link surviving basically through economic expediency as suggested earlier.[44] Exhibitions contributed to these aged forms of entertainment by exaggeration through technology. That is, the modes already at work in society were simply made bigger. Sporting challenges, such as tests of strength or ball games between rival villages, were transmuted first into ordered sporting events and eventually into Olympiads. Freak shows, foodstalls, gambling, musical and comic troupes became amusement arcades, native villages, brass band concerts and joy-rides. The evolution in each case was due to the vast numbers using the facilities and the concern of the perpetrators to make profits well beyond the level of subsistence. The result was usually a cosmopolitan blandness as one site gradually came to resemble another. In a similar way to other artforms, the exhibitions heralded the end of vernacular entertainment and the beginning of mass international popular culture.

It would be a mistake to assume organizers carefully sought out traditional modes of popular enjoyment with a view to integrating them into the workings of the site. Much rather, in the first instance, it was the entertainers who sought out the exhibitions, setting up illicit booths and stalls outside the official areas. Indeed, at the first few international events legislation was passed to prevent entertainers of all kinds gaining access. It was only the realisation that the crowds came specifically to be entertained which led to the inclusion of amusement areas into overall plans. Before then, visitors would expect to walk through acres of fairground activity outside the exhibition perimeter, including everything from merry-go-rounds to gambling dens and brothels. The move from unofficial to official status naturally entailed the 'cleaning up' of entertainment and the re-presentation of it into acceptable forms for the bourgeoisie, since they comprised the largest single group visiting the sites. By 1889, the exhibition medium had created and institutionalised the notion of 'family entertainment', this aiming to harmlessly satisfy the curiosities and desires of all genders and ages. Thus it was from the last decade of the nineteenth century, the middle classes attended exhibitions to enjoy filtered versions of the types of entertainment preserved through peasant and working class culture. In this regard at least, the working classes had led the way. In sad contradiction to the Utopian dreams of educationalists, for the majority, cultural enlightenment with regard to fine art and science was infrequently sought after and more rarely achieved; in some cases the possibility of such enlightenment could well have been reduced not increased by the exhibitions.

By 1890 it was thoroughly understood that the appearance of site itself was the single greatest factor in entertaining the crowds, and hence generating a profit. The site became subject to complex landscaping plans and extraordinary pieces of fantasy architecture in order to delight and amaze the casual stroller. Again, the Chicago Columbian made the pace, with a neoclassical dreamland, artificial lake, monumental sculpture and its uniform, brilliant whiteness. This Fair took the accepted medium for site architecture, plaster (or staff) facings on wood or iron frames, to new heights of grandeur, which all successors sought to mimic or surpass. Buffalo in 1901 achieved an unearthly effect through the use of a bright colour scheme in conjunction with classical plan and monumental sculpture. In 1904 the Louisiana Purchase Exposition had the advantage of a vast 1,272 acre site to sprawl over, the effect being of a classical scheme loosened by a picturesque approach to garden design. Perhaps the two most aesthetically resolved American exhibitions were the Panama–Pacific (San Francisco 1915) and the Panama–California (San Diego 1915–1916). The former, by far the largest of the two, used a classicism tinged with a romantic nostalgia; the intention, as always, being to carry the spectator away from reality:

The most striking court, in its mysteriousness, is Mullgardt's Court of Abundance, particularly so on a foggy night. Large volumes of vapor are lazily rising from huge bowls and torches, below, and in the tower, suggesting the early days of the cosmic All, cooling off from the turbulent period of its creation. The fogs sweeping from the bay add more mystery, and with the gorgeous perfume of the hyacinth carpet in the garden spaces, the effect is almost narcotic. The whole court, under these conditions, seems heavy with the atmosphere of abundance, of physical well-being, of slumbering natural powers . . . At the same time, it is truly religious in its effect of turning the mind away from the ordinary world into the realm of the mystic and the supernatural.[45]

At San Diego, the notion of the picturesque was at the forefront of the site planners minds, as they attempted to create something different from previous exhibitions:

As the Chicago, the St. Louis and the Buffalo expositions were a glorification of the monumental in city planning, so the San Diego Fair is the apotheosis of all those elements of charm and variety that we associate with the cities of Italy and Spain. It has the varied symmetry and underlying order of the Latin cities, without the squalor of the crowded quarters; it is the glorification of the romantic in city planning as the gothic cathedral was in building.[46]

In Europe, an intention from 1851 onwards had been to suspend the harshness of reality. Up to 1880, this had been brought into effect through promises of material progress for all. The visitor was encouraged to dream of an imminent better life. Toward the turn of the new century however, the exhibitions sought to escape reality not so much through the myth of progress as through the creation of a fantasy land. As with the theme of Education, 'Progress' was overtaken by the desire to entertain; there were fewer promises to the visitor about improving life off the site and a heightened insistence on having a good time whilst on it. The maleability of the plaster and the availability of new technologies, especially electric lighting, enabled designers to create spectacular effects. The Paris show of 1900 was the most developed example of the exhibition as an unreal paradise. It was the first in Europe to extensively use electric lighting to evoke a fairy-tale environment, invariably in conjunction with water cascades, glass and mirrors. A large number of the buildings had an Oriental feel to them:

On the right hand side of the Eiffel Tower, upon a rock overlooking a little lake, stands the Luminous Palace . . . An opium smoker might have conceived this fairy palace after reading the Arabian Nights. All the forms, aspects, and prisms of which glass is capable have been utilised in the design of this unique edifice, and its effect is crowned by a pretty cascade.[47]

[47]

The Franco–British Exhibition took its lead from American and French forerunners, combining water, electric lighting and oriental detailing to create its atmosphere. Even the driest commentator the Architectural Review could muster was forced to acknowledge the success of this pastichism: '. . . the waterways, catching the reflection of the buildings by day, and half a million lights by night, and throwing them back distorted and broken, adds not a little to the effect'.[48] Whatever grievances with the world the crowds had when they arrived, they cannot have left the sites in anything less than a state of confused euphoria.

Normally, the exhibitions managed to pay for themselves; overheads were more or less met, excessive loss or profit was quite unusual. In the sense of direct profit in relation to lay-out, the Great Exhibition of 1851 was the most successful, followed by the Paris 1867 and the London White City series 1908–1914. In terms of loss, the famous disasters were the Vienna 1873, Paris 1878, with the St. Louis 1904 Fair probably having the greatest deficit in the American tradition. These were the exceptions, the majority of shows making slight losses after gate receipts were counted. Debts were made good by subscribers and government.

Simplistic assessments however are deceptive, as the economic ambitions of exhibitions cannot be clearly discerned from the immediate takings. Government, for example, did not expect to profit from exhibitions as they were considered a source of publicity and propaganda which would have to be paid for whatever the medium. For the thousands of participating manufacturers, the winning of new orders was the economic rationale of exhibitions, not gate-money. As Henry Chardon explained in the Revue de Paris:

> Expositions secure for the manufacturer, for the businessman, the most striking publicity. In one day they will bring before his machine, his display, his shop windows, more people than he would see in a lifetime in his factory or store. They seek out clients in all parts of the world, bring them at a set time, so that everything is ready to receive them and seduce them. That is why the number of exhibitions increases daily.[49]

The economic consequences of exhibitions in terms of custom won by manufacturers cannot be calculated but in many instances the good done to a national economy must have compensated handsomely for any immediate loss on the site itself. More than this, the service industries at work in the host city made profits regardless of the overall success of the event. Conservative estimates in 1908 suggested every million visits to the Franco–British Exhibition generated three million pounds business for the hotels, transport systems, restaurants and post offices of London.[50]

Most events left permanent features behind, such as galleries, museums, general exhibiting areas, railway stations, sports stadiums, parks and even mass-housing. Often these were counted as part of an overall expenditure, yet they continued to provide service to the city for decades after. For example, the audit figures for the Paris Expositions Universelles from 1867 onwards tend to reveal considerable short-falls – some forty million francs in the case of 1900 – yet buildings still giving service at the present time were part of that apparent loss; the expositions added substantially to the amenities of the metropolis.[51] The Palais de l'Industrie (1855 to 1900), the Palais de Trocadéro (1878 to 1937), the Eiffel Tower, the Galeries des Machines (1889 to 1910), the gardens of the Champs de Mars and the Parc de Vincennes,[52] the Grand Palais, the Petit Palais, the Pont Alexandre lll, the Musée d'Art Moderne de la Ville de Paris, the Palais de Tokyo, Palais de Chaillot, housing in Montmartre and the first Metro stations were all built for the expositions. When these permanent features are taken out of the deficit, losses in most instances become negligible. The same pattern repeats itself across America, where the Fairs resulted in the development of land into parks, where museums and galleries were built and roads and sewage systems were provided to accomodate the influx of people. In Britain, the whole of the museum complex surrounding Exhibition Road in South Kensington is in the debt of the temporary events staged there when the area was still an under-developed suburb. Until recently, the White City Stadium was a reminder of the events of 1908–1914 and Wembley Stadium remains the premier sporting venue of the English. Glasgow's superb art gallery, Kelvingrove and Balahouston Parks continue to serve a public oblivious of the exhibitions they were developed for. Indeed, throughout Europe useful edifices remain. As the author writes, Barcelona has been chosen to host the 1992 Olympiad; apart from the debt the event itself owes to the exhibition tradition, Montjuic, the area of Barcelona where the Games will be sited, was the result of development undertaken for the 1929 International Exposition, including the main stadium itself. Looked at in this light, exhibitions were of considerable material worth to urban dwellers.

Due to the invisible earning capacity of exhibitions, they were seen as a remarkably efficient medium for the conducting of commercial, political, industrial, military and artistic business. Throughout the nineteenth and twentieth centuries, they were the only events capable of bringing such a wide selection of people to the same place for the purpose of edification and entertainment. They were intended to distract, indoctrinate and unify a population; as the electorate swelled toward the turn of the century these three intentions swelled also, their realisation being hoped for through concentration on particular themes.

Perhaps the single most persistent of these was that of empire, as it contained all the political, commercial and social ingredients capable of preserving the progressive-liberal order of things. It is to this our attention turns next.

Notes

1 The vast majority of histories put forward the idea that the exhibitions were part of a continuing phenomenon beginning with Roman markets or mediæval fairs. Such suggestions fundamentally misunderstand how and why they came into being.
2 I have not concentrated to any degree on the activities of Henry Cole as other histories of the Great Exhibition and virtually all design histories deal with him in depth. My ommission is not intended to suggest he was unimportant but is simply a recognition of the thoroughness of other secondary sources.
3 This was the famous Colonel Sibthorp incident. See chapter Six.
4 Sources vary on exactly what was contributed by government. It appears that one tenth of the initial cost was contributed in order to get the project underway, although this figure is disputed.
5 Quoted from Aaron Scharf, *The Crystal Palace and the Great Exhibition* in *Art and Industry*, Unit 33 of Course A100, Open University Press 1971.
6 Quoted from C.H. Gibbs-Smith, *The Great Exhibition of 1851*, London 1981, H.M.S.O. press.
7 Quoted from *The Opening*, in Humphrey Jennings (ed.) *Pandæmonium*, London 1985, pub. André Deutsch.
8 Surprisingly Henry Mayhew is also guilty of this error.
9 Gideon Mantell, quoted from *Pandæmonium*, see note 7.
10 Henry Mayhew, Ibid.
11 *The International Exhibition of 1862: The Illustrated Catalogue of the Industrial Sections*, London 1862.
12 Ibid.
13 Ibid.
14 See chapters 3 and 4.
15 By far the best source for the finances of the 1889 and 1900 Expositions Universelles is Richard D. Mandell,*Paris 1900: The Great World's Fair*, University of Toronto Press 1967.
16 See, for example J.M. Richards, *The Problem of a National Projection*, Architectural Review 1937.
17 See, Paul Greenhalgh, *Art, Politics and Society at the Franco–British Exhibition of 1908*, Art History December 1985.
18 Raymond Isay, *Panorama des Expositions Universelle*, Paris 1937, Gallimard.
19 Raymond Rudorff, *Belle Epoch: Paris in the 1890's*, London 1972, Hamish Hamilton.
20 Quoted from Mandell, see note 15.
21 Figures used are from Kenneth Luckhurst, *The Story of Exhibitions*, London 1951, Studio Publications.
22 See Chapter 5.
23 *Frank Leslie's Illustrated Historical Register of the Centennial Exposition 1876*, Philadelphia 1876. Facsimile copy now available, New York 1974, Paddington Press.
24 Ibid.
25 Ibid. I am unsure as to what exactly these sums refer to. They were probably in part advances given to the Exposition to pay for the materials and labour for the national pavilions.
26 In fact this was an over optimistic belief, the exposition made a small loss.
27 The best account of this is in Reid-Badger, *The Great American Fair: The World's Columbian Exposition and American Culture*, Chicago 1979, pub. Nelson Hall.
28 Ibid.
29 Ibid.
30 Ibid.

31 The company later changed its name to *Shepherd's Bush Exhibitions Ltd.* and finally the *Great White City Ltd.* See Donald Knight *The Exhibitions*, London 1978. I am grateful to Mr. Knight for the kind help he has given me with the White City exhibitions, his personal collection of catalogues and ephemera being a vital source. See also my own article on the Franco–British Exhibition, note 17.

32 Ibid.

33 Newspapers are the most informative source for these exhibitions, notably the Daily Mail, Daily Mirror, the Times, Manchester Guardian, Pall Mall Gazette and the Telegraph. The best French source on the Franco–British is Le Figaro.

34 See chapter 4.

35 Quoted from Reid-Badger, note 27.

36 *Official Guide Book of the New York World's Fair 1939*, New York 1939, Exposition Publications Inc.

37 Ibid.

38 Ibid.

39 Ibid.

40 Ibid. Shortly after the New York World's Fair Andre Breton, leader of the Surrealist organisation, invented the anagram Avida Dollars from Dali's name, and permanently excommunicated him from the movement.

41 The Times, May 21st. 1909.

42 *Latin–British Exhibition, Official Daily Programme, 1911*

43 The White City was sadly demolished in 1985.

44 This obviously contradicts the view that the exhibitions had general roots going back to Roman or mediæval times. See note 1.

45 Eugen Neuhaus, *The Art of the Exposition*, San Francisco 1915, pub. Paul Elder.

46 C. Monroe-Winslow, *The Panama–California International Exposition*, San Francisco 1916, pub. Paul Elder.

47 Alex M. Thompson, *Dangle's Guide to Paris and the Exhibition*, London 1900.

48 R.W. Carden, *The Franco–British Exhibition 1*, Architectural Review, Volume 24 1908.

49 Quoted from Rosalind Williams *Dream Worlds: Mass Consumption in Late 19th. Century France.* University of California Press.

50 Anon. *Do Exhibitions Pay? Some Surprising Facts and Figures*, Answers Magazine, May 23rd. 1908.

51 See Mandell, note 15.

52 The Parc de Vincennes was used as the site for the Paris Internationale Coloniale Exposition of 1931, and was to be the site for the 1992 Olympiad had the French bid been successful, which it was not. Interestingly enough, the winning bid, from Barcelona, proposes to hold the event on a former exposition site.

CHAPTER THREE

Imperial display

When Eric Hobsbawm entitled his classic work on the modern British economy 'Industry and Empire', he brought together in a phrase the two forces which have most decisively divided off the modern world from previous history.[1] For whilst both of these existed long before 1760, it was after that date the face of the earth was dramatically changed by them. Industry in itself would have restructured European life, but harnessed to the cause of imperial conquest, it was destined to transform life everywhere by 1940. Imperial achievement was celebrated to the full at international exhibitions. Any study of them that would exclude or underplay this aspect would run the risk of misrepresenting their overall flavour. In their presentation of industry and empire, they reflected more profoundly than any other cultural institution the driving forces behind Western society up to the Second World War. It was both logical and inevitable when governments backed events attempting to reflect the contemporary achievement of mankind that empire would be an uppermost consideration. At some exhibitions the imperial theme was made to dominate to the exclusion of all others. Virtually every Western nation with overseas territories, however slight they might be, participated in imperial sections of exhibitions; even the Americans by the end of the century lauded the idea of empire at World's Fairs, mimicking their European forebears with grim effectiveness. At later British exhibitions empire gushed out of those areas allocated to it, spilling over into every activity on the site. It was so pervasive at the White City Exhibitions for example, that the 'Times' indexed them not under the standard heading 'Science, Art, Music and Drama', or even 'Politics and Home Affairs' but under 'Empire and Foreign Affairs'. The extent of participation by any one nation would normally be gauged by the political, economic and strategic importance of the colonies involved. In the first instance, Britain set the pace for imperial display, before the French took the genre to its extravagant peak in the closing decades of the nineteenth century. For other nations, the evolution of imperial displays quickened after the scramble for Africa. London would therefore seem the logical place to begin the discussion.

The empire the British had acquired affected the total wealth of the mother country far more than was the case with any other imperial nation. By 1849, when the Great Exhibition was in its planning phase, British life was already difficult to conceive of in the absence of overseas resources, the maintenance of these being at the core of foreign policy. On the domestic front, power groups within British society increasingly saw the need to educate the population on the merits of the empire and to encourage the idea of a 'Greater Britain' in terms of one which included imperial gains. Empire was to be 'naturalised' for the British public, settled into their way of life in order to make them feel comfortable with the thought of Africa, Asia and India. If the population at home could be swayed into believing Africa was theirs, the problem of sending troops and resources to defend it would be considerably reduced. Popular pride in empire must be viewed as an emotion that was, in the first instance, artificially generated to facilitate governmental policy abroad; the Great Exhibition can be seen as one of the earliest and most effective examples of this artificial generation.

Virtually the first organizational task that the Royal Commission controlling the Exhibition set itself was the orchestration of colonies, dominions and dependencies into a huge imperial display. The produce of every possession that could be economically transported was to be there; the final list of exhibited colonies was staggeringly impressive: the East Indies, Indian Archipelago, Jersey, Guernsey, Ceylon, Ionian Islands, Malta, Cape of Good Hope, Natal, West Coast of Africa, Canada, Nova Scotia, Newfoundland, New Brunswick, St. Helena, Mauritius, the Seychelles, St. Domingo, Grenada, Montserrat, St. Kitt's, Barbados, Antigua, British Guiana, the Bahamas, Trinidad, the Bermudas, South Australia, Western Australia, New Zealand, New South Wales, Van Diemen's Land, Labuan and Borneo.[2] From the beginning the centrepiece of the imperial sections were to be the contributions of the East India Company. J. Forbes-Royle was appointed to conduct initial negotiations with the Company, which resulted in his 'Papers referring to the proposed contributions from India for the Industrial Exhibition of 1851.' (London 1849). These contained extracts from a report by Henry Cole to Prince Albert on the proposed contribution of India: 'Before concluding this report, we would inform your Royal Highness that, . . . it appeared likely that the East Indies would be able to contribute very largely to the division of the Exhibition proposed to consist of raw materials.' Cole's conception was to present empire as a treasure-house, a vast reservoir of tappable wealth that in itself had little shape or sophistication – hence the label 'raw materials' – but one which could

c

nevertheless stagger the visitor with its extent and opulence. With the Prince of Wales' consent, Cole and his committee determined that the British empire, especially India, would appear as an Alladin's cave to the general public, showing them the full extent of their national belongings.

A dual aim can be detected in the reasoning behind the imperial displays at the Great Exhibition. The grandeur of the material wealth of British possessions was to be made clear; and the necessarily alien nature of the empire was to be reduced and the whole melted into the average British consciousness. The exhibition was to simultaneously glorify and domesticate empire. These goals were potentially contradictory in terms of display, as overpowering exotic wealth was not easily presented so as to not alienate the average British artisan or office clerk. Consequently it was decided to separate out certain centre-pieces for lavish treatment, most notably the Indian Court, and then to largely blend the rest of the empire into the plethora of national exhibits making up the British (western) side of the Crystal Palace. The effect must have been an extraordinary confusion, as the description in the Art Journal Illustrated Catalogue suggests:

> Crossing the transept, and pursuing the course to the left, we enter the western division of the nave. We have here the Indian Court, Africa, Canada, the West Indies, the Cape of Good Hope, the Mediaeval Court, and the English Sculpture Court . . . To these succeed Birmingham, the woollen and mixed fabrics, shawls, flax, and linens, and printing and dyeing. The long avenue leading from the Mediaeval Court to the end of the building is devoted to the general hardware, brass and ironwork of all kinds, locks, gates etc . . .[3]

Unfortunately for the Royal Commission, this dispersal reduced the overall impact of the colonies; only the East Indies appear to have left lingering memories in the minds of visitors.

Like everything else at the Great Exhibition, Empire was a commodity, a thing more important than but not dissimilar to shawls, ironwork, flax, or indeed, sculpture. This point was reinforced by the way the countries within the empire were exhibited, as quantifiable batches of produce rather than as cultures. Only India was partly spared the dissection of its heritage into numbers and types of disposable wealth, but even here the crudely material outlook of the English mind toward its subject-nations manifested itself. India was divided along the lines of the four main categories of the whole exhibition, Raw Materials, Machinery, Manufactures and Fine Arts, with the first of these subdivided into three sections, the 'Animal, Vegetable and Mineral Kingdoms'. The types of produce on display included coal, petroleum earth oil, saltpetre, silex, various types of clay, jasper, marble, precious stones, all kinds of herbs, seed, grain, spices, fruits, ivory, medicines and various types of craftwork. The machinery and manufactures were strictly non-industrial and mainly concerned with agriculture; the catalogue to the Indian section noted the machines (ploughs, seed-drills etc.) were 'of extremely rough workmanship'.[4] By many accounts the most impressive parts of the assemblage were the silks and the metalwork, although on the whole art received a far more generalised assessment than other areas of Indian production; an exception was the praise accorded to the pastichism of the Indian Court itself. Despite a quasi-educational slant, the overall attitude and feeling was one of stocktaking, of an accountant's inventory of a company's possessions. The full significance of 'the jewel in the crown' was being shown off to an awestruck British public and an envious Europe, with every aspect of the prize carefully itemised.

The imperial theme at the Great Exhibition, and most British events following it, was supported by national associations operating in conjunction with government. The earliest of these was the Royal Society of Arts, which had involved itself in colonial affairs from its inauguration in 1754. Its original areas of interest were America and the West Indies, a committee being formed to encourage trade and industry there. Benjamin Franklin was chairman of this committee when he was resident in Britain. Later in its history, the Society clarified its intentions in relation to empire:

> In addition to offering rewards for encouraging the industries of the colonies, the Society rendered them valuable aid by the transmission of seeds, machinery and models, and supplying information. From the correspondence which has been preserved, it is clear that the colonial officials and others were eager to obtain information, and the Society was ready to collect and supply it . . . As the British Empire expanded it was considered advisable to establish a special section of the Society to deal with its varied interests. This is now known as the Dominions and Colonies section.[5]

In 1851 the central rôle the Society had in the organisation of the Great Exhibition guaranteed empire a high profile amid the acres of exhibits. Its continued interest in exhibitions through to the First World War ensured that effective use of imperial resources would always be a main topic of debate at every major international event. Up to the final demise of empire, the Journal of the Royal Society had a regular section on colonial affairs and would involve itself in exhibitions in different colonial centres. For example, exhibitions were supported (and partly sponsored) in Calcutta, Delhi, Victoria, New South Wales, New Zealand and Nova Scotia between 1880 and 1914. Its published reasons for supporting all forms of imperial displays at exhibitions were: '1) To show the resources of the colony off, 2) To awaken local interest and to encourage emulation, and 3) To enhance British trade there.'[6] Thus the Society saw empire as essentially an economic affair and its own self-generated rôle as being one of helping the cause of industrial culture wherever it could be shown to pay the mother country. Throughout its reign as one of the foremost British art institutions, it saw empire, industry, art and design not as unrelated things but as united accoutrements of a powerful, centralised, imperial state.

At the turn of the century the power of the Royal Society began to wane with regard to exhibitions and a new set of institutions came to the fore as guiding spirits. Prominent among these were the various imperial associations, notably the 'British Empire League', the 'Primrose League' and the 'Imperial Federation League'.[7] The first of these had a particularly strong grip on the organisation of the White City Exhibitions, having a power base in the House of Lords which ensured governmental support. The Earl of Derby and Viscount Selby for example, were President and Chairman respectively of both the Central Committee of the Franco–British Exhibition and the British Empire League. Thus imperialism acquired a cultural platform totally lacking a critical dimension.[8] In the decades before the Second World War, it was various bodies associated with the Board of Trade which took care of the British profile at exhibitions, as the age of empire crept unwillingly to its final close.[9]

Following the precedent of 1851, the produce of colonies, dominions and protectorates was carried to exhibition sites all over the world in vast bulk, causing the amount of space afforded to imperial displays to increase from event to event. The key development after the Great Exhibition came when visiting nations as well as the host country insisted upon huge imperial sections. In 1851 the only colony on show outside the British areas was Algiers, taken there by France. By 1855, when the first Paris Exposition Universelle opened, every nation with possessions wished to show them off. The British took an enormous imperial display to Paris, including exhibits from the East India Company, the Bahamas, Barbados, British Guiana, Canada, Cape of Good Hope, Ceylon, Jamaica, Mauritius, New South Wales (Sydney), New Zealand, Van Diemen's Land and Victoria (Melbourne).[10] Nor were they the only ones, for the Dutch exhibits were generally noted to be as impressive. Naturally enough the French, as hosts, outstripped all others both in size and exotic flavour. A precedent was set at this exposition in the form of an 'Imperial Pavilion', a government-built structure separate from the rest of the exhibition housing much of the imperial produce, as well as providing a centre for dignitories to gather. The idea of wholly separate structures for the housing of colonial produce gathered pace from this; by 1876 lavish Colonial Palaces began to appear and larger colonies began to merit their own buildings. By 1890 one would normally expect to find individual palaces to India, Tunisia, Algeria, Canada etc. on the site. Into the twentieth century dominion and colonial palaces became standard features of most exhibitions, occasionally the genre being pushed to extreme proportions until the site resembled a bizarre city of exotic edifices. Amongst the most stunning of the earlier examples were the extraordinary palaces erected by the French to house their Algerian and Tunisian exhibits at the Exposition Universelle of 1889. Built in authentic materials in hybrid North African styles, their apparent grace overcame even the bigotry of English critics reporting on the Exposition. The largest example of the exhibition as an imperial city came in 1924 at the British Empire Exhibition at Wembley, where every colony and dominion able to afford it built a palace to house its exhibits. Some of these covered several acres and cost enormous sums to erect, transforming what had been a drab London suburb into an imperialist's dreamland. Amongst the nations erecting palaces were Canada, India, Australia, New Zealand, Malaya, Burma, Newfoundland, South Africa, West Africa, East Africa, Palestine and Cyprus, Fiji, West Indies, Hong Kong, Ceylon and Sarawak.[11]

Examining British exhibitions from 1851 to 1940, the type and shape of imperialism at work in them can be seen to alter qualitatively much in the way empire changed in the world in general. Because of this, exhibitions can be used as a socio-political gauge for attitudes toward empire throughout the period. A major debate within British imperial studies concerns the nature of continuum in empire. Following the lead of Sir John Seeley, working at the end of the nineteenth century, many historians have depicted the development of the empire as phasal, whereby three discernable periods can be seen to straddle the imperial age: the 'mercantile' (up to the 1830's), the 'anti-imperial' (to the early 1870's) and the 'new imperial' (1870 onwards).[12] The new imperial period, inaugurated by Disraeli's famous Crystal Palace speech of 1872, was the aggressive sequel to a supposed period of 'acquisition by accident' when, in Seeley's words, Britain seemed '. . . as it were, to have conquered and peopled half the world in a fit of absence of mind'.[13] This view came under increasing attack in the 1950's from historians who detected a far more continuous development of empire than the anti-imperial phase would suggest. These historians stressed the economically abrasive edge to British imperial policy through the second half of the nineteenth century and attacked the idea that empire was received as an unwanted burden at that time.[14] The major function of such a view, it has been suggested, was to humanise and underplay the real nature of British imperial ambition and to deny the essentially economic rôle of British policy. Within the debate, the exhibitions become interesting indicators of the real intent behind empire, for they reveal the extent of the value government and major economic forces placed on it through the period.

Most importantly, the unfolding of the exhibition tradition from 1851 does not support the idea of an 'anti-imperial' phase as being anything more than a fluctuating Parliamentary debate. From 1851 onwards empire was proudly and exhaustively displayed. In 1862 at the London South Kensington exhibition thirty-five colonies and dominions were shown; a similar number appeared in 1871, 1872, 1873 and 1874 at the International Exhibitions also in South Kensington. Parliament, Crown and private enterprise lent support to all these events, the last two of which should have evidenced the beginnings of a shift from 'anti' to 'new' imperialism, which they did not. They simply showed the proud bombast with which the British regarded their empire, a bombast that did not fade into the twentieth century. Neither was there anything in British exhibits in foreign exhibitions showing an anti-imperial stance from government or the private sector at any time. Anti-imperial speeches in Parliament carried far less weight in the outside world it would appear, than many future historians accorded them. Into the 1880's however there was a distinct shift in emphasis at exhibitions. The aftermath of the scramble for Africa left the British wary of the imperial ambitions of her European rivals and worried for the safety of her own empire. The Colonial and Indian Exhibition (London 1886) revealed a move from complacent pride in empire to a propagandistic defence of it. Empire became proportionately more a topic for abrasive forms of entertainment and less one for quasi-educational displays. By the time of the 'Greater Britain Exhibition' (London 1899), a climate of jingoism had evolved, with most exhibitions both reflecting and fueling this. After the Boer War, into the twentieth century, exhibitions became increasingly vocal about empire, as its permanence was for the first time at issue. Imperial propaganda grew as Britain declined, the vulgarity and violence of exhibitions in this regard becoming markedly more noticeable. What had always been assumed in the nineteenth century now had to be justified and defended in the twentieth, as the demise of British industry made empire all the more vital for the maintenance of her position. Literally dozens of substantial National Imperial exhibitions were held in different cities in the British Isles after 1900, presenting empire to the public in the form of museum-like displays, constructed environments and popular entertainment. Among the most impressive of these were at Edinburgh (1886), Bradford (1904), Wolverhampton (1907) and Newcastle (1929).[15] Larger shows at the White City (London 1908–1914), Wembley (London 1924–5) and Glasgow (1901, 1911 and 1938) carried the imperial theme onto an epic scale. This activity brought an irony to the exhibition tradition, in that the century which saw the disappearance of empire was also the one that lauded it most lavishly.

From 1851 to 1940 then, committment to empire at exhibitions never slackened or lost its fervour, it merely changed emphasis. This could be said of British concern for empire in general; during the brief period between the scramble for Africa and the Boer War, the calm expansiveness of British imperial policy foundered and an attitude of 'benevolent' appropriation became one of increasingly paranoic defence. The ambition to consume as much as possible became a frenzied desire to hold on to what had already been won. Exhibitions became a propaganda ground for imperial justification, attempting to reinforce the unity of empire and to imbue the British public with an imperial pride. In the second of these, they undoubtedly succeeded.[16]

The British imperial policy at exhibitions was most clearly demonstrated with regard to India. India was the most carefully displayed possession at the Great Exhibition and continued to be so throughout the period under discussion at home and abroad. The Indian Court in 1851 filled 30,000 square feet; the South Kensington Exhibition of 1862 was a smaller but more extravagant affair than its predecessor, covering a total floor space of 10,000 square feet. At the Paris Exposition Universelle of 1867, 8,700 sq.ft. were filled at a cost of £4,562; in London again, at the four events in South Kensington between 1871–1874, 8,000 square feet were filled at a total cost of £7,351. At Vienna in 1873, 10,000 square feet cost £12,342 and at the Paris Exposition Universelle of 1878 an Indian Court covering 20,000 square feet cost £3,278. From 1880 the trend was an upward one both in cost and size. In 1886 Indian exhibits at the Colonial and Indian Exhibition filled 103,000 sq.ft. at an expenditure of £22,000.[17] At least twenty-four further Indian Palaces and Courts were erected in foreign exhibitions between 1886 and 1939. Large teams of administrators and skilled workmen were constantly employed all over the world to build and fill these expensive temporary buildings. No evidence has emerged so far to indicate whether the buildings were ever taken from one exhibition site to another, the usual pattern being to demolish and dispense with them completely and start afresh at the succeeding event. The funding for the Palaces normally came from three sources, the Indian government, the British government and private enterprise. Of the three, the Indian government paid the lion's share, normally about half to two thirds the total cost. The usual branch of private enterprise to fund the Indian exhibits were the tea companies, notably the Calcutta Tea Syndicate. There were exceptions to this pattern, for example the Colonial and Indian Exhibition, where the total bill of £22,000 was divided as follows: Indian

Government £10,000, Royal Commission (effectively the British Government) £3,000, Bombay Exhibition Grant £6,850 and the Royal Commission Screen Grant £2,500. The origin of these last two authorities is unclear, but it does appear that they were officially appointed, indicating that on this occasion all the money came from governmental sources.[18]

The exhibiting of India developed onto its grandest scale in the twentieth century, beginning with a grand palace at the Paris Universelle of 1900. Following the established pattern this was a treasurehouse full of opulent produce, complete with beautifully dressed Indians serving as exhibition attendants. For one of the first times in recent imperial history however, some were prepared to criticise what they saw as a gross distortion of the Indian story. The revelling in conquest which had seemingly undergone no public challenge during the previous century now had its detractors. Maurice Talmeyr, a catholic writer reviewing the Exposition for the 'Revue des Deux Mondes' attacked what he saw as an India presented by British overlords:

> ... why is starving India incarnated in well-coiffed, well nourished, well clothed Indians? Because famine is not and never can be an Exposition attraction ... The notion ... of an India warehouse, so magnificent and so partially true as it may be, is true only partially, so partially as to be false, and these overflowing rooms ... speak to me only of an incomplete and truncated India, that of the cashiers. And the other? That of the famine? For this land of enormous and sumptuous trade is equally that of a frightening local degeneracy, of a horrifying indigenous misery. A whole phantom race dies there and suffers in famine. India is not only a warehouse, it is a cemetery.[19]

Impervious to such criticism, British organisers continued to expand the scope of Indian displays. At the Franco–British Exhibition of 1908, a splendid building, complete with minarets, towers and domes housed a huge selection of produce which undoubtedly had an effect on popular taste at the time. In addition to this, various entertainments were provided to explain Indian life since British rule to an inquisitive audience.[20] Perhaps more interesting than these latter pieces of jingoism was the centrepiece of the exhibition, the Court of Honour. This was to remain virtually unchanged through all the exhibitions held at the White City up to 1914.[21] A critic at the time remarked that the style of the Court appeared not to reflect the theme of the exhibition, the Entente Cordiale of 1904:

> Here we have a village of steel and stucco palaces raised to commemorate the falling on each others necks of two great nations, and, the last thing the architect seems to have thought of was to make his buildings reflect the situation. The Court of Honour is neither French or English, but

Mohamedan-Hindoo, and the other buildings have more in common with the architecture of Spanish America or of an ununited Germany than with anything in the two countries involved.[22]

In actuality, the Court of Honour intentionally had little to do with France, but was a bizarre mixture of India and Britain, a mingling of minarets, onion domes and Indian tracery with the then fashionable 'Edwardian baroque' style. The architect, Commissioner-general Imre Kiralfy, had achieved in architecture what the British government sought to achieve in other spheres of British life, the irretrievable fusion of Britain with India. Eastern exoticism gave drama and excitement to facades composed in a staid English classicism. In the architectural fabric of the Court of Honour, empire was displayed to fulfill its two essential rôles at exhibitions. It showed off the epic scale of the wealth India brought to Britain, and it settled India into the English scene, harmonizing it into English vision in a way which felt natural, even permanent.

The last significant Indian Palace to be built in Britain was also the most impressive, in 1924 at the Empire Exhibition at Wembley. As with many of the exhibitions held in Britain after 1880, the Wembley show was international only by virtue of its empire, as other countries were not invited to participate. Thus the imperial theme saturated the whole site in a fashion rivalled only by the last great imperial exhibition, in Glasgow in 1938.[23] At Wembley, the Indian site covered five acres, the Palace itself three acres, with a total expenditure of £180,000. The Official Guide described the apparent effect of the Palace, which was the second most expensive and by far the largest present:

An Anglo–Indian who has devoted many years of his life to the civil service, said as he came from the Indian Pavilion one afternoon in May that he had now seen India for the first time . . . He had travelled upwards of thirty years along the main roads of Indian administration, seeing much, but inevitably missing more, while at Wembley all India swam into his gaze . . ..[24]

One of the main functions of the building was to show all that Britain had done for India since her arrival there. This had been a rôle of Indian Palaces since the 'Colonial and Indian' exhibition, the theme often meriting an area of its own by the turn of the century. At the Festival of Empire of 1911 (London, Crystal Palace), for example, the Official Guide pointed out that 'a small section has been arranged to show the progress which has been made in India under British rule in the past sixty years.' At Wembley, British help to India was assessed more passionately,

. . . we must realise, even if we have no more than a little imagination, how ceaselessly Britain has wrought for India, how much has been accomplished, how much remains yet to do . . . To understand the resources and variety of India as set out in the Pavilion, and to grasp the part Great Britain has played in developing one and unifying the other, is to understand why the title of King Emperor is the first of all titles throughout the world.[25]

Obsession with India obviously had its basis in economic dependence, the extraordinary attention given to the Indian continent at exhibitions exposing both a pride in possession and a terror at the thought of loss. As has already been suggested, India was widely thought of as a reservoir which could be drained into the British economy, an inanimate 'thing' to be used as one used coal or flax. In varying degrees the analogy could be made across all British territories. It was no coincidence that the Indian and Colonial Exhibition of 1886 came at the end of a sequence of four annual international exhibitions, the others of which, Fisheries, Health and Inventions, were not cultures but types of produce.[26] The sequence revealed a good deal about British attitudes to empire; it was variously considered as a resource, as a commodity, as something the British had created, as an abstract concept; it could be many things in fact, except people with lives and traditions of their own. Such an admission raised the issue of exploitation, a topic which never emerged throughout the history of British exhibitions.

The approach to dominions and colonies other than India was usually below this intense level, depending upon the status and value of the nation involved. The standard format in Britain and in British contributions to foreign exhibitions from 1893 onwards was one whereby colonies and dominions were displayed according to their economic usefulness. A total colonial section would usually involve the creation of a single composite display of lesser territories and a small number of separate pavilions and palaces to larger ones. Thus, in 1938 at the Glasgow International, a 'Colonial Avenue' was built, containing within it individual national pavilions and a multi-nation Colonial Court, described in the official catalogue:

> Represented in the Colonial Court are Malaya, the West Indies, and a composite group of Colonies, Protectorates and Dependencies, including Cyprus and Malta, Ceylon, British North Borneo and Sarawak, Hong Kong, the Falkland Islands, Somaliland, Bechuanaland, and others. They are grouped around a central exhibit which illustrates their trade with Britain. In the background are tropical forests, fields of rice with maize, and a strip of yellow sand, with caravans winding down toward the sea which occupies most of the foreground. In the immediate foreground are the ports of Britain, and between them and the distant tropics, fleets of ships sail.[27]

A 'diorama' such as this was a normal display method, two central themes being evident. First the 'lesser' territories were to be seen as a single concern, a grouped resource fused together as an economic unit with Britain as the common factor to link them. Despite their very different geographic locations and traditions, they were fused into the proverbial 'over there', with Britain at the centre of their world focus. Second, Britain was depicted as being in close physical proximity to its possessions in order to make them 'feel' British in popular consciousness. The message to the average British person visiting Colonial Court was clear, 'this is yours, see how naturally it fits into your own way of life.'

The major white dominions, colonies and commonwealth territories were normally separate from other nations of the empire after 1870; increasingly from the opening of the new century they showed a willingness to build substantial pavilions to house their exhibits. The economic motives behind this willingness were trade, which could receive noticeable stimulation from a good showing, and emigration. By 1908, a spirit of rivalry had grown between these nations, revealing itself in an eagerness to rent the best areas of sites and to erect the largest building. Australia, Canada, New Zealand and South Africa were the principal rivals, newspaper reports showing that exhibition jealousies could become openly aggressive. At the Franco–British Exhibition for example, the Australian organisers took the Commissioner-General to court because he had allowed a building to be erected partly across the frontal facade of their building. The claim was that they had paid an exceptionally large rent on the understanding that the view of the Pavilion facade would be completely unobstructed. The Commissioner, Imre Kiralfy, failed to appear to explain his position, the case being settled out of court by a refund of part of the Australian rent.[28] At many of the twentieth-century events the urgency of the new nations to excel came out of a desire to show Europe they had achieved a cultural respectability to match their more utilitarian accomplishments. Splendid classical pavilions from New Zealand, Canada, Australia and South Africa stood as confirmation that the colonial stage had been transcended, and independence had been gained not only materially but culturally also.[29]

British imperialism, as a vital force at the centre of the British way of life, was bound to appear at exhibitions in a more thoroughly conceived way than the imperialism of her major European rivals. This is not to say other nations cared less about the presentation of their foreign acquisitions but that the range of messages they carried were not so extensive or so subtly constructed. As late as 1925 many European displays carried a 'spoils of war' flavour with them, an implicit glorying in the rich pickings of foreign campaigns and a revelling in military power. The only consistent exception to this pattern were the Dutch, who concentrated almost exclusively on the history of their empire and its raison d'être in trade. Whilst the approach of Portugal, Belgium or France to the acquisition of territory was no more or less brutal or even tactically different from that of the English, there was a tendency to be more 'matter-of-fact' about it at exhibitions. The British had a long-term concern to tie empire into the national economic fabric using means other than the force which initially acquired it. Domestication and reconciliation were persistent elements in her exhibitions from 1851. These were less important to most other nations, who, despite the vicious way they tended to hang onto their gains, regarded empire more as an economic bonus or as a symbolic indicator of power than as an economic life's-blood. Only into the third decade of this century did reconciliation and harmony within colonies become a major concern of European powers at exhibitions, when economic depression made empire all the more important. The pattern for most nations was set by the French, who gloried in empire at the Expositions Universelles more brilliantly but in a less deeply constructed way than the British.

It was the French in fact who first displayed imperial gains at exhibitions when they brought produce from Antilles to the 1839 National Exhibition at the Champs Elysées. In 1844 at the tenth National event, also held at the Champs Elysées, Réunion, Pondichery and Guadeloupe appeared. At the Exhibition of 1849, these three were once more presented and for the first time Algeria was shown to the French public as one of their national possessions. Whilst the very first national displays had carried Napoleonic imperialism within their scope, with the showing, for example, of art objects taken from Italy, the displays of 1839, 1844 and 1849 were the real forerunners, probably providing the English with food for thought as they prepared their own imperial sections for the Great Exhibition.[30] When the first Exposition Universelle opened in 1855 the imperial theme was immediately evident from two sources. As has already been noted, an Imperial Pavilion marked French gains, but more than this, foreign nations had by now grasped the imperial potential of exhibitions after the Great Exhibition, where only the host country was fully aware of its intended rôle. Virtually every imperial possession in the world was represented on the site, making the event an appropriate show piece for its main sponsor, Napoleon the Third. Algeria was the centre-piece of French efforts, effectively being the equivalent of India for the English. The scale and opulence of the displays and the heavy presence of the French imperial armies led historian Raymond Isay to comment 'L'Exposition Universelle, d'abord envisagée comme une fête de la paix, devint, du fait des circonstances, une manifestation de guerre'.[31] The French sense of rivalry with the English had a direct bearing on the imperial sphere, in the care and expense they went to in the presentation of their empire; from this point in time the two nations were to persistently attempt to out-do each other in their imperial exhibits until the outbreak of the Second World War. The statistical inferiority of the French territories did not prevent them from spending vast sums on display, and the undoubted excellence of the pavilions they erected did not prevent the English from indulging in snide comments upon them. The exhibitions came, by 1889, to expose both countries as spoiled children attempting to out-boast each other with their vast and priceless toys.

In the Exposition Universelle of 1867 the French empire received considerably more space than in 1855, as Napoleon III attempted to give full meaning to his title. Tunisia and Morocco joined Algeria as the main centre-pieces, these three meriting their own sections and organising juries. The Exposition was untypically systematic in its presentation of empire. Following the British pattern, displays went well beyond the finer end of the cultural spectrum, providing exhaustive economic and demographic information. Morocco for example was divided into the following sections: geography, population, government, imports, the military, principal towns, agriculture, commerce abroad, commerce at home, industry, science and art.[32] Whilst statistical analysis was always a part of French display, organisers normally preferred to put these elements in side rooms or annexes in order to leave the central spaces for large splashes of exotic produce and decor. In 1878 this was the case, the emphasis being more on oriental romance than on learning. Here the imperial displays were put in facilities on the Chaillot Hill leading up to the Palais de Trocadéro, the French taking half the space with other nations filling the rest. The larger French colonies had their own buildings, the rest being in a single colonial palace; other nations had national buildings to house their possessions. This was the largest space so far given up to empire at any exhibition anywhere and was the beginning of the genre whereby imperial sections were presented as exotic cities of pavilions and palaces. The sloping site in front of the Palais de Trocadéro was kept for the imperial sections at the two following Expositions Universelles, when the scene blossomed into a baroque exhuberance of different cultures.

Despite the care taken by French organisers to show overseas territories as exciting and viable additions to French holdings, empire was not always popularly acknowledged with the unrelenting awe it received in Britain. After the Franco–Prussian War many Frenchmen had come to regard African and Asian gains as being minor side issues compared with the real European loss. Indeed, there can be no doubt the government in 1878, and in the following Exposition of 1889, used the empire to detract from widespread desire to regain Alsace-Lorraine. Celebrating the gains in Africa, it was vainly hoped, would compensate for losses nearer home and help rebuild French national confidence. With this rationale, vast sums were spent in 1889 on displays that were to provide the model for all imperial exhibitions which followed, including those held in Britain.

Several sources indicate that it was the London Colonial and Indian Exhibition of 1886 which inspired the massively enhanced imperial Parisian display in 1889; [33] this may be the case but the decision to build a town of pavilions and palaces remains a wholly French one. The pavilions sprawled over one hundred acres between the Champs de Mars and the Trocadéro and were so positioned as to form the core of the Exposition. A reporter working on the site for the English publication the 'Pall Mall Gazette' was particularly enlightening on the display, not only for his eloquent description but for his pronounced sense of envy and rivalry:

> As you pass palace after palace and pagoda after pagoda, you seem to gain a continually increasing conception of the grandeur of France outre mer, which contrasts curiously with the impression produced by studying the colonial question before a map. The French chef who produced a dainty banquet out of the sole of an old boot has been out done by the genius who conjured up this phantasmagoria of a colonial empire out of the few out-of-the-way-bits of territory over which, Algeria excepted, the Tricolour is flying... Palace succeeds palace each reproducing the salient features of tl e architecture of the country represented: gay and gorgeous pagodas, like architectural parrots, add vivid outlandish colour to the scene, while native temples and colonial pavilions create a pleasing sense of bewilderment and magnificence.[34]

Such a report did more than simply confirm the continuing existence of competition between the two nations – soon to be exacerbated by the Fashoda crisis – it also highlighted the disproportionate emphasis the French placed upon empire at that time, an emphasis welling out of political expediency rather than economic reality. As large as French gains had been up to 1889, this imperial weighting betrayed politically motivated exaggeration. Predictably, the most impressive palaces according to newspaper reports were those of Algeria and Tunis, the latter being described as 'a graceful oriental edifice'.[35] French Indo-China also provided French pastiche architects with rich source material. A Colonial Palace was filled with surplus produce, where those territories too small to erect a building for could be found. French India was heavily presented here, mainly in the form of Pondichery, while other notable exhibits came from Senegal (mainly skins), New Caledonia (nickel and other mined produce), Cayenne (mostly the manufactures of convicts), the French West Indies (sugar and rum) and miscellaneous raw materials from Obock, Nossi-Bé, Mayotte, Tahitti and others. Statistical information could be found in the side-rooms of this building. Adjacent to the imperial pavilions in the Palais de Trocadéro itself there was an extensive ethnological exhibition. Aboriginal, African and Oceanic objects of various types and periods were present in quantity and pre-Columbian artefacts were shown in Europe for the first time. The Trocadéro was soon to become associated with non-Western art and was to be the venue for many important exhibitions up to its demolition in 1937. The site is still the main centre for anthropological exhibitions in Paris, the successor to the Trocadéro, the Palais de Chaillot, now housing the Musée de l'Homme.

At the Exposition Universelle of 1900 the colonial area was expanded still further, becoming the most impressive aspect of the site. This was indeed a feat for the show as a whole has commonly thought to have been the most spectacular ever held. The Hachette Guide described the scene as it appeared looking west from the first stage of the Eiffel Tower:

> The Trocadéro, with its symetrical fan-shape, envelops the mass of pavilions. To the left, recalling the Byzantium of the empresses and the Moscow of Ivan the Terrible, rise the gilded ridges of the Siberian Pavilion. At the top a large heraldic bird begins its flight of conquest over Asia, which lies out at its feet like a tame leopard... Lower down, the sculptured structures of the Dutch Indies display their red and blue masses. Sumatra, Borneo and Java... Roofs, curved at the corners in the form of ships prows, cover the sanctuary with elaborate freizes where Buddha, with eight arms and eight legs, rests on the immortal lotus. Nearby, to the right, rises the graceful spire of the pavilion of the Transvaal and in the background, beyond the masses of greenery, the inextricable entanglement of the Chinese roofs bears witness to the active presence of the children of the Celestial Empire.[36]

A bristling panoply of steel, stone and plaster structures, curiously resembling a massive set for an epic silent film, the colonial sections at the 1900 Exposition saw Europe at its presumptuous, confident peak, long before the nightmare of the First World War brought the curtain down on the era. Empire here was transformed from military and commercial conquest, from the brutal control of other peoples for cynical economic purposes, to propagandistic entertainment, to a fair. The gaiety of the pavilions was purposely meant to hide the darker side of the gloried conquest, the near genocide which had at different times occurred all over the imperial world, the destruction of cultures, the appropriation of wealth on an unprecedented and greed-ridden scale. The

Exposition was in every way a harlequin's mask hiding brutish, heavy features beneath. This of course did not prevent it from transfixing its audience. Across the cultural range this swirling mass of minarets, palm trees and pagodas exerted an influence and provoked admiration.

After 1900 there was a gap of twenty-five years before Paris staged an event of comparable stature, but successive French governments took great care to maintain an imperial stance at all major foreign events, usually providing a lavish publication for their imperial sections, separate from the main catalogue. The beautifully produced guide to the French Empire on sale at the New York World's Fair in 1939 was testament to the fact that interest had by no means slackened, even with the German war looming.[37] Pride in the African empire, in part generated to detract from the loss of Alsace-Lorraine, would eventually lead France into one of the last and bloodiest of imperial conflicts. The expositions played their part in convincing Frenchmen that possession of Algeria was worth dying for. French displays in foreign exhibitions, as with the English, became distinctly more propagandistic as the twentieth century progressed. One of the more interesting efforts came in London in 1908, at the Franco-British Exhibition, when French and British empires appeared head on, with no other nations present. The British felt themselves able to revel in the statistical side of things:

> In no other country do the theory and practice of colonization receive more careful attention than in France. The French colonies, dependencies and spheres of influence, second in number only to those of Great Britain, have an area of over four million square miles and a population of over sixty million.[38]

It was generally acknowledged however, despite the competitiveness of the English, that the Palaces erected to Tunisia and Algeria comfortably equalled the one built for India, making the significance of the two empires indistinguishable in the eyes of the exhibition visitor.[39]

The Expositions Universelles of 1925 and 1937 maintained the colonial element despite the insistence both had on positive aspects of modern life, although it had shrunk back somewhat from the excesses of 1889 and 1900. The 1925 show was more centrally based around the visual (decorative) arts than any international exhibition before or after, and so understandably a main issue was the definition of 'colonial art' as a type. The main catalogue provided a definition which was surprisingly wide:

> There are three types of colonial art. The first, in the exact meaning of the word, is the indigenous art; another is the art practiced by the colonials of European origin, who incorporate or juxtapose their own needs, their own science and aesthetic with the primitive civilizations. Lastly the same

name is convenient for works of Europeans influenced by exoticism. The three types of art figure in the exhibition.[40]

The third type was not shown with the indigenous forms it was inspired by but was with other European art-forms spread through the public and private pavilions. In retrospect the categorization of it as 'colonial' does seem to be a bizarre eccentricity.[41] Having defined colonial art, the catalogue asked another potentially interesting question, 'Comment peut-il être moderne?', but for this there was no immediate answer.

In 1937 an extensive French colonial section was located west of the Champs de Mars in pavilions built on huge pontoons floating on the Seine. There were separate buildings to Morocco, Tunisia, Guadaloupe, Indochina, Martinique, Madagascar, Algeria, Réunion and Corsica. Foreign nations had their colonial exhibits within their own pavilions. Whilst the overall imperial flavour was perceivably not as strong as it had been at the turn of the century, this was not particularly due to a slackening interest in empire. On the contrary, the drift from excessive imperialism at the last two Expositions Universelles was caused by the growth of alternative expositions based entirely on the imperial theme. Huge colonial expositions were held in Marseilles in 1906 and 1922, where the usual bias of French events toward the arts was virtually forgotten. Marseilles staged these expositions because 'In Marseilles, everybody – high and low, big and little – thinks colonially. Very few of France's overseas possessions are not linked directly with this port . . . Marseilles . . . owed a duty to itself to call attention to its efforts and its results in the colonial sense.'[42] More spectacular than the Marseilles shows was the Paris Exposition Internationale Coloniale of 1931, held in the Parc de Vincennes.[43] Appearing in some ways to be a response to the British Empire show at Wembley six years previous, Vincennes bristled with dozens of flamboyant pavilions in the form of temples, pagodas and mosques. A permanent Musée des Colonies and large botanical gardens were also built on the site. Unlike the Wembley show the empires of other nations were included, Britain being the only major absentee.[44] The French contribution included separate buildings to Madagascar, Indochina, St. Pierre-et-Miquelon, French Guiana, the French Indies, Oceania, New Caledonia, Martinique, Réunion, Guadeloupe, French Equatorial Africa, North Africa, West Africa, Morocco, Tunisia and Algeria.[45] This was the most spectacular of French imperial displays since 1900. In comparison, the floating pavilions of 1937 seemed noncommittal and ephemeral; for the French the Internationale Coloniale was the climax of their colonial displays. As with the empire itself, every effort after then seemed to hint at decline.

Vincennes focused Western imperialism more dramatically than any exhibition before or after it; only the absence of the British prevented it from being the most comprehensive event of its type in the tradition. Large pavilions were erected by Belgium, Holland, Portugal, Italy, Denmark and the U.S.A.. The desire to have an imperial profile was such it seems, that any claim was worth display space. Denmark exhibited Greenland; Italy, whose empire was diminutive at the time, played heavily on her glorious imperial tradition as established by the Romans. The other nations had more significant contributions to make, their appearance in the Internationale Coloniale being part of well established policies by 1931. Belgium, Holland and Portugal had been active displayers of empire since the last decade of the nineteenth century, when the scramble for Africa brought empires to those least expecting them.

Portugal had been surprisingly prominent as an imperial exhibitor throughout the twentieth century. A lavish display in her national pavilion at the Paris Exposition of 1900 and a further one at the Imperial International Exhibition of 1909 in London established a trend which developed to a high pitch in the 1930's. At the Paris Coloniale Internationale no less than three separate buildings were erected, designed to reflect her long standing as a colonizing power. The Guide explained:

> The first two pavilions of Portugal evoke this glorious past. The first, in its architecture, follows the inspiration of Portuguese constructions of the fifteenth century, where the influence of the Moors lingers, mixed with the austere ruggedness of Henry the Navigator, initiator of so many overseas enterprises. This pavilion contains evidence of the oldest Portuguese expeditions ... The second pavilion is devoted to Alphonso of Albuquerque, who died at the beginning of the sixteenth century, after having given to his country, among other marvellous lands, Ormuz, Goa, Malacca ... Such men are the vital force of a nation ... And now, dear Visitor, let us return to the Grand Pavilion, which houses the exposition of the two African territories; Angola and Mozambique. These two territories are the most important from the territorial viewpoint; within them are to be found the greatest possibilities for economic development.[46]

The Guide also noted other Portuguese possessions on display, including the Cape Green Islands, Portuguese Guiana, the islands of San Tomé and Principe, Goa in India, Macoa in China and Timor in Oceania. In its completeness it represented the high-point of Portuguese imperial exhibits, although there were significant displays to follow before the outbreak of the Second World War. At the Paris Exposition Universelle of 1937, for example, a 'Salle Outre-Mer' was created in the national pavilion, centring on Angola and Mozambique.[47] A large photomontage display explained the economy of the two territories, alongside examples of the extensive range of raw produce extracted from them. In

1940 a Colonial Exhibition was held in Lisbon itself.[48]

Holland and Belgium were the most consistent European exhibitors of empire throughout the exhibition tradition after Britain and France. Both sent colonial exhibits to major events and occasionally had exhibitions of their own with an imperial dimension. The Dutch was one of the oldest and most lucrative of all world empires, a fact they themselves were keen to acknowledge in international company. Displays were taken to all the Paris Expositions Universelles, to the South Kensington Exhibition of 1862, the Imperial International Exhibition of 1909 (both in London) and to numerous other exhibitions in Europe. Quite surprisingly, they still exuded a proud imperial spirit in 1931, at the Internationale Coloniale:

> Today, the Netherlands consider that they belong, not only to countries with overseas possessions, but that the Dutch West Indies are so important in world economics that they can be considered as a great colonial power. The Netherlands are not wrong. We must rank them among the first colonizers of the world.[49]

Belgian imperialism was a more recent phenomenon, belonging almost entirely to the last decades of the nineteenth century when Leopold the Second benefitted his country out of the scramble for Africa. At the Internationale Coloniale his rôle was heavily emphasised in the official literature, which gave an overall impression of the Belgian Congo as a giant business speculation. Three pavilions sheltered exhibits on the history, economy, demography and geography of the single possession.

Perhaps a better guide to Belgian imperial consciousness is provided by their own events; after the French, British and Americans they had the most consistent policy for the holding of international exhibitions. It was here the Belgian empire received its greatest embellishment. Expositions Universelles in Brussels in 1897 and 1910, in Liége in 1905 and 1930, and Antwerp in 1894 and 1930 all had extensive imperial sections. The last two in Liége and Antwerp in 1930 were held simultaneously as a joint celebration of the centenary of independence. Antwerp had Colonial, Maritime and Flemish Art displays, Liége had Science, Industry, Social Economy, Agriculture and Music; between them, as it were, they made up one large Exposition. The colonial display in Antwerp was the most ambitious Belgian effort ever and the largest held outside Britain or France. It is deserving of more historical attention than it has hitherto received. The major European Empires could be found on the Avenue de la Colonie, including Britain, France, Holland, Portugal, Italy and, in pride of place, Belgium. The main Belgian building, named the 'Palais du Congo', had a curiously hybrid appearance the General Report of the Exhibition felt itself bound to explain:

Externally, the pavilion has a more oriental than Congolese character. One could not find in Congolese art the inspiration for the great architectural forms of this palace, the artist has used very advantageously, in the ornament, engravings certain populations indigenous to the Belgian Congo use on their weapons and utensils, and characteristic geometric drawings one can find on the mats of certain tribes in our colony.[50]

In his ethnocentricity the architect decided the Congo could not provide a suitable form for the pavilion housing its produce, it could only aspire to provide decorative trimmings. In exhibition architecture, African building forms were only used when the designer sought an authentic setting. It would then serve in the manner of a stage set in an attempt to mentally transport the visitor away from northern Europe.[51] In 1924 at Wembley and 1931 at Vincennes for example, the British, French and Belgians all constructed mock African fortresses and meeting houses, in the absence of any serious architectural considerations. If a permanent or significant building were needed, the furthest move from a European construction one could expect would be a pastiche of Indian, Arabic or Eastern architecture. The architect in charge of the Palais du Congo at Antwerp went as far as racially determined stylistic conventions would allow him.[51]

The Antwerp Exposition took a more rigorously rational approach to display of empire than many before it, having a long list of categories for exhibits which visiting nations were requested to adhere to. This was out of character with most exhibitions held after the First World War, being reminiscent of British Victorian events and the Paris show of 1867. The categories were: the history of colonization, geography and cartography, indigenous population, indigenous politics, government and administration, the judiciary, medicine, hygiene, medical assistance to the colonies, missions, development in labour, civil engineering, transport, commerce, financial organisation, agriculture including breeding, hunting and fishing, agricultural industry, heavy industry, mining, and diverse products. It is not recorded as to whether the other nations followed this pattern with any exactitude but it is likely they did, as prizes were awarded for the best displays in any one subject area.

Everything indicates the participants considered Antwerp an important imperial event. The French, Dutch and British all built substantial structures, the Dutch one being the most unusual of these in that it was designed in what was a late and eccentric version of art nouveau, which must have seemed strangely uncomfortable in surroundings of such pomp. Aware they were not going to participate in the Paris Internationale Coloniale, Britain made a special effort at the Antwerp Exposition.[52] The General Report recognised this, and acknowledged also the progressive display techniques used:

> Great Britain has supplied us, with great success, with a model of the new
> style exhibition . . . more than a fair intended to entertain the crowds who
> come to idly stroll: a parade of dioramas, models and electrically lit maps
> are put under the eyes of the curious, without requiring on their part any
> effort to understand, a suite of images at once concise and living of her
> history, her navy, her aviation, of her dominions, a striking synthesis of
> her imperial strength.[53]

It is difficult to ascertain who exactly applied these technologically
enhanced display methods to imperial exhibits first, but by 1930 they
were widely used. The British appear to have been early masters of the
techniques, showing a progressiveness strangely out of step with retrogressive attitudes evident elsewhere in their design practices. French
and Portuguese efforts in Antwerp were less exciting than the British. In
the case of the former the decision to participate at all was taken mainly
as a courtesy to the Belgians, as the Internationale Coloniale was less
than a year away. For the latter the General Report tells us the decision
to take part was made late, preventing anything but the meagrest of
buildings to be erected. Even so, the colonial sections as a whole bulked
large, proudly showing to the Belgian population the riches that
European imperial exploits had brought.

There were a number of European nations which did not take part in any
committed way in the imperial sections of exhibitions. Most notable
amongst these were Spain, Germany, Russia and Austria. In the case of
the first two, explanations are simple enough. Spain lost much of her
South American territory by 1900, just as the temperature of imperial
propaganda rose generally, and her other holdings were negligible. For
her, imperial displays could do little more than remind her of a former
glory that could never return. Germany had won a reasonable slice of the
African cake as it was divided at the end of the century but still had only
a tiny overseas empire compared to her two major rivals, Britain and
France. By her own standards there was little to gain in terms of prestige
from an imperial display. A small nation could enhance its world image
by displaying its empire, no matter how small, but a nation already
believing itself great stood to gain nothing by drawing attention to its
meagre foreign possessions. In any case, neither Spain nor Germany had
much of an exhibition tradition and so the idiom had little opportunity
or real need to evolve. This latter point holds for Russia and Austria.
Both held large events in the nineteenth century, in Moscow (1872) and
Vienna (1873), but there was no consistent policy after that date. Moreover, the nature of their respective empires rendered them generally
unsuitable for most exhibitions. The flavour of imperial displays was

non-European, that is, in the nineteenth and twentieth centuries empire usually suggested overseas conquest. Imperialism referred to the colonization of the non-Western world through trade and technology, which tended to exclude the old European based empires, epitomised by the type of control Austria and Russia exercised over their territories.[54] Particularly in the case of Austria, most of her empire was on the European land-mass and was of a different type from the progressive and voracious exploitation practiced by other nations. The notion of empire at the exhibitions was not linked so much with feudal domination as with scientific and economic progress. At the end of the nineteenth century industrial hardware and political shrewdness counted for much in the race to carve up the undeveloped portions of the globe. The 'new' empires were a result of free trade, industry, speculation and mobile, unoccupied armies. Relatively few European nations possessed all or even any of these resources at any one time. The time was therefore ripe for some but not others to claim an empire overseas.

Outside Europe there were forces progressively active in world politics at the end of the nineteenth century that had all the necessary resources for expansion. Of these, Japan and the United States of America were most powerful, and also most eager to show off their gains at international exhibitions. Japan's modern imperialism came strikingly to the attention of Europe after the Russo–Japanese War of 1904–5, when Russia's humiliating defeat made the rest of the world thoroughly aware of the strength of the Japanese war machine. Japan had been a major exhibitor in European and American exhibitions since 1862, but it was only after 1905 that empire was a properly discernable feature. At the Japan–British Exhibition of 1910 at the White City, the full weight of her imperial pride was brought to bear. The Official Guide acknowledged there was 'sufficient to justify the Eastern empire's claim to respect as a colonising power'.[55] A sizable display in the Japanese Colonial Palace was eloquently described:

> The whole of this building has been taken by the Japanese government to show what they have accomplished in their colonies and in Formosa, Korea and Manchuria . . . We pass into the Palace under a Drum Tower, typical of those erected on the South Manchuria Railway on the Trans-Siberian Line. We can ascend the tower and glance down at the magnificent array of stalls, exhibits, tableaux and pictures which have been gathered here for our inspection . . . Korea, of course, is not, strictly speaking, a Japanese possession, but there is such a strong affinity of interests . . . that this attempt to portray Japan as a colonizing power would not be complete if Korea were not represented . . . Formosa . . . is, of course, a possession of Japan in every sense of the word, and secured by her in 1895 as a fruit of the Chinese War . . . the natives were savages, . . . whom the Chinese had been unable to subdue. It was naturally with no

little misgiving that Japan assumed control over the new possession and started to colonize it.[56]

The Japanese Imperial Army was also subject of a sizable display at the exhibition, a spectacle which must have aroused the anxiety of those worried by the possibility of further Japanese expansion.

The socio-political structure of Japan was conducive to the ambitions of an imperial power. This was not the case with the United States, whose imperial yearnings were constantly challenged by the democratic process. There was always an amount of principled opposition to the establishment of an American empire. As Democrats pointed out, the nation had fought to escape one imperial regimé, making the voluntary creation of another a morally perverse act. Nevertheless, by 1900, an empire had come into being. Awareness of itself as a nation with an international rôle to play dated from 1823 when the Monroe Doctrine was issued, this effectively sending Europe a directive to recognise the hegemony of the United States of America over the whole American continent. It was soon to imply also much of the Pacific region, although it was not until the last decade of the nineteenth century that the United States could count themselves thoroughly able to back their demands with real military force. In 1880 the American navy ranked only twelfth in the world, by 1900 it was third. Such an escalation of arms, as history has often demonstrated, usually breeds a desire to use them. It was quite natural that the growth in military hardware was accompanied by one of imperial ambition:

> How did it happen that the destiny which necessitated American control of the Caribbean in the eighteen-nineties was not manifest in the eighteen-sixties? The Americans of the eighteen-nineties had come to share with the British, Germans and French a willingness to take up the 'white man's burden[57]

In 1898, on the eve of the war the Americans fought to drive the Spanish out of Cuba, the 'Washington Post' commented: 'We are face to face with a strange destiny. The taste of Empire is in the mouth of the people even as the taste of blood in the jungle.'[58] Islands in the Pacific had come under the control of America with regularity from the mid-century, but by 1900 an expansive imperial policy was to regulate and speed the process. By 1898, the Hawaiian Islands, part of the Samoan group, the Philippines and many other smaller island territories had come into the American sphere. In South America, Cuba, the Dominican Republic, Haiti, Puerto Rico, the Virgin Islands, Nicaragua, and Panama became either possessions or protectorates. By the opening of the First World War, the supremacy of the United States over the Pacific, Caribbean and the South American continent was undisputed.

The first evidence at an exhibition of a desire to be part of the imperial world-scheme came in 1893 at the Chicago Columbian. As part of the Fair's celebrations, a naval review was organised to take place in New York harbour. All the great naval powers were asked to send ships of war to this, which was presided over by the President. Contemporary accounts leave no doubt that America wished to see itself as being in league with the other imperial powers:

> ... thirty-five vessels of war ... from the caravels of Columbus to the swiftest and most powerful of steel-plated cruisers. Other reviews there have been on a larger scale, as at Spithead in the Jubilee year of England's queen; but never before had the squadrons of England and France, of Russia and Germany, of Italy and Spain, in line with those of other empires and monarchies, passed in parade before a President of the United States.[59]

Additionally, a full entourage of American military hardware and man-power was at the Columbian as evidence of America's physical abilities. In 1893 however, there was little empire to celebrate. It was not until the turn of the century the World's Fairs acquired an imperial element proper, when actual possessions could be brought to the site for popular appraisal. This was when the idea of a 'Pan-American' Fair was born, beginning with the Buffalo Pan-American of 1901 and coming to a rapid maturity at the Louisiana Purchase Exposition of 1904. Essentially, 'Pan-American' stood for empire in the sense that America possessed some but not all of what was displayed, but could simulate imperial control via her economic and military position. Power relations became increasingly clear through the World's Fairs, the treatment of some nations being tantamount to a recognition of colonial status. The American public was thus informed of the position the Republic occu-pied in relation to its geographical neighbours. It was much the same with the so-called Pan American Conferences, an international forum formed in 1889 to discuss trade relations between the Northern and Southern continents. Often held to co-incide with World's Fairs, the conferences had the merest semblance of equality, as America flexed her imperial muscles on a global stage. In all her dealings with the Southern American nations, the United States talked from a position of absolute power.

In 1901 at the Buffalo Pan American World's Fair, for the first time there were worthwhile possessions to display. In 1899 the organisers had written to the Federal Government suggesting 'the desirability of a special governmental display of exhibits from Cuba, Puerto Rico, Alaska, the Hawaiian and Philippine Islands, showing not only products, resources and possibilities of these possessions, but also ... the ethnological features available.'[60] This, the organisers believed, would satisfy the 'intense interest felt by our people to learn all about the peoples and territories which have come under our charge and there has not been so good an opportunity as will present itself to reach the many millions expected to visit us, as will be afforded at our exposition'.[61] It was proposed that the centre of the display should be the Philippines. F. P. Hilder, an English ex-India soldier, was sent there to gather exhibits once the principle of the display was accepted. Ultimately the imperial sections covered a large area of the site, taking the form of a landscaped town of pavilions much in the fashion of its Parisian forerunners.

At the St. Louis Fair in 1904 the Buffalo experience was dramatically expanded as America settled into its imperial rôle. It was decided by statute at the onset to make the most of initiatives already taken. Once again the Philippines were chosen for centrepiece of America's empire. The Official Report on the Fair noted that a 'Philippine exposition board was created by Act 514 of the Philippine Commission, passed for the purposes of collecting and installing a distinctively Philippine exhibit at the Louisiana Purchase Exposition of 1904 at St. Louis.'[62] $125,000 were put to one side for the exhibit immediately by the Louisiana Purchase Company (the controlling body of the Fair), with a further $250,000 to follow from sponsorship. The appointed board had numerous full-time members, two of whom were Philippinos. For reasons as yet unknown, one of the two, a Dr. Pedro Paterno, resigned in 1904 before the Fair opened. Forty-seven acres were given over to the Philippine display, south-west of the main exhibition, the whole virtually constituting an independent exhibition. The 'Committee on Industrial Exhibitions Report' of 1906 described the site:

> The work of construction consisted of building a miniature city, with streets and parks complete with sewerage, water and electric light, and fire alarm systems. The ground plan included a central park or plaza, the sides of the quadrangle being occupied, respectively, by the Cathedral or Education building, the typical Manila house, the Commerce building and the Government Administration building, each of these beautiful structures being filled with appropriate exhibits.[63]

There were separate buildings to forestry, mines and metallurgy, agriculture and horticulture, fish and game and ethnology, whilst the arts and crafts of the Philippines were in the Government building. There were reproductions of the 'Ancient Walls of Manila' and the 'Bridge of Spain', which straddles the river Pasig in Manila. The whole display constituted one of the most lavish manifestations of its type ever devoted to one territory, outdoing in size and scope anything the British produced on India or the French on Algeria. Apart from the Philippines, Cuba received special attention, meriting total expenditure of $130,000.

The architecture of the building was described as 'Florentine Renaissance, from the last half of the fourteenth century',[64] being a porticoed pavilion covering 7000 square feet. Most other possessions were absorbed in various ways into the site, usually being presented thematically amongst the entertainment sections.

Unlike its British and French equivalents, American Imperialism at World's Fairs did not particularly grow as the century progressed, rather it maintained a constant, unfluctuating presence. This is possibly explained by the general nature of imperial propaganda. In Europe, the twentieth century saw the British and French empires come under increasing tension and attack, necessitating a constant expansion of the propaganda and publicity rôles of the exhibitions. In America, the steady increase in real power made the propaganda element far less vital. It was enough to recognise Pan-American control, it did not need to be artificially inflated or justified. In 1904 at St. Louis, America felt it important the world saw her imperial potential; after that date imperialism remained but the urgency to present it was less intense. Nevertheless, most World's Fairs maintained an imperial element and out of this, as the next chapter will show, blossomed a vibrant racism. Perhaps only the New York World's Fair was free of overt American imperialism, as the theme of the Fair, 'Democracity', simply did not allow for it. Elsewhere in the 1930's the imperial idea emerged in varying degrees. America took part in the Paris Exposition Internationale Coloniale in 1931, showing Puerto Rico, the Virgin Islands, the Hawaiian Islands, the Philippines and the Samoan Islands. The Golden Gate International Exposition (San Francisco) of 1939 separated the various regions coming under the military and economic aegis of America into a Latin-American Court and a Pacific Basin Area. A third area was designated 'Foreign Pavilions', implying that the Latin-American and Pacific areas were not foreign to the United States. For some reason Brazil and Argentina were located amongst the foreign pavilions and not the Latin-American ones. Included in the Latin-American Court were Mexico, El Salvador, Panama, Chile, Ecuador, Colombia, Peru and Guatemala, all heavily bound to the American economy via loans or investment.[65] In the Pacific Basin section, the Philippines and Hawaii were the main areas of American interest to be shown.

A unique twist was put upon the imperial theme at the Texas Centennial Exposition of 1936, held in Dallas, for here an imperial show was presented by a power with no empire. Texas chose to present itself at its celebration of a hundred years in the Union as a separate nation inside the United States with an imperial past. Governor James V. Allred explained in the Official Guidebook:

... the Texas Centennial is dedicated to the Great past of the Lone Star State, ... to you, on behalf of Texas and her people, I say, welcome to an Empire on Parade ... In the Texas Centennial Exposition the story of Texas will be told. No chapter of American history is richer in romance, dramatic highlights and stirring events. The saga of the Southwest, as written by men and women who built a great empire, is an epic setting for a World's Fair that traces the development of a people and a land.[66]

The jealousy of the peoples of the New Land for the empires belonging to the old were occasionally manifested on a spectacular scale, as at this festival of regression. If empire was a chimera here, the obese materialism was real enough; the obsession with money expressed everywhere on the site led to its officially adopted nick-name of the 'twenty-five million dollar Fair'.

The empire displays at exhibitions fulfilled a rôle which has been persistently underplayed or romanticised since the demise of the tradition. In the post Second War period, when the very word 'imperial' can be a cause of embarrassment, the imperial element of exhibitions casts a cold shadow over them, reducing their cultural respectability and the depth to which they are studied. Nevertheless, it is an aspect that not only improves our vision of them as events but which also increases our understanding of Western culture as a whole during the period. The coming together of contradictory values at the exhibitions, whereby positive notions of progress were buttressed against organised oppression and exploitation, says much about the plural morality in operation throughout European culture at the time. Ultimately, as with a vast number of cultural artefacts, it must be concluded that the exhibitions embodied neither good nor evil in any simple sense but were a complex mixture of both.

Notes

1 E. J. Hobsbawn, *Industry and Empire*, London 1969, Pelican.
2 *Great Exhibition 1851, Official Descriptive and Illustrated Catalogue*, Part 1 of 4, London 1851.
3 *The Crystal Palace Exhibition Illustrated Catalogue: The Art Journal Special Issue*, London 1851.
4 A. M. Dowleans, *Catalogue of the East Indian Productions Collected in the Presidency of Bengal, and Forwarded to the Exhibition of Works of Art and Industry to be Held in London in 1851*. London 1851, Thacker and Son.
5 *The Story of the Royal Society of Arts*, London 1934.
6 Journal for the Royal Society of Arts, *Colonial Exhibitions and their Uses*. October 22nd. 1909.
7 For the best discussion of these see John M.MacKenzie, *Propaganda and Empire: The Manipulation of British Public Opinion 1880–1960*, Manchester University Press 1985.
8 Paul Greenhalgh, *Art, Politics and Society at the Franco–British Exhibition of 1908*, Art History December 1985.

9 See Chapter 5 and also P. M. Taylor, *The Projection of Britain: British Overseas publicity and Propaganda 1919–1939*, Cambridge University Press 1981.

10 *Reports on the Paris Universal Exhibition.* 3 Volumes, Presented to both Houses of Parliament by Royal Command, London 1856, H.M.S.O. Press.

11 *Official Guide, British Empire Exhibition 1924.* London 1924, Fleetway Press.

12 For the best recent summary of these issues see C.C.Eldridge (Ed.) *British Imperialism in the Nineteenth Century.* London 1984, Problems in Focus Series, MacMillan 1984.

13 R.E. Robinson and J.A. Gallagher, with A.Denny, *Africa and the Victorians: The Official Mind of Imperialism*, Second Edition London 1981.

14 Ibid.

15 The most detailed survey of the British Exhibitions can be found in MacKenzie, see note 7.

16 Ibid. Also see John MacKenzie (Ed.) *Imperialism and Popular Culture* University of Manchester Press 1986.

17 The figures come from disparate sources. Particularly useful was Samuel Digby, *India*, from *The Royal Commission for the Chicago Exhibition, Official Catalogue of the British Section.* London, William Clowes and Sons, 1893.

18 Ibid.

19 The quotations from Maurice Talymeyr's articles in *Revue des Deux Mondes* come from Rosalind H. Williams, *Dream Worlds: Mass Consumption in Late 19th. Century France.* University of California Press.

20 See Chapter 4.

21 See Greenhalgh, note 8.

22 Sir Walter Armstrong, *Art at the Exhibition.* Guardian June 3rd. 1908.

23 The organisers of the Glasgow exhibition wished their event to be properly international, but were prevented by the 1928 Convention (see Chapter 1). Thus the imperial flavour was not as intense or entrenched as the Wembley show.

24 *British Empire Exhibition 1924, Official Guide.*

25 Ibid.

26 See Chapter 8. Also *Official Catalogue Great International Fisheries Exhibition.* London 1883, William Clowes and Son; *The Story of the Royal Society of Arts.* note 5.

27 *Empire Exhibition Scotland, Official Guide.* Glasgow 1938.

28 Pall Mall Gazette, May 15th. 1908.

29 The colonial stigma was also a factor in American displays. See Chapter 5.

30 There is controversy as to which French colonies appeared up to and including 1849. The most plausible source has proven to be Paul Dupays, *Vie Prestigieuse des Expositions Historiques.* Paris 1939, Published by Henry Didier.

31 Raymond Isay, *Panorama des Expositions Universelles*, Paris 1937, Gallimard.

32 Auguste Beaumier, *Notice sur Le Maroc*, Paris 1867, Mogador Press.

33 For Example see *Paris and its Exhibition.* Pall Mall Gazette Special Issue, No. 49 Friday July 26th., 1889.

34 Ibid.

35 Ibid. For all the later Expositions Universelles Le Figaro and its Special Editions provide the most colourful descriptions.

36 Quoted from Philippe Julian, *The Triumph of Art Nouveau: Paris Exhibition 1900.* Phaidon Press 1974.

37 *France Outre-Mer: Guide Officiel.* Paris 1939.

38 *Official Catalogue, Franco–British Exhibition.* London 1908, Published by Bembrose and Son.

39 It seems likely that lessons were learned from these pavilions for the following White City shows, and possibly also for the Wembley exhibition seventeen years later.

40 *Encyclopaedie des Arts Decoratifs et Industriels Modernes au XXeme Siecle* 12 Volumes, Paris 1925. A facsimile edition has now been produced by Garland Publishing, New York, 1977.

41 Possibly the categorization was an attempted integration of empire into the cultural mainstream. Little evidence for this exists outside certain areas of the decorative arts however, regardless of the debt French artists obviously owed non-Western practitioners.

42 Quoted from *Paris 1931 Internaional Colonial Exhibition, Your Guide.* Paris 1931.

43 Vincennes had held the over-spill of the Expositions Universelles from the Champs de

Mars since 1878. Sporting and agricultural sections had been housed there.

44 It is difficult to see why Britain was absent. It would be most unlikely that the responsible bodies in London would refuse to participate in an event of such use as propaganda. The likeliest explanation is French jealousy and the desire to be the largest empire on site.
45 Official Guide, see note 42.
46 Ibid.
47 See *Portugal: Exposition Internationale de Paris 1937*, Paris 1937.
48 At this time I know little of this exhibition and so am unaware as to whether it included other European nations.
49 Official Guide see note 42.
50 *Rapport Général, Exposition Internationale Coloniale, Maritime et d'Art Flamand, Anvers 1930*. Produced by the Commissariat Général du Gouvernement, Brussels 1931. See also *L'Exposition Internationale de Liége 1930* by Léon Michel, Brussels 1929, Published by Goemaere.
51 See also Chapter 8 for social Darwinian strategies in the defining of the fine arts.
52 See note 50.
53 Ibid.
54 Obviously there are examples within Russian imperialism in the nineteenth century which run against this summary. Generally speaking however the characterisation of non-participation remains valid.
55 *Official Guide Japan-British Exhibition 1910*. London 1910, Published by Bembrose and Son.
56 Ibid.
57 Morison, Commager and Leuchtenburg, *A Concise History of the American Republic*. Oxford University Press 1977.
58 Ibid.
59 H.H.Bancroft, *The Book of the Fair, an Historical and Descriptive Presentation of the World's Science, Art, and Industry, as Viewed through the Columbian Exposition at Chicago in 1893*. Chicago 1893. Reprint Facsimile in Bounty Books, New York.
60 Quoted from R.W. Rydell, *All the World's a Fair: America's International Expositions*, Phd. thesis, University of California Press 1980. An exemplary study containing useful ethnographic material on a number of events.
61 Ibid.
62 *Louisiana Purchase Exposition Commission 1906, Committee on Industrial Expositions*. Washington Government Printing Office, 1906.
63 Ibid.
64 Ibid.
65 *Official Guide, Golden Gate Exposition, 1939*. San Francisco 1939.
66 *Texas Centennial Exposition – Dallas. Official Souvenir Guide*. Dallas 1936.

CHAPTER FOUR

Human showcases

The international exhibitions are normally given a place in history because of the range of objects they assembled on a single site. The art and design historian cannot afford to exclude them from detailed study on this ground alone, because they brought together disparate types of produce in a way that no cultural manifestation before them could ever contemplate. Thus they reflected and influenced taste and attitudes in their respective times. The focus on objects however has tended to detract from a feature of central importance to the exhibitions held from the closing decade of the last century. This was the displaying of peoples. Between 1889 and 1914, the exhibitions became a human showcase, when people from all over the world were brought to sites in order to be seen by others for their gratification and education. The normal method of display was to create a backdrop in a more or less authentic tableau-vivant fashion and situate the people in it, going about what was thought to be their daily business. An audience would pay to come and stare. Through this twenty-five year period it would be no exaggeration to say that as items of display, objects were seen to be less interesting than human beings, and through the medium of display, human beings were transformed into objects.

When the specific discourses which surround and justify this extra-ordinary genre are examined they usually reveal an imperial rationale at base. However, it would be incorrect to assume imperialism was always an underlying motive behind human exhibits, or that these displays were always in some sense immoral. Looking at the exhibitions as a whole, human exhibits fell into types, two of which were not necessarily imperial or immoral. For the purpose of analysis, I shall identify four types, and label them the Imperial, the Educational, the Commercial and the Ambassadorial. Having chosen these headings, and having shown reserve on the imperial aspect, it must immediately be made clear that some displays had the features of all four types, that most had pretensions to the first two, and those which escaped the influence of the first were often afflicted with a dubiously abrasive nationalism.

1 Interior view of the Crystal Palace, Great Exhibition 1851

2 View of the Exposition building and Grounds, Paris 1867

3 Interior view of the Main Building, Philadelphia Centennial 1876

Paris Exposition Universelle 1889 **5** Interior of the Palace of Fine Art, American Sections
6 The Galeries des Machines, rear view during construction

Chicago Columbian Exposition, 1893   8 Interior view of the Women's Building, showing the North tympanum and a view of Mary Cassatt's mural 'Modern Woman'
9 Dahomeyan Villagers parading on the Midway Plaisance

Paris Exposition Universelle 1900   **10** [*below, left*] Neo-baroque lamp-posts and balustrade of the Pont Alexandre III, with the Grand Palais in the background
11 [*facing*] View of the Rue des Nations from the Pont Alexandre III, featuring, from left to right, Belgium, Norway, Spain, Monaco and Sweden
12 [*below, right*] Art nouveau style Metropolitain Railway Station Entrance

The Franco–British Exhibition, 1908 **13** The Senegalese Village
14 The Court of Honour at Night **15** [facing] The Palace of Women's Work

18 The Indian Pavilion at the Empire Exhibition Wembley, 1924
19 The Pavilion of the U.S.S.R., Paris Exposition Universelle 1937

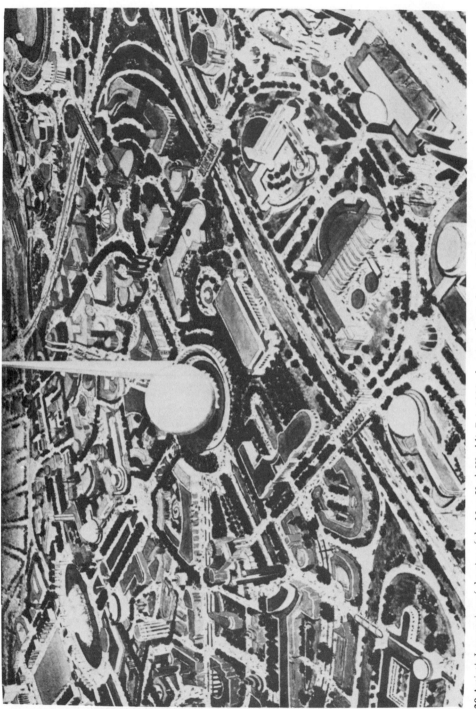

20 Artist's Impression of the site of the New York World's Fair 1939, showing the Trylon and Perisphere

Imperial displays of people were the most numerous and lavish at exhibitions; perhaps this type, as the single most significant one, should be discussed first.

Alex M. Thompson, a visitor to the Exposition Universelle of 1900, noted as he sat in a café in the middle of the colonial sections, that 'here are shown not so much specimens of produce, as of humanity brought from the colonies to be exhibited. . . .'[1] In making such an observation he was merely recognising what had come to be a prominent feature of French expositions by that date, the 'native village'. Brought from all areas of the French empire, groups of people would be settled into an appropriate surrounding where they would live, night and day, for the six months of the exposition. Often they were given the materials to build their own dwellings and invariably they were supplied with foodstuffs and raw material to prepare their own meals and make their own clothes. They would usually be situated near other 'native villages' on the site, they would be expected to perform religious rituals at set times each day for the visitors and to give demonstrations of their various arts and crafts. After the first month or so, the majority of the people in the villages adapted to their extraordinary situation, developing a mode of existence which was manageable for themselves and showy enough for the visitors. Often whole families were transported to an exhibition site, including cousins, uncles and aunts; occasionally the social mix was more random. Anything up to two hundred people might be resident in a single village although the likely number was fifty. Some villages were moved from exhibition to exhibition due to their popularity, eventually being able to boast appearances all over the world. Non-Western people would also be brought to exhibitions to work in ethnic restaurants and theatre facilities. At the Expositions Universelles of 1889 and 1900, the atmosphere in this area of the site could only be described as utterly bizarre, as the noises, sights and smells of dozens of totally different cultures vied for attention. Alex Thompson described the scene he saw before him in 1900:

> Here are the multi-coloured dwellings of the various Asiatic and African natives subject to the dominion of France . . . Here one may sit and take tea or coffee, served by men of strange tropical nationalities, whose faces look as polished as your fire-grate at home, while for music there is the monotonous chant which accompanies the 'Danse du Ventre' droning from the closed jalousies of the Algerian palace, and the gruesome dirge, which usually accompanies the walloping of the earnest but misguided tom-tom . . . Some of these people have never before worn clothes, and even now wear them much against their will. Amongst the many different villages of huts or Kraals built here by each tribe according to its native custom, that of the French dependency of Senegal is probably the

one that attracts most visitors. In this little village of jet-black negroes are men and youths of different ages, several women, and even children.[2]

A chaos of colour, a riot of superficial jollity, with crowds bustling to stare at people who only weeks before had been sitting in real villages with the sound of nature around and no conception of what was about to happen to them. One can only speculate on what the Senegalese man thought, as he looked back at the gaping expressions of the Parisian crowd, a pale and unhealthy looking mob shrouded in their gaudy dresses and frock-coats, laughing and sneering at what they undoubtedly considered the just spoils of war. Perhaps the culture gap was to wide for him to ponder upon anything more than the eccentricity of the garb, the dullness of the climate and the predictability of the crowd's response to him. He may even have enjoyed the attention he was given – there are instances where this is known to have been the case – in probability unaware that even as he stood there, the fabric of the culture he belonged to was being torn apart.

For the European nations who controlled an empire, the showing of native villages had several aims. It placed hitherto unrelated peoples of different parts of the empire together, physically and psychologically, and it centred the empire on the controlling imperial nation. The public could see at a glance the extent of the imperial pickings and feel in a real sense that they belonged to them. More importantly, it 'revealed' the apparently degenerate state the conquered peoples lived in, making the conquest not only more acceptable but necessary for their moral rescue. The Senegalese or Dahomayan man became less than human, a pitiable part of an untamed environment who had not yet begun to ascend the ladder of civilization. The village he had built for himself and his companions in Paris was proof not only of his intellectual inability but of his proximity to nature. He lived so as to be more comparable, in the eye of the visitor, to animals rather than European man. His animal state made him a fair subject for development, as one might develop crops, livestock or land.

Few who visited these exhibits intellectualised what they saw in order to fully comprehend the exploitative nature of the enterprise. More usually a romantic vision of another world was all the visitor could or chose to see, an exotic explosion of peoples and dwellings, a vehicle to transport the mind from routine and hardship. Indeed, the mingling of Chinese, African and Asian peoples in colourful ethnic dwellings, against a backdrop of the grand imperial pavilions, aided many to rise to hitherto unachieved heights of literary eloquence:

> I made a thousand extraordinary journeys almost without moving; under the Eiffel Tower, near the little lake, was hidden the Tonkinese village

with its junks and its women chewing betel; sometimes I watched the old Cambodian elephant sent by Doumer and called 'Chérie' drinking there. The Indo-Chinese theatre adjoined the reproduction of the strange temple which had just been discovered and was called Angkor . . . The entire hill was nothing but perfumes, incense, vanilla, the aromatic fumes of the seraglio; one could hear the scraping of the Chinese violins, the sounds of the castanets, the wailing flutes of the Arab bands, the mystical howling of the Aissawas more heavily painted than De Max, the cries of the Ouled Naïl with their mobile bellies; I followed this opiate mixture, this perfume of Javanese dancing girls, sherbets and rahat-lakoum, as far as the Dahomean village.[3]

As an experience of the senses, the whole was undoubtedly a delight, certain to influence artists and writers of a symbolic, romantic or escapist bent. Lodged peculiarly between high and popular culture, displays of colonial peoples legitimized imperial conquest across a remarkably broad spectrum, justifying European expansion without troubling the minds of the spectators with economic or military factors. Urchins from the streets of Paris went to stare alongside the nation's leading intellectuals; on the Champs de Mars shop-girls, stevedores and clerks revelled, as Gauguin and Debussy formulated new art-forms from their discovery of the Orient and Oceania.[4]

The actual presence of peoples of empire at exhibitions went back to 1851, when representatives of most nations of the British empire were constantly in attendance at the Crystal Palace. The first time people could properly be called part of the exhibit though was in 1867, at the Paris Exposition Universelle, when various North African exhibits were presented as tableaux-vivants. An Egyptian Bazaar contained crafts people and vendors, a camel stable had real camels and Arabic attendants, an authentic Tunisian Barber Shop was open for business. Various Egyptian, Tunisian and Algerian Cafés were staffed with specially imported waiters and chefs. It was also noted at the time that visitors to the site were more fascinated by foreign workmen finishing off incomplete pavilions than they were by the pavilions themselves. In Philadelphia in 1876 the novel success of the Paris show was capitalised on by the installation of Chinese, Arabic and Japanese craftsmen in facilities on the site and the creation of a Turkish Bazaar and Café.[5] After this the genre blossomed. Back in Paris in 1878 an Algerian Bazaar and a Cairo Street formed the core of extensive peopled displays on North African and Arabic themes. From the early 1880's the British set up Ceylonese and Indian Tea-houses with Asian waiters in their own and foreign exhibitions. It was the Paris Exposition of 1889 however which inaugurated the practice in a more specific sense, whereby colonial peoples were not brought to serve as exotic vendors, waiters and servants, but simply to be looked at. This Exposition was unprecedented in its presentation of colonial peoples, setting the pattern for the ensuing twenty-five years.

The 1889 Exposition had a different approach to peopled exhibits not explicable merely in terms of expanded scale. An intellectual shift had occurred which changed the emphasis of the event. This was largely due to the rise of anthropology as a discipline in Paris between 1878 and 1889. In tandem with imperial expansion – and frequently as a justification of it – anthropology had gained its first foot-hold on the slopes of academia during the 1870's, the foci of attention being primitive cultures of Africa, Oceania and Australasia. Imperial institutions and the general public were invited to take part in (and hence fund) anthropological research by visiting exhibitions of various kinds. The most important of these were the ones held at the Jardin d'Acclimatation in Paris. The Jardin was established in 1859 as a centre for the study and popularization of botany and zoology, with permanent displays of animals and plants being open to the public throughout the year.[6] In 1867 due to the Exposition Universelle there was a marked rise in public attendance at the Jardin, though this was curtailed in the 1870's by the slaughtering of livestock during the Commune and the loss of public funding. The search for patronage led to an expansion of the exhibiting programme, until it occurred to the curators in 1877 to include people amongst the exhibits of plants and animals. At first this appears to have been an after-thought, most certainly inspired by the 1867 Exposition and by the generally known intention of bringing foreign peoples to the one of 1878. Girard de Rialle, a member of the Paris Anthropology Society, reported of the first peopled display at the Jardin that:

> The convoy belongs to a foreign merchant whose speciality is furnishing interesting specimens to the zoological gardens of Europe and who is supplied in these countries from which he draws his animals by paying local hunters. This time, instead of leaving them in Africa, he wanted to bring them to Europe, and if we can believe those who say so, he will not be poorly rewarded.[7]

The scheme had the backing of the Parisian academic community. Fourteen Nubians were presented to a fascinated Parisian public, whereupon attendance increased markedly, guaranteeing the Jardin's future. Later in the same year six Eskimos were shown and from then onwards peoples were brought from all over the world to be displayed alongside the animals. Between 1877 and 1887 Lapps, Gauchos, Fuegians (Tierra del Fuego), Galibis (Guyana), Kalmouks (Siberia), American Indians, Ceylonese and Ashanti were taken to the Jardin.[8] Scientific acumen soon began to give way to financial considerations and the anthropological worth of the displays became questionable. Into the 1880's, scholars who had initially welcomed the displays began to voice misgivings about them, as the atmosphere around began to change from one of learning to a circus parade. Leonce Manouvrier, an early supporter, was not untypical:

> At the Jardin d'Acclimatation what information can we obtain? These individuals, in effect, are transported to an environment where they can no longer, so to speak, be themselves. Everything is changed in their way of life; they must contend on the one side with the administration of the Jardin, on another with those who brought them, on another with the crowds of the curious, and on another side with a committee that comes out to examine and measure them by means of little trinkets.[9]

Such misgivings fell mainly on deaf ears as the Jardin went from success to success. In 1889 when the largest Exposition Universelle to date opened, it became apparent that the organisers had taken careful note of it and had expanded its activities onto a grand scale. For the first time before an international audience people were degraded to the level of zoological exhibits. Regardless of its motives, the anthropological community had invented a genre at the Jardin d'Acclimatation destined to debase and defile non-Western cultures in a way barely conceived of before.

The importance of the 1889 Exposition for its imperial exhibits was noted in the last chapter, but only when the display of native villages erected on the Chaillot Hill amongst the imperial pavilions is taken into account, is its significance fully recognised. For innovation in the presentation of all aspects of empire it was unequalled. It created the prototypes for imperial sections of all international events following it, including those in Britain. As with other areas of the show, the imperial dimension was underpinned by the belief that it was possible to present a complete knowledge, to create a physical encyclopædia capable of capturing and explaining a total world view.[10] Thus every aspect of empire had to be portrayed, as realistically as possible, making the presence of the conquered peoples imperative. The nineteenth century had added a material dimension to the rationalism of the Encyclopédie, giving scientific credence to the idea that everything on the face of the earth was measurable and knowable. Faith in the idea of a finite world led to a quest for empirical totality at the Exposition, in the belief this could simulate absolute truth. The native tribes were there not only to reveal the extent of French territories but also to show the human race in its every aspect, so that human life could be instantly understood through all its evolutionary stages. The native villages therefore answered to imperial, scientific, philosophical and moral discourses all at once, making their emergence as a phenomenon at that time understandable if not predictable.

The main attractions at the 1889 show were the Senegalese, the Congolese, New Caledonians, Gaboonese, Dahomeyans, a Cochin-China and a Kampong–Javanese settlement. A visitor described it in colourful terms:

> A popular feature of the show is the street, not of an ancient civilised city, but of aboriginal savages. In the back settlements behind all the gorgeous finery of the pagodas and the palaces of the further East the ingenious French have established colonies of savages whom they are attempting to civilize. They are the genuine article and make no mistake, living and working and amusing themselves as they and their kinfolk do in their country. Some day an enthusiast promises us we shall have a great anthropological exhibition of living samples of all nations and tribes and peoples that on earth do dwell. That may be the next Universal Exhibition. That it will not be without deep interest and instruction this street of colonies of natives suffices to prove. Each village is built in its own grounds, enclosed by a fence, and inhabited by its own natives . . . All these natives have been specially imported for the exhibition. They have brought with them the materials for their huts, their tools, and everything necessary for them to reproduce in the capital of the civilised world the everyday life of Africa, the Pacific, and the Further East. To add to the attractiveness of this anthropological collection there is close to the street of aborigines an Annamite restaurant. The garrison consists of one hundred and eight men, drawn from all special corps serving in the colonies – namely ten Indian Sepoys, . . . ten Senegal tirailleurs – coal black negroes. Six Senegal Spahis, seventy-six Sakalava, Annamite, Tonkinois tirailleurs.[11]

The concern of the writer that these were the 'genuine article', in conjunction with constant reference to anthropology, reveals an attitude of mind which indicates the age of the museum was well underway. The obsession with the authenticity of the object and the rationale for its collection in science, not in plunder, would soon encourage and justifify the acquiring of objects from all over the world by Western museums. More powerful than anything else in this passage however, is the dismissive arrogance of the writer, whose confidence in the inferiority of the people on display has an aura of absolute unshakability. These 'articles', 'savages' or 'samples' as he variously refers to them, are the stuff of good exhibitions, fodder for scientific, philosophical enquiry and, as a biproduct, entertainment. They emerge in his total discussion of the exposition as less serious or interesting than the fine arts, machine technology or the Eiffel tower, having the status for him of a fascinating distraction.

The composition of the displays was, as far as possible, based around the family unit. The Senegal village had eight families, the Congolese seven, the new Caledonian six, and the Kampong–Javanese a larger but unspecified number. If the intention was to create a socially harmonious unit however, this most certainly did not occur in the case of the Senegal village, as the families came from several distinct regions, meaning that they had no common language. The three races, the Peulps, Goloffs and Bambaras, also had independent cultural and religious traditions. Whatever the performances they were asked to execute for the crowds were, they certainly did not represent the customs of the majority of the people in the village itself.

Most of the villages were part of the French empire, but not all. The Belgians funded the Congolese one; the Kampong–Javanese, recognised as the most impressive on the site, was a private undertaking. The subtitle of this village was 'Life in the Dutch Indies', implying perhaps that the Dutch government had some interest in it, but so far evidence to prove this has not emerged. The manager of the village was a M. Bernard, who had lived in Java for seventeen years. He was responsible for selecting the villagers, who consisted of four nationalities, Javanese, Sundanese, Malays and Batavians. There were twenty-two houses on the site, built with bamboo and covered with palm leaves. M. Bernard was largely responsible for a little booklet of explanation containing his own prosiac anecdotes on the setting up of the exhibit; '. . . they like the climate now . . . but when we arrived in April last, they almost revolted and cried master, master, take us home, you have brought us to a country where there are no leaves on the trees. I had to explain to them how the leaves would come by and by, and gave them a lesson in botany'.[12] He also gave guided tours of the site, during which he would inform the crowd of the cultural and personal habits of his exotic wards:

> They are a very clean people, and bathe twice a day. That thickset, powerful fellow, making bamboo hats with his little son, is a Malay. The Malays are stronger than the others. These women in the next house are Batavians. Their skin is lighter than the Malays. That man sitting running paint onto a piece of cloth is from Java. That is how they paint their dress and napkins.. Sometimes it is done with wax, sometimes with paint. It takes nineteen months to finish one robe . . . These are the dancing girls . . . they are lent by the emperor Solo, who has twenty-six at his court. I have telegraphed for three more. The jewelry they wear is real, and belongs to the emperor.[13]

The attitude of M. Bernard toward the people in his village fell somewhere between how one might normally regard animals or children. Simplistic but strong, he casts them collectively as pleasant buffoons, incapable of looking after themselves, in awe of their white governor, but strangely capable of making art objects. In effect, he sees them as a mixture of animal and human, his text giving off a feeling that he is describing the bahaviour of well trained dogs.

As has already been noted, the 1900 Exposition Universelle maintained the native village element, if anything expanding it slightly. In 1906 at the Exposition Coloniale in Marseilles the villages were an important part of the whole event, by this time being a natural and essential ingredient in any exposition even of modest size. At the second Exposition Coloniale in Marseilles in 1922 villages from most of the African territories were erected, at a time when the genre was beginning to lose popularity elsewhere in Europe. In 1931 at the Paris Exposition Internationale Coloniale in the Parc de Vincennes, for the last time anywhere, a large area of villages appeared specifically within an imperial context. By this time such things began to attract widespread criticism, as opposition to both imperialism and racism grew.[14]

In Britain, the idea of the native village only became attractive to exhibition organisers after they had seen its potential at the 1889 Paris Exposition. From that date it became a regular feature, reaching a high-point in terms of frequency at the White City (1908–1914). The popularity of the genre after 1890 is largely due to one man, Imre Kiralfy, who was Britain's premier exhibition organiser from the closing years of the nineteenth century until his death in 1919. Kiralfy was the driving force behind the White City Exhibitions and before that he was responsible for numerous events at the Earl's Court and Olympia arenas in London. Born in Budapest in 1845 of Jewish parentage, he had a colourful career as an entertainer before becoming the premier entrepreneur of his generation. He started life as a music hall prodigy, appearing on stage as a musician at the age of four and having some of his music published at thirteen. Through the first thirty-five years of his life he toured Europe and America as an all-round entertainer, apparently entering a new sphere as an organiser of events by chance. The move took place when he was asked to take over the organisation of a pageant he was appearing in in Brussels, because the manager had been taken ill. He subsequently went on to set up countless grand events in different cities around the world, making himself famous in the process. His first major success was 'Nero, or the Fall of Rome', an extravaganza held at London's Olympia arena in 1889. Vast sets which collapsed to order, hundreds of actors, extras and animals were orchestrated into what was essentially a tableau-vivant of special effects. In 1891 and 1892 he staged 'Venice, Bride of the Sea' again at Olympia, touring it then to Paris. This event was partly on water, partly amongst exact copies of famous Venetian buildings, with a choir of one thousand Italians. In 1894 in Chicago, a year after the Columbian Exposition, he produced a 'Grand History of America' and in New York in 1895 he was once again on water, with

'Our Naval Victories, an American Naval Spectacle.' From 1890 he often worked in conjunction with Barnum Circus Enterprises, it probably being Barnum's advisory rôle at the Columbian which first made him aware of the exhibition as a medium for entertainment and money-making. He returned to London after the New York naval show and settled there more or less permanently to the end of his life. It was then that he developed the two obsessions which occupied him through to his death: exhibitions and empire. His last extravaganza show in 1895 at Olympia was significant in its move toward imperial concerns, 'India, a Grand Historical Spectacle.' In the same year, he formed 'London Exhibitions Ltd.' and staged the 'Empire of India' Exhibition at the Earl's Court arena. In 1896 he organised the 'India, Ceylon, Borneo and Burma Show', in 1897 a 'Jubilee Exhibition', in 1899 the 'Greater Britain Exhibition' and most notably the 'Savage South Africa Spectacle'. By 1905, when he started plans for the White City Exhibition site in Shepherd's Bush, he was acknowledged as the foremost authority on large international exhibitions in Britain and was constantly employed as a government advisor on British exhibits in foreign shows.[15]

Kiralfy's rise to pre-eminence in Britain meant several things for the exhibition genre. It meant empire would be a constant source of subject-matter for events and that the tableau-vivant format would be in regular use. Under his influence, international exhibitions in Britain changed emphasis, the educational and philanthropic flavours of the earlier South Kensington shows being decisively replaced by those of theatre and fairground. Kiralfy did not seek particularly to educate or improve his audience so much as entertain and propagandise them with his special effects. Many sections in his exhibitions were virtual replicas of the extravaganzas he had staged in the first part of his career. Once he had realised its potential, the native village as an idea came to suit him perfectly as a dramatic medium to express his imperial beliefs through. The Savage South Africa and Greater Britain events prepared the ground for his first international exhibition, the Franco–British of 1908, in this regard. Far more like huge fairground spectacles than exhibitions, they brought African and Asian peoples to Britain explicitly as exhibits for the first time. Reconstructions of the African Wars, tableaux-vivants of life in Africa and Asia and crude parodies of other cultural activity were presented with real Africans and Asians acting out various rôles.[16] In 1908 at the Franco–British, he organised a Ceylonese Village and booked the Senegalese one from the French empire. The Official Guide to the Senegal exhibit left the visitor in no doubt as to the considered cultural and intellectual status of the Senegalese people:

In a cruel-looking stockade over a hundred men and women from the borders of the desert are now living exactly as they do in their native

Africa . . . Take a hasty glance at the interior of this hut . . . and make a rapid inventory of the contents. That will not be difficult. Inside you will see a bed of straw and nothing more. These people have not yet adopted all the fashions and utensils of the luxurious life.[17]

The Ceylonese Village had a number of jugglers, magicians and other entertainers amongst its residents, Kiralfy obviously feeling that in itself ethnographic curiosity might not guarantee good attendance figures. Most impressive at the Franco–British though was an open air theatre capable of holding three thousand spectators, where an 'Alfresco Spectacular' entitled 'Our Indian Empire' was staged. Hundreds of Indians and Ceylonese and a wide range of wild animals were brought to London for this show, which took just two hours (on a twice daily basis) to explain how the British civilized India.

At following shows on the White City site the native village remained a constant feature. The Official Daily Programme of the second, the Imperial International of 1909, was at pains to reassure the public that the natives were being well catered for, following questions in the House of Commons about unsatisfactory conditions the year before:

A number of typical native villages are being set up, for the pleasure side of the Imperial is to possess as distinctly an international scope as the commercial sections. There are many little-known peoples dotted about in distant latitudes, whose customs and habits would undoubtedly prove of boundless interest to their more civilised brothers and sisters. Where it is possible, the lives of these people will be shown by miniature villages, built in the same manner as the originals and occupied by the natives, who are being brought over for the purpose . . . Here will be represented the daily life and excitement of the natives, including the War Dances, Ceremonies, Forms of Worship, etc., etc., Their introduction to the West will take place under favourable auspices, those who have charge of them taking every care that they do not suffer by their altered circumstances.[18]

The full number of villages at this exhibition has still not been ascertained, or the identity of funding sources which brought them, as the official literature contained no detailed catalogue. In probability Kiralfy booked some from foreign governments, notably the French, Dutch and Belgians, and paid for those from the British empire out of his company funds. It is to be assumed that the peoples in the exhibits were paid something for appearing, although at this time in no instance anywhere is it known what these payments consisted of or how they were made.

The villages attracting most attention at the Imperial International were the Dahomeyan, Irish, Scottish and a Kalmuck Camp. The latter was brought by the Russians as part of their imperial display and soon became a most popular exhibit. It polled by far the heaviest numbers on the day of the largest ever attendance on the site, May 21st. 1909. The

'Camp' was peopled by (very bemused) nomadic Tartars from the Kal-muck region, described romantically in the Official Guide: 'Here, within the borders of civilization, you may find a tribe of Kalmuck Tartars, actually encamped, with their tents and their camels, their women and children, their priests and their praying wheels.[19] The year after at the Japan–British Exhibition on the same site, the last village ever to be brought to Britain by a foreign power as part of an imperial display arrived, when the Japanese brought a 'Formosa Hamlet';[20] one other village appeared, this being a repeat of the Irish one. The relative lack of villages was probably due to the fact that Kiralfy was planning a dramatic expansion of his peopled displays for the year after, at the Coronation Exhibition. This was to have more native villages and related displays than any before or after it in Britain.

1911 was the year Kiralfy chose as the most fitting for his largest celebration yet of empire, with the British monarchy the subject of attention everywhere due to the crowning of George V. His personal obsession with the imperial achievement of his adopted country rose to new heights of epic melo-drama at the Coronation Exhibition, as this strange man continued his quest for national acceptance. It was as though his Jewish origins, in a country which was part of an unstable empire, had filtered through to the very core of his pyschological make-up, to surface in a manic involvement with the empire of his adopted home. He had made himself part of a stable, powerful nation by lauding it in a way it had never been lauded before. By 1914, he was more responsible perhaps than anyone for the vivid and vulgar understanding the British population had of its foreign territories. The Coronation Exhibition was, in imperial terms, his greatest achievement.

The native villages present in 1911 were not as numerous as those at the larger events in France or America, but the range was unusually exotic. A Somali Village featured, having already been to the Bradford Exhibition of 1904 and Dublin in 1907. It appeared for the last time in Britain as a holiday resort attraction in Douglas (Isle of Man) in 1912.[21] Apart from this well travelled group there was a tribe of Iroquois Indians from Canada, a Burmese village and theatre, a Ceylon Village with entertainers, an unspecified 'African' village, and a Hindoo Settlement with a Temple of Magic. By far the most popular and unusual attraction though was a Maori Village and theatre. The Official Daily Programme felt it needed to provide some historical background to this exhibit:

The Maoris are a most interesting race, they being the original inhabitants of New Zealand where they arrived from the island of Hawaiki, in the Pacific, more than seven hundred years ago. Since the occupation of New Zealand by Great Britain in 1814, there have been many Maori outbreaks, the most serious of which started in 1868, under a chief named Te Kooti,

and was not finally quelled until 1875. There have been minor insurrec-
tions since, but the Maoris are now a most peaceful race, and among the
most loyal subjects of King George. Their population has diminished since
1846, when they numbered 100,000, to about 45,000, but is now station-
ary. The party consists of fifty warriors and maidens of the Arawa tribe . . .
and it also includes Mita Taupopoki, the veteran chief who fought for the
British against Te Kooti in 1873.[22]

A fascinating passage, treating clinically and lightly the genocide of the
Maori's and the desperate struggle for freedom they had fought in their
own country, merely in the hope of a right to share it. Displayed with
pride was a chief who turned against his own nation to side with the
British; even he, despite the service he rendered his conquerors, was
presented as an anthropological exhibit. The willingness to accept
imperial violence as a natural order remains perhaps the most disturbing factor in the whole of these barbaric celebrations of conquest.

By 1908 by far the most famous of the native villages were the
Senegalese and the Dahomeyan, both from the French empire but both
operating in a quasi-independent way from the French government by
that time. Both groups decided to take their fates into their own hands
by placing themselves under the control of various entrepreneurs, leas-
ing out their services to exhibitions and holiday resorts, although they
still appeared in a more official rôle as part of French imperial sections.
Little is known about the entrepreneurs in question. An Xavier Pené
organised Dayomeyan villages, notably the one at the Chicago
Columbian, and Messrs. Bouvier and Fleury-Tarnier ran the Senegalese
Village at the Franco–British Exhibition.[23] They were independent of
government but clearly controlled by them in certain ways. It is not
known either whether the same group of Dahomeyans and Senegalese
moved around Europe and America or whether different people took
over from venue to venue. It does seem likely that the composition of
the group operating in America was different from the one in Europe.
Within the two continents personnel appears to have remained reasonably stable. Dayomeyan and Senegalese villages featured in the most
unlikely of places between 1889 and 1931. The Senegalese were in Paris
in 1889, 1900 and 1931, in Marseilles in 1906 and 1922, in Edinburgh in
1908, in London in the same year and in Newcastle for the North-East
Coast Exhibition in 1929. They also toured resorts in France. The
Dayomeyan's most impressive appearances were at Paris (1889, 1891,
1893 and 1900), Chicago in 1893, and London in 1909.[24] The latter
appearance, at the Imperial International Exhibition, produced a Guide
which painted a familiar picture of how the Dahomeyans had benefitted
from French conquest:

Order and decency, trade and civilization, have taken the place of rule by fear of the sword. France has placed its hand on the blackest spot in West Africa, and wiped out some of the red stain that made Dahomey a by-word in the world. Today Dahomey is a self governing colony of France, with a revenue which exceeds its expenditure, a line of railway, rubber and cotton plantations, exporting palm oil and copra, maize, nuts, dried fish, cattle, sheep, pigs and fowls. The days of savagery are passing away . . . one day the European tourist will go to far Dahomey as he now goes to Egypt in search of sunshine and merriment in the winter months. Until that time comes he must seek his amusement, instruction, and entertainment in this Dahomey Village.[25]

Exhibitions insisted upon the advantages of empire for those who were conquered, it being common to find in official literature a scenario suggesting the peoples on show had been violent not only toward their white overlords but also toward other African peoples, and that the 'civilizing' process they had been subjected to was welcomed by Africa as well as Europe. There was an additional implication that psychologically they had found peace from their barbaric past. The Dahomeyans were particularly popular at exhibitions because of their reputation as warriors, the village revealing at the same time their 'savagery' and the extent to which they had been broken by the victorious French army. The Maoris were seen in a similar light, as a docile people who had once been savage. Moreover, John MacKenzie has pointed out the tendency of organisers.to seek out recently conquered peoples for village displays in order to make their appearance topical; undoubtedly this was a source of morbid pride for the crowd.[26]

After the decline of the White City as an exhibition ground in 1914, the displaying of peoples in British exhibitions became something of a rarity. Perhaps the only exhibition to come anything near the exotic excesses of the 1908–14 period was the Wembley British Empire Exhibition in 1924, although the way it presented these sections was markedly subdued. The inherent racism of the displays was becoming difficult to justify, with an empire on the edge of becoming a commonwealth. A single mention at the back of the Official Guide expressed the sober mood:

Races in Residence. Every section of the empire is represented at Wembley. Many of the colonies have representatives of their local inhabitants at work in local conditions. The following list gives the name of the races and the approximate numbers actually living in the exhibition: Malays 20, Burmans 30, Hong Kong Chinese 160, West Africans 60, Palestinians 3. In addition there are Indians, Singhalese, West Indians, and natives of British Guiana, who live outside the exhibition, but attend their respective pavilions daily. [27]

It would be a mistake of course to suggest this implied a generally less racist approach by Britons to their colonies and dominions, rather, it revealed a shrewd reluctance to parade racism as openly. Whilst the inhabitants of exhibition villages were no longer referred to as 'samples', 'articles' or 'savages', scant evidence existed throughout the exhibition to suggest economic or cultural attitudes toward the empire had shifted any.

The educational motive behind the displaying of peoples shaded into the imperial one, often to the extent that the two were indistinguishable. Whilst the professed aim was to teach the curious crowds about the peoples of the world, the net result was normally a biased, racist degrading of all peoples who were effectively outside the canons of white, Western culture. The popularity in academic and popular circles of social Darwinism led to its continuous presence as an idea at exhibitions from the 1870's onwards. Essentially, followers of social Darwinian theory subscribed to the existence of a human evolutionary chain which placed some races nearer to the animals than others. Obviously, Aryan races derived from Western stock represented the pinnacle of development, Aborigine and African tribesman the nadir, with the various Indo-Eurasian races filling the intermediary stages. Measured on the sacred yardstick of Progress, all races showed themselves hopelessly behind the white man:

> Everywhere the keen, bright, energetic Aryan race excited other races to a higher civilization, and only the races in which the Aryan element is pure or predominant have proved progressive; those in which it was overwhelmed by the Turanian races having always been unprogressive, as in India, Egypt and Assyria.[28]

In this way, predominant attitudes in educational circles facilitated themselves nicely to the imperial cause. Recent work on the history of British anthropology has shown, as with the French, that in order to acquire establishment recognition, research often strayed a long way from any objective basis in order to support predominant views in imperial circles on the degeneracy of non-white races.[29] Between 1878 and 1914, anthropological displays at exhibitions used a variety of means, including the use of phrenology, in order to 'prove' white superiority. The popularity of phrenology outside academic circles, as a source for party games, enabled organisers to feign scientific objectivity whilst courting the crowds.[30] Occasionally there were awkward moments; for example, when the Japanese rose to respectability as an imperial power, the British had to carefully adjust previous anthropological and phrenological calculations when they organized the Japan–British Exhibition in 1910:

> One curious similarity runs through the whole, that is, the striking

similitude between Japs and our own people. This resemblance manifests itself in manner, physical stamp and shape of head. To anyone acquainted with the principles of phrenology the resemblance is very marked. This last point is indicated by the large proportion of the brain in front and above the ear. The structural conditions are distinctive indications of considerable mental power, and are emphasised by the portraits of some of the most highly placed representatives. Taken as a whole, they constitute a good augury for the growth of sympathy between east and west.[31]

With most Asian and all of the African races though, the 'scientific evidence' was overwhelming. The white man's burden would have to be endured for a considerable time into the future, until the inferior strands of humanity evolved into races capable of ruling themselves.

The insistence upon the proximity of African and Asian peoples to the animal state was given weight by the character and arrangement of exhibitions themselves. Paris provided the classic example of the abrupt contrast evident on sites everywhere. The Eiffel Tower leaned over the site of the native villages, casting its shadow over them like a giant Triumphal monument. A culture/nature juxtaposition of terrifying simplicity, the vast, gaunt tower represented the power that had enabled the imperial take-over of the lands the villages stood for. Struts, pillars and cables of iron begged comparison with the mud, sticks and leaves the people of the villages had constructed their dwellings with. The whole can be seen as an exercise designed to show that there existed not only differences in qualities of life, but differences in type. The Tower was contextualised so as to be a yardstick to measure Western supremacy by. The unyielding linearity of the philosophy of 'progress through science' condemned the peoples of Africa and Asia in advance, the Exposition serving as evidence in the judgment.

After France and Britain, the exhibiting of peoples occurred most frequently in America. These displays had all the dimensions the European ones had, but the essential make-up of American culture meant there were additional factors at work which were absent in Europe. The Chicago Columbian began the genre there, in what was most certainly a response to the Paris Exposition of 1889. No less than seventeen villages were built altogether, eight of which were associated with empires, the Dahomey, Chinese, Javanese, Soudanese, Alaskan, Arab, South Sea Islanders and Algerian. Although the literature of the Fair suggested the motive of all the villages and associated ethnic displays was educational, their proximity on the site itself to the Midway Plaisance, the entertainments area, immediately transformed any atmosphere of learning into a fairground side-show. Indeed, the villages were the closest in spirit to 'freak shows' that the genre had yet been, probably because pleasure was the main rationale behind most exhibits. In Chicago displays of people suffered more than ever before from exaggeration and caricature. Each day, the people from the villages, accompanied by various Arab groups from other exhibits, were paraded up and down the Midway Plaisance before returning to their display areas to commence their day of public living. The humiliating racism of this spectacle, apart from fulfilling a propaganda rôle for co-operating foreign nations, had a distinct purpose for reactionary elements within American society.

At virtually all of the great World's Fairs, America experienced racial tensions of a kind at that time insignificant in Europe, caused by large indigenous populations of coloured peoples. These tensions were not reduced by an insistence on the primacy of white culture over all others, or the ingrained belief that white Americans alone had been responsible for the success of the nation. In his opening speech as Chairman of the National Committee for the Chicago Fair, J. T. Harris actually named the specific racial strand which had 'created' America, citing it as the one being celebrated at the Columbian: '. . . it remained for the Saxon race to people this new land, to redeem it from barbarism, to dedicate its virgin soil to freedom, and in less than four centuries to make of it the most powerful and prosperous country on which God's sunshine falls.'[32] The very title of the exhibition, evoking the name of the explorer sponsored by Spain, was thus rendered a nonsense, in this festival of 'American Saxons'. Identification of Anglo-Saxons by Harris at the onset was not however intended to alienate the Spanish speaking minorities; they were the least of the organisers worries. The reference was really made in relation to the Negroid and American Indian peoples. In most European events non-white races had normally been the subject of exhibits and had never been afforded any kind of equality in the creating of them; America decided to follow suit. Nevertheless, the American Negro and Indian presented grave problems to the organisers, who pushed freedom and democracy as the ideals of the Fair, yet who had no wish to give either race a position of equality at any level. The plan from early phases of the organisation had been to ignore the black population altogether, allowing them a rôle only as menials in the construction work on the site, and to exhibit the Indians much in the way the Dahomeyans were displayed, as a primitive foreign race. In the end, this did in fact happen, but not before both races fought for a better representation on committees. After a congressional struggle, blacks were denied any places on the two hundred and eight person national commission for the exhibition and black women were denied any part in the Women's Building. The Lady Board of Managers refused to acknowledge any representation from them, an irony, since the Women's Building actually contained a fine collection of craft work from women of all races. Appeals for a separate Negro Building were refused, the only concession in the end being the declaration of a 'Coloured Peoples Day' on August 25th. Against such a background of racial intrigue, the Dahomey Village suddenly acquired a significance it had had nowhere else in the world, as contemporary commentator Frederick Douglass recognised: '. . . to the coloured people of America, morally speaking, the World's Fair in progress is . . . a white sepulchre . . . as if to shame the Negro, the Dahomeyans are also here to exhibit the Negro as a repulsive savage.'[33] The degradation the Dahomey Village brought upon its own race was thus expanded to degrade all coloured peoples.

After the Columbian, several World's Fairs did come to acknowledge the existence of the American negro in cultural terms, although obviously this did not imply a recognition of equality. At the Buffalo Pan-American just the opposite was strongly suggested. Amongst the various native villages an exhibit called 'The Old Plantation' could be found, showing the life of the black populations in the South. A key-note was the difference between Southern and Northern Negroes:

> It is easy to pick up coloured people of the North and draft them into show business . . . but the darkies of the South do not take so kindly to the rogue box . . . the Southern Negro is a stay-at-home darkey, not so much through the dislike of publicity as through the inherent laziness that will not run the risk of a nomadic life.[34]

Many of the Fairs in the South erected Negro Buildings, integrating the black population into the structure of Southern life and economy. The Atlanta Cotton States and International Exposition (1895), the Tennessee Centennial (1897), the Trans-Mississippi and International Exposition (1898), the South Carolina Inter-State and West Indian Exposition (1901–2) and the Jamestown Tercentenary Exposition (1907) all included Negro sections.[35] At Jamestown an impressive building was erected, but the emphasis was on segregation, not recognition. Dedicatory remarks predicted that 'The showing we will make in this building will startle the world, it will astonish those who are unfamiliar with the condition of the Negro and it will be stimulating to our race.'[36] A public relations exercise funded and controlled by the Federal Government, the Negro Building avoided the issues which most concerned America's black population at the time. The building, designed by one of America's first black architects, W. Sidney Pittman, was, ironically, reminiscent of the classicism of the Southern plantation mansions belonging to those in America who had kept the black population so cruelly repressed. Included or excluded, the black populations of America were never considered as more than a socio-economic issue by their fellow Americans. Later in the century the situation had changed little. At the Texas Centennial of 1936 a 'Hall of Negro Life' was built which treated coloured people as a useful economic resource rather than as a culture with a part to play in the future development of the American continent.[37] The vulgar presumptiveness of the racism in this pavilion was in keeping with the regressive spirit to be found everywhere at the Centennial. This was never likely to be an arena for debate about equal rights; if anything, it was just the opposite.

The American Indians first featured at a World's Fair in Philadelphia in 1876, where extensive displays in the Government Building attempted to assess the progress of their assimilation into white American culture. Some Indians were actually part of the exhibition, but preference was for mannequins. The overwhelming effect of the Government Building was to cast the Indian as an immoral savage, one observer even seeing the superb examples of Indian art as indicating 'most conclusively that the moral standard of the aboriginals must have been at the lowest possible grade'.[38] The portrayal seventeen years later at Chicago showed that if anything, attitudes toward the Indian had deteriorated. Here they were widely treated by white Americans as the 'enemy within', a primitive, amorphous race defying Western ideas of decency and civilization. At Chicago the decision was taken to present the American Indian as a savage who had only recently encountered the rudiments of humanity. Henry Pratt, founder of the Carlisle Indian School, was asked to organise the exhibit. A humanitarian and worker for the Indian, he quickly realised the intent behind the display and refused to have anything to do with it, going as far as to object altogether to the inclusion of the Indian unless the context were right.[39] He was ignored, and various Indian races were settled into tepees, given canoes to row on a man-made lake and obliged to perform various famous ritual ceremonies.[40] They were a long way indeed from realising their rights as equal citizens. Adjacent to the tepees was the Buffalo Bill Show, an entertainment which outlined the standing of the Indian in American life in the most crude and derogatory of ways. In its vision of the Indian as a broken race best suited to serve as entertainment, the Columbian outlined the pattern for Fairs to come. At Buffalo an 'Indian Congress' served up the Indians to the American public as a type of animal rather than human life: 'No such lesson in history can be gleaned from books as is here shown by 'Native Americans' – long haired painted savages in all their barbaric splendour'.[41] The animal analogy was often directly made: 'A wild west Indian, at the Exposition, was observed absorbed in contemplation of a wolf. It was like meeting an old friend in the strange east. The wolf's howl too seemed to carry with it a note of recognition'.[42] At succeeding events in the twentieth century, up to and including the New York World's Fair, the Indian continued to fulfill the rôle of entertainment, a spectacular but expendable extra in a world conducting itself as though it believed the narratives of cowboy films then enjoying popularity. The reality of genocide and land sequestration were hidden by the pastiche of carefully arranged tepees, totem poles and trinket sellers.

Buffalo followed the Chicago pattern and presented an impressive range of exotic villages from different areas of the world. Japanese, African and Eskimo villages all proved popular with the crowds. Xavier Pené won the commission to build the African settlement, which most probably comprised of Dahomeyans. Most interesting at Buffalo though was the presence for the first time of villages from the American empire. Cuban, Hawaiian and Philippino villages celebrated American gains, the Philippino display being the largest with one hundred people on an eleven acre site.[43] A living display of peoples from all over the American continent was also presented. Its aim according to its organiser A. L. Benedict was to make 'an exposition of the living natives of Pan-America' containing 'only the aboriginal races of the Western continent and the islands geographically or politically associated with it'. Benedict's main problem was in keeping 'discipline and sanitation in a large population of uncivilised tribes, each possessing its own pecularities and religious prejudices'.[44] Describing his function as a farmer or zoo keeper would, he showed fully the extent to which anthropolgy itself was a victim of prejudice and misconception. Indeed, the major fascination for us now is not found in the types of life non-Western peoples created for themselves, but in the collective psychological condition of those who felt justified in creating displays of other peoples, in order to try and prove they were less than human.

Three years later at the St. Louis Fair the Philippines were the main part of the ethnographic display, villages of various different tribes being intended to show human development 'from the lowest grade to the better class'.[45] The committee reports described the arrangement:

> Vast quantities of bamboo and ripa brought from the archipelago, were used in the construction of the native villages ... The exhibit was an honest one. There were the least civilized people in the Negritos and the Igorrotes; the semi-civilized in the Bagobos and the Moros, and the civilized and cultured in the Visayans ... In all respects the exhibit was a faithful portrayal.[46]

In this particular exhibition, the authenticity of the exhibits could hardly be doubted, the Igorrotes causing a scandal by spearing and cooking the pet dogs of some of the local inhabitants. To complicate the anthropological picture, it was discovered that some of the dogs they ate were brought to them by local boys for a small fee. The organisers had taken the wrong advice on the dietary preferences of some of its most notable guests.[47]

The social, economic and political situation of the indigenous coloured populations of America gave social Darwinian theory added significance. 'Proof' of the degeneracy and genetic underdevelopment of the Negroid and American Indian populations gave justification to the status they were accorded. The first Fairs in the twentieth century became obsessed with evolutionary theory in an attempt to give scientific credence to the legalised racism present everywhere in American society. Buffalo was the extreme case, where the layout of the whole site was intended to show the visitor the shift from low levels of humanity to higher ones. It was hoped the visitor would sense the evolutionary flow of mankind as he/she walked through the Fair. The sculptural decoration and colour scheme of the buildings was intended to suggest a pattern of human development. The artistic directors of the Fair arranged its formal characteristics to illustrate social Darwinian theory: 'an ethical significance is aimed at, in the chromatic arrangement as in the architectural plan; the whole symbolising progression from a less civilized age to a higher. Thus the strongest, crudest colours are nearest the entrances.'[48] As the visitors entered the grounds through the Triumphal bridge, they 'would come upon the elementary conditions, that is, the earliest state of man suggested on one side and primitive nature on the other . . . The strongest primary colours should be applied here'; further along 'the colours should be applied refined and less contrasting, and the Tower which is to suggest the triumph of man's achievement, should be the lightest and most delicate in colour'.[49] Thus pure colour was natural, simple and brutal, mixed colour, particularly pastel shades, was synthetic, complex and hence civilized. Nowhere else in the history of international exhibitions – or in any other sphere – was there a more carefully constructed contrivance with the specific aim of high-lighting differences between racial types. The Buffalo Fair and many which followed it was intended to reinforce the racial structure of American society by driving wedges between the various ethnic groups.

The native village was only one form of human display common to exhibitions, there were several others, these normally being reserved for races considered higher up the evolutionary ladder. The foreign 'street' was a regular feature of exhibitions after 1880, the most famous one of all being the 'Rue de Caire'. The first Rue de Caire appeared at the Exposition Universelle of 1878, a modest affair with shops, a bazaar and a liberal number of North Africans. In 1889, as with all peopled displays, the scale was dramatically increased, making the street into a long, winding passageway full of shops, bartering Egyptians and irate camels. Visitors could buy artefacts made on the spot or consumables such as tobacco, perfume and spices brought from Arabic countries. Initially appearing when the French had strong interest in Egypt, the 'Rue' out-grew the imperial dimension to become more an exotic piece of entertainment. It would be a mistake however to suggest that at any time that was all it was, as European interest in Egypt and the Near East remained intense until well after the Second World War. After 1889 it was a feature of various exhibitions including the Chicago Columbian, the Greater Britain (1899), Paris 1900 and St. Louis. Of all of these, the Chicago and Paris 1900 ones were thought to be the most complete. In both the Cairo theme was made vague in order to allow most Arabic cultures some space, in what became genuinely thriving commercial centres. Dozens of craft shops, food stores, shoe shops and barbers lined the street, which gained an authentic feel from the sheer numbers of Arabic people present. At Paris an estimated thousand people worked on the Rue de Caire through the six month period. It became a place where one might while away a whole day, the pleasures available going well beyond those of simple sight-seeing. Restaurants and drinking shops were crowded, usually with men, as were the small theatres where one could see erotic belly-dancers perform in a way Paris was not normally accustomed to. Contemporary accounts hint at pleasures to be had even beyond these:

> In the Egyptian theatre the derboukhas purr; reed-flutes whine, the harsh and strident flute of the Arabs already heard in the Sahara, on the fringe of oases, mingled with cries, guttural and rhythmic, in a chant which tries to be gay and which hums sadly, so sadly and monotonously, so desperately . . . At the Cairo café where we are seated in front of steaming cups, a delicate, frail Egyptian girl, barely fourteen years old, with a finely modelled face of light amber, smiles at us with all her enamel teeth and her large, green eyes; she is sheathed in reddish-brown silk which makes her look like a gleaming serpent. She stands beside us, immobile and silent, having been brought by a negro at our request . . . A horrible matron, of a thoroughly Levantine puffiness, with swarthy eyes and sunken cheeks, watches her from the counter, wrapped in an ill-fitting coat of a sapphire-blue plush of a vulgar modernity.[50]

Achieving a realism the organisers could not have anticipated, the Rue de Caire seemed to escape all intended categories to become an independent force in itself. Hardly a celebration of imperial success, it could not be described either as an educational exhibit even in the most liberal of senses, though doubtless many learned things there they certainly did not know about before. Perhaps the only real way it justified its existence and earned its continued reappearance was through its commercial

E

potential. Not only was a large amount of produce sold from the Street but it also brought thousands through the turnstiles who would otherwise not have bothered. This was certainly the case with the Cairo Street in the Chicago Columbian where, though the sensual delights of Paris seemed to be absent, the money-making angle certainly was not. This Street contained sixty shops, all commercially viable and competitive. Apart from this, one could buy a donkey or camel ride or pay to go into a Muslim Mosque.

The financial aspect of human displays was important. They guaranteed attendances, they often produced a useful spin-off in sales of craft and food produce and they proved perfect venues for Western firms to advertise their goods. Maurice Talmeyr, in exasperated tone, questioned the ethics of a French manufacturer in connection with an 'Andalusia at the time of the Moors' display at the Paris 1900 show:

> Why does Andalusia – at the time of the Moors – recommend Menier Chocolate to us? Because the authentic Moors and the authentic Andalusia do not, according to all appearances, sufficiently allow for advertisements, and an exposition is not going, and never has gone, and never will go without advertisements.[51]

The most commercially considered presentation of peoples were the Indian and Ceylonese Teahouses erected by the British at countless exhibitions from 1880. Paid for mainly by the Indian Tea Syndicate, the whole point was to popularise tea among the Europeans; in order to do that dozens of Indians and Ceylonese people were brought to Europe to work in authentically styled Teahouses. Up to 1900, the British government took an active part in the Teahouses with the Syndicate, often subsidizing them so heavily that the tea could be served free. The bulk sales which might emerge if tea became fashionable in Europe were the incentive, there being sufficient evidence to suggest the ploy was a success.[52] The free Teahouse at the Amsterdam International of 1883 caused a stir amongst the suspicious Dutch gentry:

> The mere idea of any refreshment being given without charge appeared so strange to Dutch notions that visitors crowded the tea-room daily, and could scarcely believe that no charge would be made. Some of the better class of visitors at first objected to placing themselves under any obligation by drinking tea without payment; but this feeling soon wore off, and the tea-room was thronged.[53]

The commercial side of human displays reached a peak of variety at the American World's Fairs, edging the whole tradition close to a fusion of departmental store and fairground side-show. The Chicago Columbian boasted the widest range of peopled displays shown anywhere up to that time, the trend moving continuously upward from then. Apart from the seventeen villages and the Cairo Street, there were Chinese and Japanese Teahouses, a Moorish Palace, an Indian School, a Persian Coffee House, a Japanese Bazaar, a Parisian Café, a French Cider Press, an English Pub (the White Horse Inn), a South Sea Islanders canoeing Lake, Highland Pipers, a Hunter's Cabin and the Buffalo Bill Show. A large proportion of these were sponsored by individual companies, whose names would feature prominently in the display. At Buffalo, St. Louis and San Francisco the entertainment and selling aspects of human display were equally evident. After the First World War however, alternative forms tended to replace human displays; in particular the use of non-Western peoples declined, the tableau-vivant aspect surviving mainly in the form of white Americans advertising new products. At the Chicago Century of Progress Exposition in 1933, the number of foreign peoples of any kind was drastically reduced, this event boasting only Moroccan, Chinese and Belgian Villages, an Old Heidleberg Inn and a Maya Temple.[54] The New York World's Fair three years later had only Cuban, Seminole and English Villages, an English Pub and the Bendix Lama Temple.[55] As in Britain, the Great War was a watershed for peopled exhibits.

There were not always racial, imperial or commercial motives behind human exhibits. Some were engaged in what could be termed an ambassadorial rôle. That is, they were there to illustrate an issue, usually to do with the type of life led in the country they were from. Most governments participating in international exhibitions wished to give off a pleasant notion of what life was like in the country they ruled over, exhibits often being geared specifically to this end. To give off a pleasant idea of ones country had the dual purpose of creating an image of national stability before an international audience and of encouraging foreign visitors. By the start of the twentieth century, tourism was an ever-growing phenomenon, the exhibitions being used to sell the beauty of the homeland to prospective visitors. From the Paris 1900 show onwards, tourism displays featured prominently at exhibitions, usually in the form of tableaux-vivants with charming people in national costume explaining the advantages of their ethnic regions. A Portuguese Street, for example, was part of a display of the holiday resorts of Europe in the Machine Hall at the London Imperial International in 1909. At the Barcelona Exposition of 1929 a huge Spanish Village was built, complete with Spanish inhabitants producing local craft objects. The aim was to sell a particular vision of the Spanish nation to a Europe which appeared reluctant to visit. The village had examples of Spanish vernacular architecture from earliest times to the present, constructed entirely in authentic materials. Its success led to its retention after the exposition closed, and it remains today, on the Montjuïc hillside on the edge of the city-centre, the only surviving village from the whole exhibition tradition.[56] The Exposition of 1937 countered the resentment much of France felt at the constant location in Paris of all major cultural events, by featuring the different regions in individual tableaux-vivants. Most of these were village settings, created not only to serve as ethnic appeasement but also as a stimulant to tourism. Included were Marseille-Provence, Loire-Ardèche, Languedoc, Franche-Comté, Gascogne, Poitou, Massif Central, Nivernais-Berry, Vallée Moyenne de la Loire, Dauphiné et Hautes Alpes, Bretagne, Languedoc-Pyrenées, Rousillon, Champagne, Normandie, Picardie and Bigorre. It is not known whether this show quietened the grumblings of the rest of France but it certainly succeeded in creating a feeling of rurality which ran against the flavour of the rest of the site.

A considerable number of 'white' villages were built from 1900 onwards, usually performing public relations rôles for the countries they came from. English villages were particularly popular in America, appearing at regular intervals up to 1939. There were German, Austrian, Belgian, Swedish, and Dutch villages erected on several occasions, again mainly in America. The image the English invariably went for was one of Tudor bliss, complete with May-pole and village green, in direct contradiction of the reality of English life as lived by the majority.[57] Similarly, realism was a low priority across the range of white villages, the normal format being one of an exaggerated vernacular, emphasising rural values rooted in tradition, language and local custom. Most nations showed themselves as residing in pleasant holiday-camps, where everybody had plenty, everyone was content, and everyone knew his or her folk-tunes by heart. The distortion of the truth could become a sinister form of propaganda, depending on the country and the time, but usually, the visual rhetoric of an industrialised Europe pretending it was still operating with mediaeval technologies and power relations was harmless enough. Essentially, these villages were a dream of the bourgeoisie, a grand version of the suburbs they were busily building for themselves. The retreat to pre-industrial life was an attempt to suspend the knowledge that the industrial age gave them their power, and that the ugliness of the urban environment was their doing.

Interesting anomalies amongst the white villages were those of Ireland and Scotland. The first to appear was the Irish village of BallyMaclinton in 1908 at the Franco–British, this being retained for the following three White City exhibitions due to its popularity. The Scottish Village joined the Irish one in 1909 at the Imperial International, making sporadic appearances after that, notably at the Cornonation Exhibition of 1911, the Scottish National Exhibition, Glasgow 1911, and the Glasgow Empire Exhibition of 1938. These were ideologically difficult villages for the British to create, especially the ones staged in London, as they raised issues as to the status of Ireland and Scotland in relation to the colonies of the empire. Moreover, BallyMaclinton was conceived of at a time when the high Tories Bonar-Law and Carson were stirring Ulster to revolt, against a Liberal government desperately attempting to find a solution to the Irish issue.[58] BallyMaclinton presented Ireland as ancient and rural, with thatched cottages, peat-burners, traditional dancing and the Gaelic language; all was wrapped in a self-sufficiency scarcely less complete than that of the Senegalese Village next to it. The Times (May 14th.) listed Irish industries as handloom-weaving, lacemaking, embroidery, carpets and soaps, implying that Ireland's industrial revolution was as distant as Africa's. The reality of Ireland in 1908 – a nation which had staged its own international exhibitions since 1853 and which was struggling for independence both inside and outside of Parliament – could hardly have been less appropriately depicted. Scotland was treated in a similar manner, with cottage dwellers singing Highland melodies, ambling around the green in their tartan kilts. In this case, the image was little more than a farcical misrepresentation of a nation boasting one of the largest docks and industrial conurbations in the world. The Highland idyll was lifted from its context and made to stand as the essence of Scottish culture.

The presentations though were less to do with accuracy or with the encouragement of tourism than with the relationship they were in with the English. Colin McArthur has discussed this in terms of a core-periphery structure,

> whereby economically strong core countries draw weaker contiguous countries (or more accurately regions) into a satellite relationship across the entire range of the forms of social life . . . In the very act of equipping themselves ideologically to be core countries, and to sustain the undoubted strains of so becoming, the core countries at the same time defined the Other, the regions they themselves were not – i.e., the peripheral countries.[59]

Ireland had to be different, as did Scotland, in order for the English to be able to differentiate themselves and rule. The core-periphery phenomenon can be applied to the whole empire, and can be found throughout the exhibitions in the tendency to emphasize rurality, backwardness and nature when discussing subject-nations, and the city, industry and culture when discussing the imperial ones. Power was achieved and maintained through industrial technology, and it was through demonstration of it that core countries maintained their hold. To juxtapose a Machine Hall with a native village was to provide the clearest possible illustration of power relations in the world. For those who wished to see it that way, it also indicated relative positions on the social Darwinian scale. By showing Ireland and Scotland as nations of hand-loom weavers and Gaelic singers, organisers at the exhibitions were relating to them as periphery nations, as part of the empire. A time-worn attitude toward the Celtic races facilitated this, an attitude which has had its derogatory nature obscured by a quasi-romanticism. Malcolm Chapman:

> Since the eighteenth century, the Celtic fringe has posed for the urban intellectual as a location of the wild, the natural, the creative and the insecure. We can often find it said, with warm approval, that the Celts are impetuous, natural, spiritual and naïve . . . Such an approval is drawing on the same system of structural oppositions as is the accusation that the Celt is violent (impetuous), animal (natural), devoid of any sense of property (spiritual) or without manners (naïve), the bracketed terms being effective synonyms of the words that precede them, that they would be used to praise rather than to deride.[60]

The emphasis on the Celtic and Gaelic languages in some exhibitions had the effect of further emphasising their 'otherness', melting them into the foreign contingent.[61] When the English presented their own Tudor village, as they often did in America, an entirely different set of values were brought to bear; their rurality was not to do with backwardness or indolence, but with tradition and stability in the face of industrial change. The English village was an historical suburbia, where humility and respect for aristocratic privilege was a part of the daily lives of the synthetic inhabitants. This was an 'olde worlde' created under the comforting wing of temporarily invisible industry. Ironically however, by 1939 when an English village appeared at the New York World's Fair, the core/periphery formation was once again in operation, but this time with the Americans at the core.[62]

Often as part of a national exhibit, a building would be erected to be filled with people acting out some aspect of their culture on a continuous basis. The most common examples of this entertaining exercise in international public relations was the 'old city'. The Austrians were the first to create an old city when they peopled a reconstructed eighteenth century Vienna in 1873. After that date, an 'Old Paris', 'Old London' and 'Old New York' made regular appearances around the world. In the 'Old Paris' of 1900 in Paris, superbly authentic streets from the mediæval period were filled with hundreds of paid individuals, who simply walked around in mediæval garb for the six months of the Exposition. Less expensive and probably more common were international concerts by performers brought to exhibitions to work either in national or communal theatres on the site. Imre Kiralfy was the acknowledged master of this form, often bringing singers and dancers from all over the world to perform in continuous spectaculars at the

White City. The Latin-British Exhibition of 1912 contained, he informed his visitors in the Daily Programme, 'troupes of male and female singers and musicians giving their national and popular songs from Naples, Venice, Sicily, Aragon, Seville, Madrid, Oporto, Brittany, Normandy, Brazil, Mexico, Argentine and other Latin-American countries, thus giving the exhibition an aspect of realism, life, light and gaiety.' [63] This was surpassed by an extraordinary parade in and around the Grand Palais at the 1925 Paris show. After a banquet, a privileged few saw a performance with over two thousand participants. Loïe Fuller and her troupe, models from leading haute couture houses, the troupe of the Casino de Paris, Eva La Galienne and her company, the Paris Opera Company, the Comédie-Française, all the clowns from circuses in and around Paris, the Hoffman girls from the Moulin Rouge, the Tiller girls from the Folies Bergère, the 'Queens of the Theatre' (sixty of the best known actresses of the day) and three hundred dancers from various Parisian ballet companies took part in this flamboyant extravaganza. The show ran from late afternoon to the early hours of the morning.[64]

The presence of thousands of people at international exhibtions as exhibits had dramatic cultural and social spin-offs. This was particularly the case with those contained within imperial displays. Many of the Senegalese, Somalis and Dahomeyans who toured the world became Westernised in some degree, could conceivably have married into local populations, and most certainly affected their own people if and when they returned home. It is known that several of the Irish girls who were exhibited as inhabitants of BallyMaclinton in London stayed there and married; it is known also that many who went over to America as part of villages from Africa, Asia and Europe stayed there. The social effect of the transformation of the individual circumstances of these human exhibits is negligible however compared with the effect it had on the masses who visited the exhibitions. The millions of artisans, clerks, shop attendants, road-diggers, miners, businessmen, bankers, writers and teachers who filed past the African and Asian villages, amazed at what they saw and openly encouraged to regard it as a lower form of life. One of the few levels where European society operated in the absence of class was in the domain of racial prejudice; messages phrased in consistent manner to all levels of society affirmed the inferiority of coloured peoples. One can only guess at the extent of the harm caused by these human show-cases, but within the bounds of speculation it can be asserted that an immense amount of damage was caused, with little good coming out of them in social, moral or intellectual terms. Fifty years after their demise, the damage remains unrepaired.

Notes

1 Alex M. Thompson, *Dangle's Guide to Paris and the Exhibition* London 1900 Published by Walter Scott Ltd.
2 Ibid.
3 Paul Morand. Quoted from Philippe Julian, *The Triumph of Art Nouveau, Paris Exhibition 1900.* London 1974, Phaidon Press. This remains one of the most complete studies in print of the Exposition.
4 See Chapter 8.
5 See *Frank Leslie's Illustrated Historical Register of the Centennial Exposition 1876,* Philadelphia 1876 (Facsimile available New York 1974, Paddington Press), for best account and illustrations of early peopled exhibits. Also John MacKenzie, *Propaganda and Empire: The Manipulation of British Public Opinion 1880–1960.* Manchester University Press 1985.
6 See W.H. Schneider An Empire for the Masses: The French Popular Image of Africa, 1870–1900, Connecticut and London 1984 Greenwood Press, for a thorough account of activity at the Jardin d'Acclimatation.
7 *Les Nubiens du Jardin d'Acclimatation,* La Nature 5, 1877. Quoted from Schneider, see note 6.
8 Schneider, note 6.
9 *Bulletin de la Société d'Anthropologie,* 1883. Quoted from Schneider.
10 See Chapter 1.
11 *Paris and its Exhibition.* Pall Mall Gazette Extra, No.49, Friday July 26th. 1889.
12 Ibid.
13 Ibid.
14 The most celebrated attack on this show came from the Surrealist Group.
15 Information on Kiralfy's life is hard to come by. Recommended are *Who's Who 1915,* Donald Knight *The Exhibitions.* London 1978, privately published, and the Daily Mail, May 14th. 1908.
16 See John MacKenzie (note 5) and Annie E.S. Coombes *For God and For England: Contributions to an image of Africa in the first decade of the twentieth century.* Art History, Volume 8, No.4 December 1985.
17 This quote appears in both publications named in note 16.
18 *Official Daily Programme, Imperial International Exhibition.* London 1909, published by Bembrose and Son. I am grateful to Mr. Donald Knight, who gave me access to his collection of catalogues, of which this was one.
19 Quoted from John MacKenzie, see note 5.
20 *Japan–British Exhibition, Official Guide.* London 1910, Published by Bembrose and Son.
21 *Official Daily Programme, Coronation Exhibition.* London 1911, Bembrose and Son, and MacKenzie (note 5).
22 *Official Daily Programme, Coronation Exhibition,* London 1911, Bembrose and Son.
23 These names came from R.W. Rydell *All the World's a Fair: America's International Expositions,* Phd. Thesis 1980 University of California, and Donald Knight, *The Exhibitions* London 1978. Much work on the administrative mechanics of these exhibits still needs to be done.
24 See MacKenzie (note 5), Schneider (note 6), Rydell and Knight (note 23). Appearances not logged by these can be found in the relevant catalogues. It is certain that there were more appearances made by both tribes which have not yet come to light.
25 Quoted from MacKenzie, see note 5.
26 Ibid.
27 *British Empire Exhibition, Official Guide 1924* London, Fleetway Press.
28 G.L.M. Birdwood, *Handbook to the British Indian Section, Paris Exposition Universelle 1878.*
29 See Annie Coombes, note 16.
30 There was a popular *Phrenology Magazine* widely available at the time, as well as cheap publications such as *Phrenology Proved,* and *The Phrenological Dictionary.*
31 Quoted from MacKenzie, see note 5.
32 Quoted from Reid-Badger, *The Great American Fair: The World's Columbian Exposition and American Culture.* Chicago 1979, Published by Nelson Hall.

33 Ibid.
34 Quoted from Rydell, note 23.
35 For information on all these see Rydell.
36 Quoted from Lois Craig, Ed. *The Federal Presence – Architecture, Politics and Symbols in United States Government Building.* M.I.T. Press 1978.
37 *Official Souvenir Guide, Texas Centennial Exposition.* Dallas 1936.
38 See H. C. Miner, *The United States Government Building at the Centennail Exhibition 1874–1877.*, Prologue, Volume 4, Part 4, 1972.
39 See Reid-Badger, see note 32.
40 *Snap-shots by an artist: World's Fair through a camera.* Chicago 1893.
41 Quoted from Rydell, note 23.
42 Ibid.
43 Ibid.
44 Ibid.
45 *Louisiana Purchase Exposition Commission 1906, report by Committee on Industrial Expositions.* Washington 1906.
46 Ibid.
47 There are several accounts of this incident, these not always agreeing on the factual circumstances. For example, see Suzanne Hilton, Here today and gone tomorrow: The story of World's Fairs and Expositions. Philadelphia 1978, Westminster Press, and Burton Benedict, *The Anthropology of World's Fairs: San Francisco's Panama Pacific International Exposition 1915.* California 1983, Scholar Press.
48 Quoted from Rydell, note 23.
49 Ibid.
50 Jean Lorrain, quoted from Philippe Julian, see note 3.
51 Quoted from Rosalind H. Williams, *Dream Worlds: Mass Consumption in late 19th. Century France.* University of California Press.
52 Tea consumption rose steadily in most European countries through the period.
53 Samuel Digby, *India* from *The Royal Commission for the Chicago Exhibition, Official Catalogue of the British Section* London 1893, William Clowes and son.
54 *A Century of Progress, Book of the Fair.* Chicago 1933, Published by the Administration Building of the Fair.
55 *Official Guide Book of the New York World's Fair 1939.* New York 1939, Exposition Publications Ltd.
56 The village is one of Barcelona's most popular tourist attractions still, for its exact location see the *Michelin Guide to Spain.*
57 See Chapter 5.
58 One of the best texts to deal with the background to the Irish issue in this period is George Dangerfield, *The Strange Death of Liberal England*, London 1935, reprinted 1983 Granada Publishing.
59 Colin McArthur, *The dialectic of national identity: Glasgow Empire Exhibition of 1938.* in *Popular culture and social relations* Edited By Bennett, Mercer and Woollacott, Open University Press 1986. I am also grateful to Colin McArthur and John MacKenzie for making me aware of the significance of Scottish village exhibits at the Art Historians Conference in Brighton, 1986.
60 Quoted from McArthur, see note 59.
61 Obviously there was a positive side to the presentation of the Celtic and Gaelic languages. This does not exclude the divisive use of the situation by exhibition organisers. The vision created of the various periphery cultures by the core often became naturalised and accepted as a true reflection of the real cultural situation by the periphery itself. There appeared to be no contradiction in 1938, when the Scots themselves presented the *Clachan.*
62 See Chapter 5.
63 *Latin-British Exhibition, Official Daily Programme.* London 1912, Published by Gale and Polden Ltd.
64 See Victor Arwas *Art Deco*, London 1980, Academy Editions.

CHAPTER FIVE

The national profile

The visitor to the 1900 Exposition Universelle in Paris would expect to spend a large part of the day exploring one of the most extraordinary streets ever constructed. Assembled along several hundred metres of the Seine were a collection of houses, pavilions and palaces designed specifically to show off the national characteristics of each of the major European and imperial powers; the Rue des Nations. A bristling panoplay of turrets, pinnacles, domes and towers, this collection of unashamedly extrovert structures served the purpose of differenciating between the various national types, exaggerating and lauding their individual peculiarities. Along the Rue, one could discover what it meant to be a German, Belgian, Swede or Finn, the architecture and decor being backed by thorough displays of cultural artefacts, industrial produce and statistical information. More than this, each nation worked hard to project a national disposition, a character that united its peoples. The Rue des Nations was not only an exhibition of art or industry, it was a flamboyant manifestation of nationalist activity which had grown steadily among advanced nations for much of the previous century. As with most nationalist institutions, the atmosphere hanging over the banks of the Seine was a strange one, an uneven mixture of bombast, pride, fear, insecurity and confusion.

In the turmoil of the first industrial age, nationalism became the principal means whereby government could ensure a unity amongst people who might otherwise have had little or no cohesion. In part replacing loyalty to monarchy or local overlord, love of nation was not in the first instance an emotion easily instilled into the masses. The generation of pride, the psychological naturalisation of politically determined geographic boundaries, and the consolidation of different racial groups into single national units, were all accomplished through what were essentially ongoing programmes of nationalist propaganda. Nationalism, as encouraged by state-machines throughout Europe, entailed the convincing of a population that it should be proud – aggressively so – of the country it lived in, and that the country somehow had a life of its own to be acknowledged and supported. 'England', 'France' or 'Italy' were not abstract concepts or amorphous pieces of land, they were things to be admired, loved and died for. The spreading of these ideas was no simple task, for whilst it was likely people would be proud of their homes, regions and indigenous cultures, it was a different proposition to make them proud of thousands of square miles of land they would never visit, these often having different climates, customs and languages. Nevertheless, between 1850 and 1940 nationalism gradually came to grip the populations of most western countries; it became an almost mystical force, one which eventually created a vulgar certainty in the minds of otherwise intelligent people, sending millions to their deaths under its auspice alone.

From the mid-nineteenth century onwards nationalist diatribe infiltrated evermore deeply into all forms of European culture, affecting education, music, the arts and literature at the highest and most popular levels. In the closing decades of the century, as the electorate came to include all male citizens, the driving force of nationalism concentrated on the new forms of popular culture. Mass circulation newspapers, pulp literature and sheet-music all felt the fervour of national loyalty. Perhaps the institution to reflect it most profoundly was the English music hall, where nationhood and empire formed the core of subject-matter for singers and comedians. In 1901 J. A. Hobson saw the music hall as little more than a sinister propulgator of jingoism:

> Among large sections of the middle and labouring classes, the music hall, and recreative public houses into which it shades off in imperceptible degrees, are a more potent educator than the church, the school, the political meeting, or even the press. Into this lighter self of the city populace the artiste conveys by song or recitation crude notions upon morals and politics, appealing by coarse humour or exaggerated pathos to the animal lusts of an audience stimulated by alcohol into appreciative hilarity . . . the glorification of brute force and an ignorant contempt for foreigners are ever present factors which at great political crises make the music hall a very serviceable engine for generating military passion.[1]

Exhibition organizers learned a great deal from such cultural forms, the entertainment areas of sites all over the world being punctuated with populist propaganda on the merits nation and empire. The exhibitions had to do more however than simply whip up general verbal enthusiasm, they had also to give a physical form to pavilions and palaces and to penetrate higher levels of cultural production with nationalist dogma. They had to cater for the educated as well as the ignorant, providing a formula and a rationale for national culture which was capable of being interpreted by a wide cross-section of the population. Between 1851 and 1939 different countries used different strategies; established vehicles for the carrying of ideas were also adapted by individual nations as socio-economic circumstances changed.

It was the French who first exploited the potential of exhibitions as carriers of nationalist ideas. The earliest national events, staged in the wake of the Revolution, emphasized the need for unity and faith in nationhood; as with most aspects of public life at the time, these struggled to effectively fill the vacuum left by monarchy. Very much establishment ceremonials, they were given the task of contributing toward the newly founded republican tradition. They were amongst the first manifestations of a new era, in which 'Frenchness' had to be redefined and then collectively loved by the population. Denied the luxury of an individual king to personify France, statesmen were forced to artificially construct an image of the Republic capable of providing a focus for popular belief systems. Throughout the succeeding century and a half the process of definition continued, the Expositions Universelles coming to serve as occasional summings-up of the condition of Frenchness and the position of France in the world.

The difficulty for those engaged in the invention and promotion of national values was in the identification of factors common to the majority of Frenchmen. Eugene Weber:

> In a lecture in 1882, Renan criticised the German concept of nationhood, as worked out by Herder, Fichte, and Humboldt, which contended that there were four basic elements of nationhood: language, tradition, race and state. Renan proposed his own list instead: present consent, the desire to live together, common possession of a rich heritage of memories, and the will to exploit the inheritance one has received in joint tenancy. One can understand why Renan would reject the German principles of nationhood. It would be hard for a Breton to ignore the absence of a common language; tradition might well be taken in a political sense where division, not community, was the rule; race was a dubious concept; and only state remained, but as an expression of power, not organic growth. Still, Renan's own desiderata served no better. In 1882 consent might be assumed from indifference, but there could be little desire to live together with people who might as well have come from another world. The heritage of memories was not held in common, but differed according to region and social stock – witness Renan's own assumptions. And there was no inheritance in joint tenancy. The Republic under which Renan formulated his idea had inherited a territorial unit but a cultural jigsaw. It was up to the Republic to turn legal formulas into actual practice.[2]

Thus Government had to invent a unity which in reality did not exist. In the absence of an actual demographic cohesion, a conceptual one was constructed, involving wide, intangible claims for the nature of Frenchness. These concentrated not on observable fact but on atmosphere and emotion. Theorists presented French culture as being the quintessence

of civilization, as an integrated and sweeping force linking all Frenchmen. Avoiding the identification of individual components, the
national profile was to be an amalgamation of vital elements in the
civilizing process; as a blended whole this was a uniquely elevating
force, a quality capable of transforming all it encountered into something of higher value. In 1832 Edgar Quinet wrote that only Frenchmen
had

> the instinct of civilization, the need to take the initiative in a general way
> to bring about progress in modern society . . . It is this disinterested
> though imperious need . . . which makes French unity, which gives sense
> to its history and a soul to the country. This civilising force, this desire for
> internal influence is the best part of France, its art, its genius, its happi-
> ness.[3]

Similarly F. Guizot had affirmed in 1828:

> . . .civilising ideas and institutions born in other lands have been in some
> way forced to undergo a further development in France whenever they
> wanted to transplant themselves, to become fruitful and general, to act for
> the common benefit of European civilization . . . There has been hardly
> any great idea, any great principle of civilization, which, seeking to spread
> everywhere, has not first passed through France.[4]

The idea of France as civilizer allowed one of the strongest elements
within French culture to come into play, the arts. Undoubtedly one of
the highest expressions of civilization and of disinterested human
achievement, the arts were particularly important for France, as she
could with reasonable accuracy claim to be European leader in most of
the major disciplines. Thus, when Napoleon III issued the decree for the
organization of the first Exposition Universelle, his insistence on the
primacy of the fine arts carried a strong nationalist sentiment.[5] France
was to realise itself through its arts, to show the world that the complex
synthesis of regions and races had given birth to a unified and glorious
culture. At all the Expositions Universelles, Frenchness was to be seen
as an essence capable of constantly producing cultural artefacts of the
first rank. Music, Poetry, Painting, sculpture, architecture, ceramic,
furniture, textiles, manufactured objects, graphics, fashion, food and
drink, in fact every type of object carrying the least cultural significance
was presented as being at its best in its French form. Louis XIV, having
realised the importance of the arts as indicators of power and civilization, had embarked on policies of encouragement which had made
French art dominant in Europe; in the nineteenth century the legacy
was fully capitalized on, until sections of French society utterly unfamiliar with art in any form were nonetheless aware they were the masters
of it. Likewise the foreigner, on the whole, accepted French artistic

primacy. The vast sums French government put into the expositions were expected to pay back through the stimulation of cultural unity and confidence; as such, they were not simply displays of produce, they were a physical manifestation of the French national character. Moreover, the exercise was meaningless when constricted to national boundaries. The proof of Frenchness only emerged when it was recognised by others, when it exerted influence – directly and indirectly – outside France. Victor Hugo made this clear when he wrote in the guidebook of the 1867 Exposition:

> O France, adieu! You are too great to be merely a country. People are becoming separated from their mother, and she is becoming a goddess. A little while more, and you will vanish in the transfiguration. You are so great that you will soon no longer be. You will cease to be France, you will be Humanity; you will cease to be a nation, you will be ubiquity. You are destined to dissolve into radiance and nothing at this hour is so majestic as the visible obliteration of your frontier. Resign yourself to your immensity. Goodbye, people! Hail, man! Submit to your inevitable and sublime aggrandizement, O my country, and, as Athens became Greece, as Rome became Christendom, you, France, become the world![6]

Attitudes toward empire at the 1867 Exposition revealed an expansive frame of mind, humanised by an insistence upon the civilizing powers of the French nation. The Notary of the Tunisian consulat for example, lauded European intervention in his country, seeing the 'benefits of their civilization', which he defined as a combination of knowledge, international understanding, industry and trade. He also cast the French as the 'enemies of isolation', a nation who saw the international perspective as the only one capable of overcoming 'hatred, ancient prejudices and war, the plague of man and the ruin of the land'.[7] More than anything else for this writer, the French were bringing a way of life. The core of his discussion begged comparison with discourses on the benefits of Roman occupation of uncivilized corners of the ancient world, so confident was his vision of his overlords.

After the shock of 1871 the material basis of French claims to world significance was severely damaged, the national profile being forced in the years after Sedan into more abstract terrain than ever before. Only seven years after defeat an Exposition Universelle was held with the express purpose of showing the world that France had recovered fully from the disaster. Here the visual arts were brought heavily to the fore as the central device for the presentation of national character. The actual appearance of the Exposition, both inside and out, was to be the basis of French claims to nationhood. A splendid semi-permanent building, the Palais du Trocadéro, was placed on the crest of the Chaillot Hill facing the Champs de Mars, to serve as the main part of the French contribution. The facade of the central core comprised of a semi-circle of giant arches, surmounted by a massive second storey in the form of a buttressed octagonal drum and cupola. Two Venetian towers flanked this and vast arcaded wings described a concave arc either side. The wings framed a garden and stepped fountain on the slope of the hill. The whole was intended to suggest the splendour of the French baroque, a previous age of power and confidence. In true conservative manner the creators of the Trocadéro reassured themselves of French standing by resorting to a distant and glorious past. It did its job well, for no innocent by-stander on the Chaillot Hill could have doubted they were in a country of importance and wealth. The literature surrounding the building dwelt on the ancient pedigree of the site: 'le Trocadéro, comme on l'a dit plus haute, fait partie du sol de l'ancien village de Chaillot, dont la première trace date du XIe siècle. Ce village appartenait à une région qui au VIIe s'etendait jusqu'a Boulogne, le bois compris, et portait le nom de Nimio'.[8] Inside the building the main vestibule was filled with an exhibition of 'Les Antiquités des Gaules', the centre of which was a tomb presented exactly as found with its treasure and bones. This was in fact a controversial display in such a context, as it implied French origins in Gallic culture, something the millions of non-Gallic French resented.[9]

As the appointed media to suggest France was a civilization in the ascendant, architecture, the decorative and fine arts were given a tremendous responsibility in 1878. It would be too crude to suggest nationalism as a sole stimulus behind French cultural policy, but a maxim of logical progression was undoubtedly everpresent, confirming the notion that France reigned supreme in art, that art dominated culture, culture evoked civilization, and hence civilization meant France. The Exposition of 1889 saw the most complete rendering so far of France as the supreme example of civilized humanity, leading the Official American Report to recognise art as a French national characteristic: 'In France there is no quality more clearly apparent than respect for the arts and works of all kinds connected with them. This trait belongs to no condition or class, but pervades alike all ranks of society'.[10] Additionally, the same report tied art not only into the French nation but also into the genetic make-up of French men:

> That there is in the human race such an intangible quality as the art instinct there can be no reasonable doubt; and that it has been more marked and strongly developed among the Latin races than among the northern people, is also indisputable. If the history of art proves one thing more than another, it is the value of this instinct in the development of painting, sculpture, and architecture among the southern races. To the influence of the Greeks, and, in later times, the great era of the Italian

Renaissance, is the northern part of the civilized world indebted for much that is good in its achievement. But in no country has that double influence taken such deep root and retained such vigorous life as in France; in no other has it produced such far reaching and beneficial results. In that country it has kept alive a natural love for the artistic, when even in these materialistic days of steam and iron, adorns every phase of national life.[11]

Thus France was the protector of Western classical culture; the organizers could not have wished for a better response from a foreign power.

By 1900 the creation of a vast expensive exposition needed little justification in government circles beyond the belief that 'France owes it to herself as the Queen of Civilization to hold a great exhibition which will become one of her many claims to glory'.[12] The organizers stated their aim as being to 'reflect the refulgent genius of France and show that, as in the past, we now stand in the van-garde of progress'.[13] When Exposition director Alfred Picard addressed the Chamber of Deputies to win support for the show, his central argument was for the need to confirm the French image of itself as a spiritual leader of humanity:

> In voting for this draft bill, the Chambers will perform an act of high patriotism . . .(the exposition) will demonstrate once again the growth of the nation's prosperity and, what is more important, add to its glory and import abroad. Paris and all of France will emerge from this solemn meeting yet more splendid. The Republic will close the nineteenth century with a suitable dignity and will attest to its desire to remain at the vanguard of civilization.[14]

The amount spent in 1900 and on the two other Expositions Universelles held in the twentieth century guaranteed their status; the sizes of the sites were steadily increased and governmental involvement was maintained at an intense level. All this testified to the fact that at international exhibitions commerical profit was never the highest priority for the French.[15]

The obsession with the civilizing aspects of 'Frenchness' led to a concentration of resources on events in Paris. From the Revolution onwards, the hegemony of Paris over the rest of France became a recognised part of French cultural strategy. Paris was to be built up into the centre of European and hence world civilization. The national exhibitions from 1798 and the expositions universelles from 1855 were inevitably and naturally held there, the capital receiving the lion's share of all government funding for cultural activities. Understandably, the jealousy of the regions became a major stumbling block for exposition organizers to overcome, a jealousy that existed in many spheres of life and revealed the tenuous nature of French national unity. Centralization, a political move begun by Richelieu and completed by the

Revolution, at times proved counter-productive in the nineteenth and twentieth centuries, as proud regions campaigned to reduce the control Paris exercised over French national life. The 1900 show was plagued in its early organizational phases by committed decentralists who wanted to abandon the concept of the international exhibition altogether, especially ones held in Paris. Maurice Barrés, predictably, led a fierce assault in 'Le Figaro', but the most vigorous anti-exposition campaign was led by the editor of 'L'Est Republique', Leon Goulette.[16] He headed a school of thought in Nancy, in existence since the first exposition in 1855, which challenged the cultural primacy of Paris and the rôle it had assumed as spiritual leader in French affairs. More than a provincial resentment at the dominance of the capital, the antipathy felt was a result of general discomfort with the national profile created for France by authorities in Paris. It was obvious to regionalists that in order to create a vision of a superior culture, money had to be concentrated into specific areas and projects, as the wealth simply did not exist to enhance every area of France equally. Thus Paris was the show-piece which drained resources in order to tell the world what it was to be French, much to the annoyance of many other French cities and areas. A lot of the anger focussed on the expositions universelles, directed mainly by middle-class business people who had a stake in promoting the regions they lived in. Thus the nationalist rôle of the expositions, whilst undoubtedly useful for impressing the foreigner with the glory of French culture, had the unfortunate back-lash of alienating the provincial bourgeoisie. The holding of State funded expositions in Marseille in 1906 and 1922 were almost certainly a result of agitation from the South. In 1937, as the last Exposition Universelle opened its gates, the problem remained unresolved despite a substantial area of the site being given over to the regions.[17]

There were theoretical problems with the identifying of the arts as a national characteristic. The most important of these was the matching of artistic traditions with other values thought to be important in the make-up of a modern industrial state. The concept of Progress for example, was a vital one to all expansive imperial economies, the motivation behind industry and capital, yet it sat very uncomfortably with long-standing ideas of artistic excellence. The arts, especially those generated by the French academies, could suggest a certain standing, sophistication, tradition and power, but they were unable to characterize with ease the voracious advance of a government committed to industrial and imperial growth. As a raison d'être behind the actual creation of art objects, the notion of progress was even more awkward. For example, in design and architecture, it implied experimentation with style and use of new materials, yet in these areas the French were reknown for classical and baroque form. In furniture the most favoured styles were those of Louis Quinze and Seize, especially amongst foreign buyers, yet adherence to these implied not progress, but regression. French cultural authorities throughout the nineteenth century were extremely reticent to even contemplate the idea of a style to represent the present or future, showing a reluctance to advance beyond artistic approaches evolved under the Louis'. Such attitudes ran against progressive industrialists, economists and imperialists, and led to awkward aesthetic and symbolic clashes, both in the arrangement and the final appearance of the exposition sites.[18]

The Revolution had forced the French into national self-consciousness at a very early date. Across the Channel, nationalist propaganda became noticeable far later, a specific vision of 'Englishness' being constructed and presented at exhibitions only after 1880. After then however, it was to be the dominant element in virtually all British contributions to international exhibitions. English nationalism, as the exhibitions exposed it, appears to have grown as a propaganda phenomenon in an inverse ratio with the decline of British power. That is to say, there is little real evidence of concern with the national profile in 1851 when industry and empire guaranteed Britain's position as most powerful country, but toward the end of the century as Europe and America caught up, the definition of Englishness had become of distinct importance. The difficulties the French encountered with the relative disunity of their regions was far less of a problem to the English, who had forged a cohesive unit long before the industrial revolution began. This is not to say England was in any real sense happily united, but merely to affirm that the state machinery had long been in place, making organised dissent along racial or regional lines inconceivable by the time Victoria's reign began. The problem for the English government lay not here but in the continuous class agitation, which showed itself capable of putting the country on the edge of revolution several times during the arduous first phase of industrialization.

At the South Kensington exhibitions of 1851, 1862 and 1871 to 1874, the national profile was so assumed it was a non-issue. In broad cultural terms there was no attempt to theoretically determine the nature of the English national character. In the arts for example there was an almost blasé acceptance of the achievement of others. The cultural produce of various European nations was widely and casually acknowledged as superior to that of Britain even in establishment circles. At the Crystal Palace exhibition it was observed that 'while in the solidity of their manufactures our countrymen were unrivalled, in the matter of adornment they were easily outstripped'.[19] In 1855, whilst in Paris for the Exposition, Victoria made plain her preference for French furniture, buying two cabinets and a table.[20] Such admissions, innocent and petty as they may appear, reveal at the highest level a lack of worry about English cultural standing which would later be unacceptable. The reality of British power between 1850 and 1880 it seems required little embellishment. Whatever other political rôles the exhibitions had, the bolstering of a national image did not need to be one of them, beyond demonstrating an awesome, intimidating power.

Englishmen identified themselves through loyalty to crown and the empire; the legendary 'stiff upper-lip' was already firmly in place by 1851, referring to the extent to which one unflinchingly did ones duty to the nation in the absence of self-interest. Empire was the vehicle for nationalism, royalty the focus, making royal and imperial presences at the exhibitions imperative for them to have any real meaning.[21] Thus, every major international exhibition held in Britain through to the First World War had extensive imperial sections and a member of the monarchy involved in the organisation. The most celebrated example of the latter was Prince Albert's activity in 1851. As personifications of nation the monarchy served a vital consolidatory rôle, rendering unnecessary any constructed profile of Englishness beyond themselves. A pamphlet written on the 1851 exhibition, entitled 'Love and Loyalty', explained English worldly success not as a result of industry, but as the natural consequence of the people's love of the monarch. Furthermore, the union of royalty with God, in the form of the Church of England, gave an eternal value to this love. Christ Himself, apparently, with Love and Loyalty at His feet, made an 'appeal to Britain to spread TRUE civilisation through the veins of the whole world through the medium of the Holy Writ'.[22] The spread of civilization for the British had little to do with the French ideal, rather it implied trade, backed by diplomacy, the force of arms and the Mission. Royalty was a sufficient unifying factor in a country which had all the evidence of its success before it. When the success began to run dry at the end of the century however, it had to be bolstered with other visions of Englishness in order to remind the population who they were.

The problem by 1900 was one of neglect. For almost a century, the monarchy, industry, the navy and the empire had said all that needed to be said about Britain. But by then this was no longer enough in a world which began to boast nations with all of these, some of them in vast excess of the English. As the new century dawned, alternative English values not only had to be highlighted at home and abroad, first of all they had to be invented. The exhibitions from 1900 onward were harbingers of this invented Englishness, until by 1939, the vision of England they put forward was so dominant that it became the mainstay of war-time propaganda.

In essence, the English national profile fabricated in the closing decades of the nineteenth century was derived from the pre-industrial world. The Tudor and Elizabethan eras were most popular for the identification of Englishness, due to their historical location at the start of English imperial history. The establishment of the Church of England, the maturing of the arts, the growth of the navy, of overseas trade and conquest, made them the perfect periods to hark back to for nationalists. After these, the later seventeenth century, and in certain instances the mediæval world, were used. At exhibitions, in the visual arts and in literature, 'Olde Englande' came to stand for a range of traditional virtues Englishmen were supposedly ingrained with. Simple, solid, quaint, reliable, unchanging and hardy were the type of adjectives used to describe the English population; more than this, they were applied to English culture in general. The sentiment was perfectly described by Chesterton:

> St. George he was for England,
> And before he killed the dragon,
> He drank a pint of English ale,
> Out of an English flagon.[23]

Higher up the class structure, more elite constructions leaned on what might be described as the Shakespearean and Royalist tradition, stressing chivalry and poetry as the characteristics of a higher kind of English gentleman. Regardless of class however, the period was marked by a widespread insistence that English power derived not from the success of industry but from innate English characteristics forged in pre-Enlightenment days. In 1900 when the organisers came to decide upon the style of the British pavilion for the Paris exposition, all these factors were taken into account. Sir Isidore Spielman, chairman of the Royal Commission over the pavilion explained:

> The Royal Pavilion on the Quai d'Orsay afforded us our only opportunity of making a distinctive national display . . . Our intention was to provide an example of the most characteristic style of English domestic architecture, fitted up and furnished in such a way as to give, as far as possible, an idea of a well appointed English house . . . The choice of architecture for the British Royal Pavilion was no easy matter, since the problem to be solved consisted in covering a space of given dimensions with a characteristic English building . . . it was finally decided . . . to take as a model the principal facade of a famous Jacobean Manor House, known as 'The Hall', Bradford on Avon.[24]

The interior of this early seventeenth century house was filled with furniture by William Morris and Company, with stained-glass windows by Edward Burne-Jones. The choice of architectural style and interior decor guaranteed a vision of aristocratic England in existence long before the industrial revolution.[25]

The return to 'Olde Englande' had long and diverse theoretical roots, giving an amount of respectability to what was in some ways an absurd vision of one of the largest and oldest industrial nations. The gothic revival in the arts had begun with the onset of romanticism at the end of the eighteenth century and had blossomed into the most significant British artistic movement in the nineteenth. The PreRaphaelites and William Morris continued the mediæval thrust through to the 1880's, from whence various revival movements in the decorative arts and architecture carried it forward into this century. Most notable amongst these was the Arts and Crafts movement. The first evidence of revivalism being used to project a national profile in exhibitions came in the Philadelphia Centennial in 1876, when Thomas Harris's two buildings for the British contingent had a haughty, half-timbered look which reminded the new nation of the age and standing of their English forebears.[26] In 1878 in Paris the English chose a heavy black and white Tudor palace style for the national pavilion along the first 'Rue des Nations'. At that stage, almost thirty years after the demise of the original preRaphaelite group and the death of Augustus Pugin, momentum was maintained in the 'pre-industry' camp largely through the exertions of the William Morris circle. By 1900, though no longer a progressive or socially aware force, arts and crafts mediævalism had become a major factor in British art and design.[27] Appropriated by conservative imperialists within the art establishment, it was reinterpreted into a national domestic style; the 1900 Paris show pavilion – designed by Lutyens – was the vision of English life as sanctioned by national propagandists. Eight years later at the Franco–British Exhibition the debate on English national style appeared to reach some kind of resolution, with an Arts and Crafts based vernacular coming into absolute ascendancy in the decorative arts and domestic architecture. In public architecture the 'Edwardian baroque' came to the fore, a dry and pompous classicism based on the work of Wren, Hawksmoor and Vanbrugh. Thus the private and public domains were divided out, Edwardian baroque being the preferred style for imperial monuments.[28] It would be a mistake therefore to associate Tudor and mediæval revivalism too closely with imperialism, rather it was a nationalist movement intended to project an image of the indigenous English population. The pattern of classical for public and vernacular for private building was repeated later in the twentieth century by most totalitarian states.

The idea that England had a better, truer and nobler past before the industrial revolution, was put forward by factions on both right and left of the political spectrum, normally in the absence of any factual back-up. On the one side, pre-industrial England appeared as an age of unalienated labour, a land of clean air and full bellies; on the other it was the time of a 'purer' Englishman, simple, obedient and untainted by the corruptions of urban life. The truth or falsehood in these positions is less important than the effect they had on mass consciousness. The image of Olde Englande came to infect British popular culture into the twentieth century from exhibition sites to fairgrounds, from graphic design to the cinema; most emphatically, it has survived to the present in the mock-Tudor trimmings of middle class housing estates.[29] In reality the worship of the ancient and rural, as opposed to the contemporary and urban, was largely explicable in terms of economic and political shifts through the period. The voracious growth which saw the expansion of cities, industries, science and empire was coming to an end; the trick after 1900, especially with the worrying outcome of the Boer War, was to hang on to what had been won.[30] George Beak, employed by the British government to produce propaganda during the First World War, emphasised this point: '. . . the spirit of British propaganda would differ wholly and entirely from the German, in that it would not be aggressive in character. Germany's aim was to secure an empire and dominate Europe; our aim is, presumably, to preserve and develop what we already have.' [31] The vibrant, progressive liberalism which had created a monument to itself in the original Great Exhibition was tattered and tired, as was the Crystal Palace itself, languishing in Sydenham and soon to be burnt to the ground.[32] Britain no longer had the power to play its former rôle with conviction. Now, comfortable, stolid values, an aristocratic quaintness, a saturation in tradition and folklore, masked the desperate struggle they were engaged in to remain a world leader. There was little to be gained in identifying English consciousness with things slipping from grasp, much rather, it was best to continue to struggle for position and deny the struggle even existed. The millions of city-dwellers whose labour had created industry and empire were bypassed in an attempt to hide the fact of English decline. In 1900 the national profile was a fabrication made by those who had enjoyed the fruits of empire and were now shocked at their own vunerability. Moreover, creation of an Olde Englande was a relatively easy task for exhibition organisers and government propagandists, as they themselves tended to emerge from the villages and suburbs of England to be educated in the most ancient of schools and universities. For them the vision felt natural and desirable. It was they who extended the national profile after the First World War to include the paraphernalia of contemporary aristocratic life.

After the rather esoteric presentation of English heritage and character at Paris in 1900, exhibition features emerged which made the point more simply. The Guide to the Texas Centennial described a typical effort. Past an English Village the visitor met with a paradigm of British cultural heritage:

> Now comes the last feature on your ticket book, the Old Globe Theatre and its Shakespearean players. Near the General Motors Auditorium, this bit of Merry Old England recalls the days of Shakespeare, Kit Marlowe, Ben Jonson and the gallant Walter Raleigh. Here, in a setting that brings back the times of Good Queen Bess, you will find a complete reproduction of the Old Globe Theatre in which the plays of Shakespeare were first produced, in London, during his lifetime. In this playhouse, typical of the Elizabethan period, the best known Shakespearean Company in the country presents the plays of the Bard of Avon exactly as he wrote them.[33]

Likewise, at the New York World's Fair 'Englishness' spilled out of the officially designated areas into the entertainment facilities. Merrie England (a reproduction village) was at the centre of a cluster of features, including Shakespeare's House, Old English Pubs, a Pageant, a Village Green and the Globe Theatre.[34]

It would be wrong to suggest that industry was wholly excluded as part of the national profile, rather, it was given a new emphasis, as a character trait of the English. 'Industrious', 'productive', 'resourceful' were the psychological attributes of the English crowd, whilst industry in the physical sense was given an historical dimension, as something the English had invented during the industrial revolution. The Machine Halls remained but they were no longer the material foci of events, their significance being continuously reduced in relation to empire, which was correspondingly raised. Occasionally a symbolic hybrid was formed; at the White City exhibitions for example, industry and Olde Englande were fused in the personage of John Bull, a figure frequently used in publicity to represent England. This comfortable, portly Englishman was at once a shrewd northern mill owner, the Lord Mayor of London, a merry wood-chopper and Sir Toby Belch; he was relatively uncultured in the highest sense, but he had the type of attitude to life that made him the perfect representative of English bourgeois values. At the Franco–British exhibition the French counterpoise to John Bull was 'La Parisienne', the two figures appearing together on much of the popular literature.[35] La Parisienne played delicacy, art and culture whilst John Bull was simplicity, industry and stalwartness. Commentator Sir John Cockburn, consciously or otherwise, recognised the intent of the two projections. Speaking on the way the national characteristics of the two harmonised for the purpose of exhibitions, he affirmed 'France and Britain possess distinguishing characteristics which admirably blend together. Each abounds in those qualities which form the complement of the other; British solidity, adorned with French grace yields a result that no other combination of nations can approach.' [36] 'Solidity' implied simple, bold, stout, honest, industrious; 'grace' implied charm, eloquence, delicacy, lightness, artistry. Whether a true or false reflection of Franco–British life and economy in 1908 – and overwhelming evidence suggests it was false – it was a vision of the two races afforded much credence on both sides of the Channel. For English propagandists, the association of honesty, simplicity and solidity with pre-industrial values stemmed from mistrust and fear of the urban working classes, the spawn of industry. Socialism and trade unionism went naturally with the city and the factory; whilst the British middle classes were quick to laud the economic value of these latter things, they preferred to escape from the social consequences of the former.

From the end of the First World War, the principle was established that there should be British propaganda produced for consumption in Europe and America, various bodies succeeding each other in the task of maintaining a particular image of Britain for the foreigner. The News and Political Intelligence Department, the Department of Overseas Trade, the Travel Association of Great Britain and Northern Ireland, the Overseas Propaganda Committee and the British Council all had specific involvement in projecting an image of Britain, this mostly corresponding with the picture created before the First World War in international exhibitions. In 1932, Stephen Tallents, working for the Department of Overseas Trade, drew up a list of subjects deemed suitable for national projection. Included were many of the eccentricities of British life Europeans would find amusing and amenable, such as London Buses, the Derby and Punch; other things were designed to emphasize British fairplay and democracy, such as the Parliamentary institutions, the Underground system and the Manchester Guardian. The majority though stressed the pre-industrial past, particularly with an accent on the aristocratic life-style and the public school ethos: the monarchy, the English Bible, the works of Shakespeare, Henley and the Boat Race, test matches, the trooping of the colour, the Lord Mayor of London, Oxford and Edinburgh, the Times, the English countryside and villages, foxhunting, English servants, English bloodstock and pedigree stock, gardening and tailoring.[37] The British masses were easily forgotten in a move to make the English the aristocracy of the world. What they lacked in real power they hoped to win back in a simulation of hereditary right. Into the 1930's, many of the items on Tallents' list were included as exhibits in British sections in international events all over the world, as the Department of Overseas Trade had taken responsibility for exhibitions in 1918. The final triumph of 'Lordly' and 'Hearts of Oak' Englishness came in the Paris Exposition of 1937 and the New York World's Fair of 1939, to be discussed later in the chapter.

Of all the Western powers, the problem of national self-identification was most awkward for America. In 1876 when the Philadelphia Centennial Exposition opened the new republic was celebrating a century of independence and, more discreetly, a decade of unity. With the Exposition the debate on the nature of American culture became collectively audible for the first time, and the first suggestions as to what it might be were proffered. The debate had polarised before 1876 around the relationship with Europe, this remaining a controversial element at the Fair. Questions of immense complexity had to be faced. At what point did the population, political institutions and culture cease to be European and become American? Was American culture wholly borrowed and if so, did this matter? Should there be new cultural forms to go with the new continent, if so what should they look like? The mixture of peoples in America made the issues all the more complex. Wilbur Zelinsky has referred to the myth of the 'melting pot', or the idea that European origins were left behind or blended once in America. The 'melting pot', he tells us 'contains a lumpy stew; . . . although ethnic groups may have thickened and enriched the All-American broth – except in the south-eastern quadrant of the pot – the lumps will not cook away, at least not for a good many years.' [38] The new continent contained not one or two races, as with most former colonies, but dozens, many of these fiercely proud of their origins. Others, by contrast, were refugees from hostile homelands. The quest for American national identity clearly did not lie in race or tradition, or even in any genuine spirit of co-operation; unity had to be sought elsewhere.

'American-ness', as it were, was formulated out of the economic-political conditions surrounding the creation of America. By the opening of the exhibition tradition three ideas had already been identified with the national character: the Pioneer Spirit, Republicanism (incorporating democracy) and Progress. All three were implied in the official literature of the Philadelphia Centennial, the exhibition having 'connected a national celebration with an international exhibition, thus identifying the Independence and history of America with the Industrial Art and progress of the world'.[39] The pioneer spirit was evident in all the World's Fairs up to and including the New York show of 1939. Exhibits where it was suggested could range widely, from tableaux-vivants showing how the land was transformed by early settlers, such as log cabins, pilgrims and old villages, to elements in the sculptural and mural decoration of the site. The Chicago Columbian was noted for its living displays of pioneers, cowboys and Indians, effectively beginning the genre at World's Fairs. The Buffalo Bill Show there gave a crude and commercialised version of 'how the west was won', particularly with regard to the American Indian.[40] Most Fairs after this had similar spectacles, usually in the entertainment areas. In terms of sculpture and mural work, the Panama–Pacific Exposition (San Francisco, 1915) provided the most famous edifice of the whole American tradition, 'The End of the Trail'. Made by sculptor James Earl Fraser, this depicted an exhausted Indian on horseback, slumped forward as if on the edge of collapse. At the Exposition it was juxtaposed against Solon Borglum's sculpture 'The Pioneer', in what was a clear indication to the visitor of the way America had gone and would continue to go. Eugen Neuhaus wrote at the time,

> The symbolism of the 'Pioneer' and 'The End of the Trail' is, first of all, a very fine expression of the destinies of two great races so important in our historical development. The erect, energetic, powerful man, head high, with a challenge in his face, looking out into early morning, is very typical of the white man and the victorious march of his civilization. His horse steps lightly, prancingly, and there is admirable expression of physical vigor and hopeful expectation. The gun and axe on his arm are suggestive of his preparedness for any task the day and future may bring.
>
> Contrast this picture of life with the overwhelming expression of physical fatigue, almost exhaustion, that Fraser gives to his Indian in 'The End of the Trail'. It is embodied in rider and horse. Man and beast seem both to have reached the end of their resources and both are ready to give up the task they are not ready to meet.[41]

At this Fair the pioneer spirit was closely associated with the notion of progress, with strong hints that the two combined would see Americans advance beyond their own shores: 'the greatest adventure is before us, the gigantic adventures of an advancing democracy – strong, virile, kindly – and in that advance we shall be true to the indestructible spirit of the American pioneer'.[42]

Republicanism and democracy were seen as the traits which most convincingly separated America from Europe. Into the twentieth century this vision was expanded to make America the 'home of democracy'. American republicanism was presented as more complete and pure than its French counterpart, Eugen Neuhaus typically commenting on 'our mighty nation, which carried to a successful ending a gigantic task abandoned by another great republic.'[43] From the Chicago Columbian onward, the American republican spirit tended to be symbolised through classicism. Classicism had the perfect historical pedigree. It had been handed down by the original democratic and republican peoples, the Greeks and Romans, it was used by the French Revolutionaries as an appropriate form and it had stood for democratic values in American architecture from the time of Jefferson. It was almost inevitable it would be used in the palaces, pavilions and site planning of the world's fairs. Between 1893 and 1915 exceptions to the classical rule were few and far between, perhaps the multi-coloured extravaganza at Buffalo (1901) being the furthest away in mood. The American pavilion at the Paris Exposition of 1900 stood austerely out on the Rue des Nations, a sober classical monument covered by a heavy dome and topped by a gilded eagle.

The move to classical form in Fairs between 1876 and 1893 did not go unquestioned, progressive architects pointing out that America was choosing to represent itself with a regressive European style when it might have been better off with new forms.[44] However, classicism fitted the requirements of the new country too closely to allow deviance. Classical form gave a look of power, solidity and permanence; it suggested a certain stature, yet its symbolism allowed it to be interpreted differently from parallels employed by European monarchies. More important than any of these in 1893 it implied, following the Roman model, not only republicanism but imperialism also. It was only in the 1930's, when European fascist states employed classicism to very different ends, that policies switched to representing America with various modernist forms. Republicanism was then more closely identified with progress of the free world, making forward-looking constructions more appropriate than classical ones. The Chicago Century of Progress Exposition of 1933 exuded a futuristic Utopian republicanism, followed emphatically by the New York World's Fair, where the extraordinary space-age centre-piece to the show was entitled 'Democracity'.

The immense size of the American World's Fairs owed a great deal to the disposition of the various authorities responsible for them, this emerging out of intense national self-consciousness. Zelinsky characterised the American race as being one obsessed with measurable achievement, arguing

> It would be difficult to imagine a culture more efficiently programmed for expediting progress towards the most advanced technologies and socio-economic organisations . . . There is an irrestistible urge to achieve – and proclaim – the quantifiably superlative – the biggest, highest, costliest, loudest or fastest, frequently without any dollar and cents justification.[45]

The Fairs celebrated the rise of America as a phenomenon; the size and expense were part and parcel of their American-ness. It was necessary for the themes carrying the national message to be expressed on an epic scale, larger than the efforts of other nations if possible. Because the French also used size and opulence at expositions to express their national identity, albeit in a different way and for different reasons, the two powers entered into a bizarre contest. The whole exhibition tradition owed its spectacular scale and lavishness to the two of them, as they persisted in expanding their efforts from the mid-nineteenth to mid-twentieth centuries. That a rivalry came to exist between them was evidenced by the attempt of the Chicagoans to out-do the Paris show of 1889, and the Parisians in 1900 to better the Columbian.[46] Likewise the organisers both at Buffalo and St. Louis, accepting the inter-state rivalry, saw the preceding Paris show as the event to measure themselves by. The effort to establish a national profile cost both dearly, as they used the exhibition medium to struggle for what they saw as a necessary supremacy. Everything came to a grand climax on the eve of the Second World War.

The French held what would be their last Exposition Universelle in 1937, in a Europe hardly conducive to an expression of international fellowship. Much of the publicity literature was so purposely unaware of the political climate as to constitute lies: 'Forty-five states responded to the appeal of France and, without jealousy or bickering, took up the task of epitomizing their culture and their individual resources. They offer,in a splendid array, the outcome of a generation's progress in the field of art, science and industry, symbolising at the same time a universal will to peace'.[47] In retrospect, such passages have a certain sad desperation about them,of hopeful pleas dressed in rhetoric and doomed to failure. Even though the organisers attempted to imbue the site with an optimistic modernism, the Exposition was saturated with an abrasive nationalism which served only to confirm the irreconcilability of major European states.[48] It was to be the cultural equivalent of the military engagement shortly to follow. The steady policies of France and Britain with regard to national profile were made to seem ambiguous and feeble compared with the confident excesses of other states. Present on the site were Germany, Italy, the U.S.S.R. and Spain, all of whom had explicit cultural visions inspired by internal political ideals. The bulwark of republicanism, America, decided not to participate.[49]

The German pavilion set the pace for all the others. Designed by Hitler's architect-in-chief Albert Speer, it was an archetypal piece of National Socialist monumental architecture. A vertical pile dominated by a tower fifty-four metres high and surmounted by an eagle on a swastica, the pavilion proclaimed loudly the presence of fascism on the site. The stripped, oversize classicism invariably used by Speer expressed fully the authoritarian power of the state; it was an architecture designed to frighten and belittle the onlooker, and it succeeded admirably. Having mounted a steep staircase under the tower the visitor crossed a projecting platform and came into a vast hall, described in the catalogue as a 'salle de fêtes'. Here was the bulk of the German exhibit:

> It is magnificently decorated with mosaic, tapestries, pictures, stained glass that, as with the groups of monumental bronze statues, were the work of the best contemporary German artists. This hall, which has no subdivision, first floor or other construction, is exclusively lit, the long walls having no windows, by the large window in the ceiling and from numerous chandeliers.[50]

Important parts of the whole were contained on a mezzanine floor at the end of the hall, the bureau of information and the cinema. Virtually every pavilion had this last item, the power of the film to project a national profile by then being fully realised. German contemporary artists did not include any of those who been declared degenerate by the party and so the great generation of practitioners who had created the German modern tradition were wholly absent. The heavy-handed, clichéd, crass classicism of those favoured by the Third Reich dominated the sculpture and painting, whilst a more Gothic flavour surfaced in the carpets, tapestries and glass. Propaganda films and information revealed fully what it meant to be a National Socialist, presumably with explanations of the State position on race.[51]

Staring across at the German pavilion was that of the U.S.S.R., an unfortunate oversight by the organisers in the siting arrangement if peace was the theme they sought to emphasize. The Soviet pavilion was the most extrovert at the Exposition, being again a building of vertical emphasis: 'The great achievement is the tower, made partly in concrete, partly in metal and covered in a rare marble from Gazan completely unknown in Western Europe. A monumental statue of a young worker and kolkhoz holding a hammer and sickle, equal in height to a six storey building, dominates the whole'.[52] Highlighted in the entrance way of this extraordinary structure were the dates 1917 and 1937, a reminder to all of how young the post-revolutionary Russia was. The pavilion had five rooms, the first containing tableau displays explaining the nature and extent of Soviet territories, natural resources, industry and the constitution of the State. At the centre of the room monumental sculptures of Lenin and Stalin cast their shadows over large electrically powered maps. The second room dealt with science and the reading habits of the Soviet populations. Large diagrams showed the authors in biggest demand by the workers; stands were dedicated to Gorky and Pouchkine. Spread between the second and third rooms were displays concerning the popular theatre, painting, sculpture and applied art, children, the peasantry and the Red Army. The fourth room dealt with all forms of transport, the fifth the architectural environment and the transformation of Moscow and Leningrad. It was clear from the pavilion that the development of an industrial economy was at the core of Soviet thinking. It was also evident that a crude and arid form of social-realism had finally swept experimentation in the arts to one side. The progressive building the Soviets had erected in 1925 at the previous Paris exposition was long forgotten, as were the heady days of the Revolution, when Suprematism and Constructivism were officially recognised movements in the arts and the avant-garde was accepted as part of the revolutionary process.[53] The struggles against capitalism and individualism were visible everywhere in the pavilion, but the embracing of Taylorism in industry and social-realism in public art-forms inevitably meant that the more fundamental problem of alienation was left totally unresolved. Stalin had made his mark, the dreams of 1917 had woken into a brutal reality. At night, the German and Soviet pavilions faced each other, flood-lit against the gloom, with the great icon of all exhibitions, the Eiffel Tower, dividing the space between them. The Parisian sight-seer might still not suspect that the builders of the one pavilion had plans for a grand return to the French capital, or that the builders of the other would be more responsible than anyone for ensuring the return would be a short one.

If anything, the Italian pavilion was more spectacular than either the German or Soviet one, reflecting Mussolini's vision of himself as a Roman emperor:

> On a grand pedestal rising from the river stands an imposing equestrian statue of Georges Gori, the genius of fascism, before a tower of forty-two metres with stacked porticoes and architraves, around which twenty-four pillars support statues. This tower, dominating the central pavilion is adjoined to the smaller construction next to it in which there is a court of honour with an Italian marble ceiling, the gardens are paved with porphyry and decorated with four ceramic fountains. Sheltered under the court portico are paintings about the various achievements of the fascist regime, and on an inner wall stands a winged Victory.[54]

The interior differed from most of the other European nations in the lack of emphasis on science and industry. The major part of the space was taken up by the various art-forms, including a whole floor of furniture and a fascinating 'ideal home of 1937', which presumably showed how the design-conscious fascist chose to live. Stands for the ministries of the press and propaganda took up a sizable area, these being combined with a 'Galerie du Tourisme'. The minister for public works organised a section on the achievements of the regime in employment and public building. On the third floor, the 'Salon d'Honneur' was most impressive, having a mosaic floor one hundred metres square and marble walls. The liberal use of mosaic, marble and bronze probably made this pavilion the costliest on the site.

Against these expressions of totalitarian might the British pavilion looked faintly ridiculous, but no less propagandistic. J. M. Richards, writing in the Architectural Review, Described the entrance.

> Beside the principal entrance in fact is a hunting scene, the riders of the stuffed horses dressed, we are told, in pink coats arranged with the advice of a real master of foxhounds, and on the other side, an autumn woodland scene, with tweed clad figures on shooting sticks . . . with the exception of a shop window displaying the coronation robes this is the only exhibition of our daily life and habits.[55]

Kingsley Martin also noticed the distinct flavour of the British section,

> When you went in, the first thing you saw was a cardboard Chamberlain fishing in rubber waders and, beyond, an elegant pattern of golf-balls, a frieze of tennis raquets, polo sets, riding equipment, natty dinner jackets and, by pleasant transition, agreeable pottery and textiles, books finely printed and photographs of the English countryside. I stared in bewilderment. Could this be England?[56]

Still refusing to portray the real Britain, the propagandists of the Department of Overseas Trade had created their best effort to date; a collage of English upper class values and habits pretending to represent the whole of British life and culture. Its flavour was different from the propaganda of Italy, Germany and the Soviet Union, in that it was vision of regression rather than progression. Britain wanted to believe that everything in 1937 was as it had been in 1837, whereas the totalitarian states were looking forward to 2037. But in its superficial falsehoods, its attempt to twist the truth in front of an international audience, the British pavilion was no less extreme than any other on the site.

The grandeur and the tragedy of the Exposition were both to be located in the Spanish pavilion, where one of the greatest works of art of all time emerged in an atmosphere of violence and anguish. Here the national profile was subject to the stress of civil war, fascist forces under Franco gradually eating into republican Spain and bringing it to its knees. The Spanish had been left to their fate by the governments of Europe and America, while Franco enjoyed the patronage of Mussolini and Hitler, in one of the more hypocritical episodes in recent European history. The cheap neutrality France, Britain and America bought themselves would soon be to no avail however, as the forces of fascism pushed them along the road the Spanish republic had been made to follow. The Spanish government attempted to twinge the conscience of Europe by taking a generally enlightened internationalist line. As part of the strategy Spain's modern artists were asked to join the struggle against Franco to help publicise the cause. Thus, the national pavilion contained monumental works by some of the greatest figures in twentieth century art, giving a remarkable profile to the Spanish nation. The pavilion itself was modernist, designed by architects J. L. Sert and L. La Casa; the sculpture was by Alberto, Julio Gonzalez, Pablo Picasso and, surprisingly, the leading American sculptor Alexander Calder. As a personal friend of many Spanish artists involved in the Surrealist movement, Calder felt strongly about the civil war and European neutrality. Inside, Joan Miró and Picasso painted large murals for the pavilion. Miró produced 'Le Faucheur' (The Reaper), the title of a Catalan nationalist song, later banned by Franco, which was a symbol of the resistance of the Catalan peoples. He also printed up small posters, sold for a franc each, which had the image of the Reaper and 'Aidez Espagne' on them. The money went toward the cause.[57] Picasso's mural caused the real stir however.

As the most famous living artist Picasso was the ideal figure to publicise any cause, and also the artist most capable of producing a masterpiece under what were extremely pressured circumstances. The dimensions of the canvas were fixed by the shape of the space it was to fill, twenty-three feet long by eleven and a half feet high; it was to be the artist's largest work to date. With three months to go to the opening of the Exposition, it appears the form and theme of the painting had not been decided, but on April 19th 1937, an event took place which shook the world, sending Picasso into a frenzy of activity. This was the saturation bombing of the town of Guernica by planes flying for Franco. The Times described the scene:

> Guernica, the most ancient town of the Basques and the centre of their cultural tradition, was completely destroyed yesterday afternoon by insurgent air-raiders. The bombardment of this open town far behind the lines occupied precisely three hours and a quarter, during which a powerful fleet of aeroplanes consisting of three German types, Junkers and Heinkel bombers and Heinkel fighters, did not cease unloading on the town bombs weighing from 1000 pounds downwards, and, it is calculated, more than 3000 two pounder aluminium incendiary projectiles . . . At two a.m. today when I visited the town the whole of it was a terrible sight, flaming from end to end. The reflection of the flames could be seen in the clouds of smoke above the mountains from ten miles away. Throughout the night houses were falling until the streets became long heaps of red impenetrable debris . . . In the form of its execution and the scale of the destruction it wrought, no less in the selection of the objective, the raid on Guernica is unparalleled in military history.[58]

The wanton destruction of a civilian population shocked the world, though by 1945 the world had seen so many things it might well have assumed the aspect of simply one more disaster of war had Picasso not chosen to paint it. The painting, from the initial sketches to completion, took around two months, a remarkable feat of energy, as hundreds of related works were produced alongside. Worked exclusively in black, white and greys, the massive swathing forms depict the horror of the town as the planes struck. Five dying women, one suckling a child, a dying warrior with a broken sword, a bull, a horse, a bird; the life of old Spain and of humanity being snuffed out by a power they could neither see or understand. No planes or bombs appear in the painting, the only symbol of the technology that destroyed the town is a light-bulb, appearing in the centre of an explosive flash (top, left of centre). The innocent, incomprehending fear of the figures is welded into a composition which, while it is violent, is also firmly held in place by a structure based around a central compositional triangle. The full flow of Picasso's cubism meets here with his classicism, both orchestrated masterfully to express his politics and his humanity. Guernica remains one of the greatest comments on the tragedy of war ever made in Western art; it is also the greatest work of art ever produced specifically for an international exhibition.[59]

The attempt of the Spanish republic to oppose fascism on a cultural level by supporting liberal and modernist art-forms won little sympathy from most European powers, the war itself causing much diplomatic embarrassment. As Sarah Wilson has observed, greater care was taken to accomodate the fascists, 'the Spanish civil war was left out of the visitors book of the exposition . . . whilst it offered to Germany a large space to lay out its social and economic performances . . . the immense nude statues of Thorak . . . gave weight to the real message of fascism'.[60] Regardless of the intentions of the organisers, the show of 1937 will remain memorable not for the French contribution but for the excesses of the Hitler and Mussolini, the crudity of Stalin and the tragedy of Guernica.

Germany was absent from the last great international exhibition in New York in 1939, as was Spain. In the case of the former, this was almost certainly due to the theme of the Fair, although by 1939 it can be assumed they were occupied with international appearances of another kind. The motto of the Fair was 'Building the World of Tomorrow', that world being epitomised by 'Democracity', a huge model of the Utopian city of the future. By 1939 the German government had made it clear they did not wish to live in Democracity. The Fair was staged ostensibly to celebrate the one hundred and fiftieth anniversary of the inauguration of George Washington as first President of the United States, democracy being central to the whole event. The classical form used to symbolise the republican ideal in earlier shows gave way to modernism, the notion of progress through technology tying into the overall ideological vision. This was not a modernism inspired by the Bauhaus or Le Corbusier

F

however, but rather by the sets for 'Metropolis' or 'Flash Gordon'. At the centre of the site stood two structures representing the spirit of the Fair, the Trylon and the Perisphere. The former was a three-sided obelisk seven hundred feet high, the latter a sphere with a diameter of two hundred feet. The Official Guide Book proudly pointed out that this was the largest globe in the world, 'eighteen stories high, it is as broad as a city block, its interior more than twice the size of Radio City Music Hall'.[61] Democracity was inside the Perisphere, the visitor being lifted into the globe by an electrically powered staircase, onto a moving balcony fifty feet above the vast model. A spectacular light-show was projected onto the inside of the sphere over the heads of the viewers, further explaining the workings of what was essentially a garden city for a million people. The whole was enhanced by electrical effects and working models, reducing the seriousness of the conception as an exercise in city planning. It would be a mistake though to see it merely as science-fiction fantasy; Democracity was a political statement made by an America grown confident in the vision of itself as the leader of world democracy. The pioneer spirit had entered the space age, the frontier having expanded well beyond American shores. The contents of the Perisphere were a direct challenge to the totalitarian powers of Europe. The political message was hammered home as crudely and abrasively as any made by Germany, Italy or Russia; the creators of the national profile had found the perfect vehicle for the expression and projection of their American-ness, and the means to explain its intentions for the future.

Italy and the U.S.S.R. were in New York in style, with remarkably similar messages to those imparted two years before. The Official Guide described the Italian pavilion as 'an ingenious synthesis of the architecture of classical Rome and modern Italy'.[62] A colonnaded front surrounded a huge tower surmounted by a statue of Roma, behind which water cascaded down a flight of marble steps. The main features of the interior were displays on social welfare, sport and recreation, the reclamation of land, the decorative and fine arts. A 'Hall of Nations' at the Fair had been built to show the international activities of participants. Here the Italians placed a statue of Il Duce and huge maps in black marble with the Italian empire outlined in copper. The Russians used the same format as in 1937, a giant statue of a worker, this time seventy-nine feet high in stainless steel and holding a star over his head. Inside were exhibits on the daily lives of the Soviet people, transportation systems, arts and crafts. A model of the Palace of the Soviets in semi-precious stones attracted a lot of attention.

The French pavilion was naturally concerned with French culture, although the modernism so prevalent in Paris two years before was far less prominent. The organisers of the French pavilions in foreign shows adjusted the flavour of 'Frenchness' to suit different audiences; here it was felt the Americans would like something a little traditional. Even though the theme of the show expressly went against historicism, once inside the swishly modern walls of the pavilion (designed by Patout), the visitor was whisked back through five hundred years of French culture. The main displays were 'French Thought', 'Five Centuries of French Art' and 'The Scenic Beauties of France'. Industry was pushed back onto a mezzanine floor and even there the largest areas went to Sevrés and Gobelins. The New Yorkers were thus given one of the richest samples of French art ever to cross the Atlantic, French insistence on itself as a civilizing force remaining consistent right up to the eve of the Second World War.

Britain had a problem in New York. The Americans were distinctly unenthusiastic about the British empire, as they were conscious they had been a part of it. Empire was usually the most important part of British exhibits, the counterpoise to the presented image of the English as a tradition-bound race of aristocrats. Whilst the American organisers could not stop the displaying of empire – most other European powers showed theirs – the British government was particularly anxious not to antagonise the American authorities or undermine the image of England for the American public. Good relations with America were crucial to British interests and they were keen not to appear as an imperial nation at a Fair where democracy was the central theme. In the end a compromise was reached by the British organisers. Empire remained a feature in the Hall of Nations, and a bizarrely complex explanation as to Britain's rôle as a raiser of democratic consciousness was provided in the national pavilion. The theme there was the Magna Carta, a copy of which was installed in 'Magna Carta Hall'. The Magna Carta it was stated, 'holds a unique position in the unending and world-wide struggle for liberty and freedom . . . It was a struggle through which and by which the Anglo-Saxon painfully learned the necessity of liberty and how to win and hold it.'[63] The English barons' imposition of con-trols over King John suddenly became a justification of empire, an example to freedom fighters everywhere and a cause for universal cele-bration. This ancient document 'proved' as it were that democracy was at the core of Englishness and that humanity reigned wherever the Englishman went. Empire was portrayed as a friendly co-operative ven-ture amongst the peoples of the world from which all benefitted. The American War of Independence was explained in a marvellous twist of logic, again with the Magna Carta as the explicatory element:

> Without this hard-won knowledge, as a solid foundation beneath them, the American colonies would have blundered hopelessly in their fight for

independence and freedom . . . The Englishman's understanding of liberty had been woven into his being by the struggle through the centuries; it was the most precious possession brought to America by the first English colonists . . . it is not claiming too much to ascribe to the heritage from the generations of struggle waged in England, the speed with which the Americans consolidated their ideas of liberty and entered upon a war to maintain their freedom.[64]

So the Americans fought successfully against the English because of their own ingrained Englishness. One may wonder why the 'Englishman's understanding of liberty' did not lead him to give the Americans their independence before they were forced to fight for it; one may wonder also what was supposedly going through the minds of Englishmen as they struggled to hold onto an empire which increasingly made vocal a desire to be free. No matter; the use of the Magna Carta to combine the theme of Olde Englande with that of democracy was clever propaganda. The rest of the exhibit was almost exclusively dedicated to monarchy. Replicas of the crown jewels were on show, amid displays showing 'how Britain's history has centred around her kings'.[65] The contradictory twists of such propaganda belonged to an age of imperial decline. These machinations would have been unnecessary and meaningless in 1851 when the national profile expressed itself in material terms.

The remarkable diplomacy of international exhibitions had allowed events to be staged in the most extraordinary of circumstances, sometimes whilst wars were being fought, often when participating nations were at political logger-heads. The Exposition Universelle of 1937 was the most extreme example of opposing ideologies coming together with the apparent motive of peaceful display, its abrasive oppositions signalling the effective end of the tradition. After the Second World War nations increasingly refused to participate in events where opposing regimes were to be present. Equally, the events themselves became muted, ambivalent affairs, where smaller budgets and rigid insistence upon diplomatic neutrality leveled out the whole into anonymity. The boycotting of sporting and cultural events has become a weapon of disruption used by most governments, ensuring there will never be a repetition of the situation like the one at Paris in 1937. Indeed, it would be patently absurd to suggest anything good came of that Exposition in social or political terms. No international understanding, no growth of human fellowship, no reconciliation of peoples or nations. The show simply highlighted the violent climax of the nationalism which had grown within the exhibition tradition since 1851. From the beginning, the contours of the national profile stood out starkly, destroying any real chance for the medium to be used to more peaceable ends. The tradition did have isolated individuals, nations and associations which genuinely attempted to foster peace and friendship. Sadly, these were all too often swamped by those with quite different motives.

Notes

1 J. A. Hobson, *The Pyschology of Jingoism*, London 1901, Grant Richards.
2 Eugen Weber, *Peasants into Frenchmen: The modernisation of Rural France 1870–1914.* London 1979, Chatto and Windus.
3 Theodore Zeldin, *Intellect and Pride.* from *France 1848–1940*, (5 volumes) Oxford University Press 1980.
4 Zeldin. See note 3.
5 See chapters 1 and 8.
6 Quoted from Philippe Julian, *The Triumph of Art Nouveau: The Paris Exhibition 1900.* London, 1974, Phaidon.
7 Soliman Al-Haraïri, *Exposition Universelle de Paris*, Paris 1867.
8 Anon, *Le Palais de Trocadéro: Le Coteau de Chaillot, Le Nouveau Palais*, Paris 1878, V. A. Morel.
9 See Eduard Fourdrignier, *Antiquités des Gaules: Exposition Historique du Palais de Trocadéro*, Paris 1878, Henri Menn.
10 *Universal Exposition 1889: Reports of the United States Commissioners*, Volume Two (of five), Washington 1890.
11 Ibid.
12 Quoted from Raymond Rudorff, *Belle Epoque – Paris in the Nineties.*, London 1972, Hamish Hamilton.
13 Ibid.
14 Quoted from R. D. Mandell, *Paris 1900: The Great World's Fair.* University of Toronto Press 1967.
15 Founding members of the Comité Français des Expositions à l'Etranger went as far as to suggest that the expositions made no money at all for French businesses, foreign exhibitions being far better in this regard.
16 See Mandell, note 14.
17 See Chapter four. Exactly the same type of national debate arose when the Centre Georges Pompidou was in its planning stages in the early 1970's.
18 See chapters 6 and 8.
19 *Handy Book to the International Exhibition 1862.* London 1862.
20 G. de Bellaigue, *Queen Victoria buys French in 1855*, Antique Collector, April 1975, Volume 46, Part 4.
21 See chapter 3.
22 *Love and Loyalty*, London 1851.
23 Quoted from John Gloag, *The English Tradition in Design*, London 1947, Penguin. Gloag makes use of several strategies for defining English design, one of which is the *Olde Englande* or *Hearts of Oak* argument.
24 Sir Isidore Spielmann, *Royal Commission Paris International Exhibition 1900: The Royal Pavilion.* Issued by the Royal Commission, St. Stephens House, Westminster, London 1900. Also see Chapter eight
25 The interiors were commissioned before Morris' death, leaving us unsure as to whether Morris himself accepted the commission or whether he understood the logic behind the choice of his firm.
26 See Vincent Scully, *The Shingle Style and the Stick Style: Architectural theory and design from Daring to the Origins of Wright.* Yale University Press 1977.
27 The move from left to right at the end of the nineteenth century of the various British revivalist movements was a critical factor in the reception later given to European modernism. Adequate research still has to be done in this area.
28 See Paul Greenhalgh, *Art, Politics and Society at the Franco–British Exhibition of 1908* Art History, December 1985.

29 See Duncan Simpson, Architectural Review 1977.
30 The significance of the Boer War as a watershed of British power is convincingly brought out in Thomas Pakenham's *The Boer War* London, 1982, Futura.
31 Quoted from P. M. Taylor's exemplary work *The Projection of Britain: British Overseas Publicity and Propaganda 1919–1939.* Cambridge University Press 1981.
32 The Crystal Palace was a probable victim of arsen in 1936.
33 *Texas Centennial Exposition, Official Souvenir Guide Dallas 1936.*
34 *Official Guidebook to the New York World's Fair* New York 1939.
35 For example see the cover of the *Official Souvenir Guide, Franco British Exhibition.*, London 1908 Bembrose and Son.
36 Sir John Cockburn, *The Franco–British Exhibition*, Journal for the Royal Society of Arts, Volume 56, 1907.
37 See Taylor, note 31.
38 Wilbur Zelinsky, *The Cultural Geography of the United States*, New Jersey 1973, Prentice-Hall. Quoted from *U.S.A. 1890–1939*, Units 7–8, Course A305, *History of Architecture and Design 1890–1939.* Open University Press 1975.
39 J. S. Ingram, *The Centennial Exposition, Described and Illustrated*, Philadelphia 1876, Hubbard Brothers.
40 See Chapter 4.
41 Eugen Neuhaus, *The Art of the Exposition.*, San Fransisco 1915, Paul Elder and Company.
42 Quoted from Elizabeth N. Armstrong, *Hercules and the Muses: Public art and the Fair.* in *The Anthropology of World's Fairs: San Fransisco's Panama Pacific International Exposition of 1915.* Ed. Benedict Burton, Scolar Press 1983.
43 Neuhaus see note 41.
44 Louis Sullivan put up one of the most celebrated arguments against classicism at the Fair, see, for example Carl Condit *The Chicago School of Architecture: A History of Commercial and Public Building in the Chicago Area, 1875–1925*, University of Chicago Press 1975. See also Chapter six.
45 Zelinsky, see note 38.
46 Many of the features of 1889 were repeated and enlarged in 1893, and many from 1893 were likewise duplicated, without acknowledgement, in 1900.
47 *Paris 1937, Wagons-Lits/Cook*, Publicity for the Exposition by major tour-operators.
48 The literature surrounding the Exposition, both official and unofficial, conducted what can only be described as a conspiracy of silence concerning the real flavour of the event. Quite rarely is the vibrant propaganda element dealt with, when it does emerge it is usually in some oblique manner.
49 I am unsure at this time as to whether there was political intent behind America's absence. It could simply have been to do with the expense involved, with their own Fair being scheduled to take place only two years later.
50 *Exposition Internationale Arts et Techniques, Paris 1937, Guide Officiel*, Paris 1937.
51 The content of the German films has not yet come to light.
52 Offical Guide, note 50.
53 See Chapter 6.
54 Official Guide, note 50.
55 J. M. Richards, *The International Exhibition*, Architectural Review 1937.
56 Quoted from Taylor, see note 31.
57 Most monographs on Miró have useful references on this topic. For a colour illustration of the *Aidez Espagne* poster see *Paris 1937–1957* catalogue for an exhibition held at the Centre Georges Pompidou, 28th. May to 2nd. November 1981. This also has a photograph of Miró working on site. By co-incidence, the Miró Foundation in Barcelona has been built on what was part of the site for the 1929 Exposition held there.
58 Quoted from *Guernica*, Catalogue to an exhibition held in Stockholm, 1956. The literature on Guernica is vast; monographs on the painting have been written by Antony Blount, Max Raphael and Frank Russell, and substantial sections of most monographs on Picasso are devoted to it. Particularly recommended are Roland Penrose, *Picasso, His Life and Work* Penguin 1971, Dore Ashton (Ed) *Picasso on Art* Thames and Hudson 1972, John Berger, *The Success and Failure of Picasso* Penguin 1965, Marilyn McCully (Ed), *A Picasso Anthology: Documents, Criticisms, Reminiscences.* Arts Council/Thames and Hudson 1981.

59 Having been cared for by the Museum of Modern Art New York for four decades while Franco reigned, the painting is now back in Spain, in the Casón del Buen Retiro, an annex of the Prado.
60 Sarah Wilson, *Problèmes de la Peinture en Marge de l'Exposition Internationale*, from *Paris 1937–1957*, see note 57.
61 *Official Guide Book of the New York World's Fair, 1939*. New York 1939, Exposition Publications.
62 Ibid.
63 J. C. Fitzpatrick, *Magna Carta Hall: The British Pavilion New York World's Fair, 1939*, Published 1939.
64 Ibid.
65 Ibid.

CHAPTER SIX

The prefabricated
and the mass-produced

Four things dictated the shape of the Great Exhibition and of every exhibition which followed it: mass-production, prefabrication, mass communications and urbanisation. All of these relate to the industrial revolution and in each case Britain experienced the force of them first. The number of man-made objects in circulation increased dramatically, the travelling speed of ideas and peoples multiplied beyond recognition and cities grew at a freak rate. The physical abundance allowed empire to expand at an unprecedented pace, until most of the known world was brought under the yoke of the industrialised nations. The Crystal Palace exhibition was nothing more than a recognition and celebration of these developments.

The economic and social jolt caused by the industrial revolution had its cultural equivalent, as practitioners in every sphere struggled to cope with new values which seemed to question the traditional basis of the disciplines they were involved with. Nowhere was the crisis more acute than in the so-called functional arts of architecture and design, simply because no factor in the whole creative process had remained a constant. The means of production, the types of material used to create objects, the numbers of objects produced, the speed of production, and the audience produced for, had all been subject to change. Moreover, the facility other arts had to challenge or comment upon developments in society was not easily duplicated in the design process. The great generation of English romantic poets could question the value of industrial and scientific advance using the same types of prose and verse they had grown up with. For them, the content of their art had changed but not the premiss of its creation or the audience who received it. Poetry had the ability to criticise, it had a basis for evolution, critique and comment without having to face the problem of transforming itself. For the designer there were no such luxuries. The mass-produced objects he or she created could not embody a critique of the world they were born into without at the same time challenging their own right to existence. Designed objects had to be positively responsive, even if the response was a pretence that industrialisation was not actually happening. Denied the luxury of negative critique, buildings and products were condemned to smilingly stare into the dark chasm of industry, picking out aesthetic and moral benefits wherever they could be found.

Design virtually invented itself in the industrial age. The very word changed its meaning through the industrial era, moving from something implying a drawing or study, to a process whereby a prototype was made for mass-production. It would be into the 1930's before the design profession existed as we now know it but most of the inherent formal and moral problems associated with it were present by the time Victoria came to power. The Great Exhibition, as a massive gathering of mass-produced objects from Europe and of crafted objects from all over the known world, gave designers, artists and critics the best opportunity to date to assess the state of the art. For this reason 1851 is often used as a starting point for the history of design. Perhaps it would be more appropriate to regard it as a starting point for the history of design criticism, for whilst relatively little in the way of innovation took place amongst the objects, a good deal of what was said was refreshingly new. Indeed, the contribution of the exhibitions in general to the development of design was mainly one of assessment and critque; they tended, with notable exceptions, not to offer design solutions but to sum up what had gone so far. They could bluntly reveal what was right and what was wrong with a generation of objects, making whole what was previously a partial vision of the profession at large.

The designed objects at the Great Exhibition caused a good deal of confusion. The critic's fraternity found little to lighten the hearts of the thousands of companies who had space in the Manufactures section of the building. A concensus of opinion seemed to believe that form and style had not developed at the same rate as production technique. Richard Redgrave, Royal Academician, summed up the situation by suggesting machinery gave the manufacturer 'the ability to produce the florid and overloaded as cheaply as simple forms, and then to satisfy the larger market for the multitude, who desire quantity, rather than quality, and value a thing the more it is ornamented'.[1] A cutlery set might take a single silversmith months to make, the time and cost growing with the complexity of the individual pieces. However, electro-plated, mold-made cutlery did not take longer or cost more in a ratio with the detailing it carried. In fact, cutlery covered with impressed detailing might cost less than a plain set, as the weight of metal used could be reduced. The social-symbolism of the detailing however continued to imply value. To the generation of upper-working and lower middle classes who had entered the market for the first time, overloaded decoration, a wide range of colour and a clearly stated narrative carried the idea of affluence and so were absolute requirements. The semblance of detailed craftwork was thus applied to machine-pressed objects not because of a failing in taste on the part of producers and public, but because both had symbolic, not aesthetic, criteria. Little thought went into what things looked like in any disinterested way, but rather into what they represented. The failure to understand this led many commentators to simply blame the production process. Critics well after the Crystal Palace exhibition continued to illogically blame industrial methods for what they believed to be a mass failure in taste. A critic at the Paris Exposition Universelle of 1867 reported: 'where manufacture has wholly triumphed in rapidity, certainty, and cheapness of production, the results are usually astonishing examples of the power of making common and really useful objects hideous'.[2] The correlation between machine production and ugliness became an assumed truth in many circles after 1851, usually in the absence of proper analysis of the motives of consumers.

The issue of style, especially an appropriate style to represent the age, was everywhere at the Great Exhibition. Style was understood as a symbolic additive emanating from accepted conventions, rendering an object meaningful to its audience. Thus, in his award winning essay 'The Exhibition as a Lesson in Taste', Ralph Nicholson Wornum found himself able to list the exact number of styles available to the designer for use, and position them in history:

> There are, of course, many varieties of very great style; but so long as the chief characteristics remain unchanged, the style is the same. From this point of view, therefore, the styles become comparatively few. We shall find that nine will comprise the whole number of the great characteristic developments which have had any influence on European civilization: namely three ancient, the Egyptian, the Greek and the Roman; three middle age, the Byzantine, the Saracenic, and the Gothic; and three modern, the Renaissance, the Cinquecento and the Louis Quatorze.[3]

All style was a copy or combination of these, Wornum posited. Furthermore, he argued that whilst all styles ultimately derived from nature, in all of them nature had been rigorously abstracted and conventionalised so that 'in no popular style of ornament have natural details ever yet prevailed'.[4] European style, therefore, transcended nature with culture and found its sources in previously credited cultural developments. It was possible to combine sources, imposing Roman on Egyptian and framing it with Saracenic; it was preferable however, for the gentleman of taste, to merely 'modernise' a single style, by neutralising its more distinctive aspects and possibly adding one or two contemporary details.

Wornum's position was the most common one of the time and can be labelled eclectic or historicist. Opposition to historicism on aesthetic and social grounds was quite common in Europe and America after 1850, though it would be wrong on the whole to see anti-historicist movements as more than isolated incidents until after the First World War. The retrospectively discernable shift from historicist to modernist forms through the period was not the logical and linear movement most histories have chosen to make it. The exhibitions reveal most historicist styles as disappearing slowly, some remaining in the marketplace long after they had supposedly died. Others were not acknowledged by critics and so have tended to disappear from history altogether. For example, Wornum casually identified the most successful style in furniture in 1851 as being 'Louis Quatorze'. Accompanied by 'Louis Quinze' and 'Louis Seize' at the South Kensington Exhibition of 1862 it dominated the French Court, which was widely praised as the best in the building: 'the French Court and its approaches form a perfect exhibition by themselves . . . everything that human ingenuity, money and taste can produce is exhibited in this court, and it will be from no want of energy if they fail to carry off the first prizes'.[5] In London, Paris and America the Louis styles maintained a presence at exhibitions throughout the century, were still thought to be a major European style in 1908 at the Franco–British Exhibition, and remained, in yet another revived form, a force at the Paris Show of 1925. This particular historicist thread therefore remained unbroken for seventy years, outlasting most of the styles dominating design histories produced to date.

Not every area containing designed produce at the Great Exhibition was concerned with style. One display concentrated on the problem of housing for the poor, this being a fully appointed 'Model house for the Working Classes' sponsored by Prince Albert. The model, designed by Henry Roberts, was constructed actual size in the proper materials and hoped to show how the masses would eventually be housed. Resembling a large cottage with gothic detailing, it featured new developments in plumbing, insulation and kitchen amenities. The ingenious part of the design was its modular format, this allowing the complete unit to be extended into rows or piled into blocks. It is not absolutely clear exactly what involvement the Prince himself had with the project,[6] but his name publicised it and so gave rise to successive philanthropic enterprises at later exhibitions. Design sections emphasising economy and efficiency were included in most events after 1851, often in conjunction with conferences on sewage disposal and household plumbing.[7]

The exhibition to deal most comprehensively with design for poverty was the Paris Exposition Universelle of 1867. Section Ten was devoted entirely to the welfare of the poor, with new designs for a wide range of produce, including the houses themselves, furniture, fittings, kitchen implements, clothes, books and tools. The subtitle to the section, 'Dwellings for the poor, constructed on sanitary principles and at small cost, and articles exhibited with the special object of improving the physical and moral condition of the people', indicated the organisers' belief in the relationship between environment and behaviour. The English report on the section affirmed, 'it is needless to repeat here the trite conclusions – which are not the least important for their triteness – as to the moral effect of such advantages upon the humbler classes of any population'.[8] An idea of the Exposition director Raymond Le Play, it was the clearest realisation of his Saint-Simonianism on the site. Somewhat surprisingly, the fittings, utensils and furniture of Europe in the section were disparagingly compared to other nations:

> It is notable that the absence of art-beauty in these homely objects is most conspicuous among nations claiming to be the highest according to the present scale of civilization. The people whom we are content to regard as semi-civilised – Oriental nations, tribes of North Africa, races from the distant part of the Russian empire – show an understanding of colour, at least, which renders their otherwise rude household goods models for the skilful European to study and strive to imitate.[9]

In this instance criticism was not being levelled at British manufacturers, as they chose not to participate in the section, but at the five hundred French firms present and assorted ones from Belgium, Austria, Spain, Italy and Portugal. The English report, apart from its slight on European exhibitors, had a prophetic warning for British producers of cheap household goods,

> . . . it is obvious that if Great Britain is to continue competing successfully with her continental rivals in the supply of articles which surround daily life of millions and which represent a trade encompassing the whole globe, her manufactures must bring to bear on her business higher qualities than are commonly deemed necessary for money making; qualifications, some of which at least must necessarily be sought beyond their own body – inventive capacity, knowledge and practice of art, wide acquaintance with new materials, and scientific skill to make them available.[10]

Six model dwellings were erected by France in Section Ten, one by Prussia and one by Austria. Reporting enthusiastically on these was English utilitarian reformer Edwin Chadwick:

> On the whole, viewing collectively the various models and collateral appliances presented for examination in the present Exhibition, there will be found in it the means of very important advances in the improvement of dwellings of the great masses of the people – in the means of relieving them from the cesspool smell, or bad drain, or sewer emanations, . . . from the foul wall smell and from wall vermin; from the damp hall; from the

smoke nuisance; and from a great proportion of the waste of fuel and from loss of heat; from stagnant and vitiated air; from the deterioration of good water supplies; from much exclusion from sunlight . . . and that too, not only without any increase but with a very material reduction of direct expense. I say of direct expense, because . . . a great proportion of the common dwellings of the wage classes, though they be cheap to construct, are indirectly and eventually dear to use.[11]

Chadwick's study talks with enthusiasm about model estates in the northern French town of Mulhouse, which were largely the work of philanthropist Jean Dolfus. Prince Albert's Model House of 1851 had been adapted and widely used there. Chadwick concludes by affirming his lifelong conviction that 'moral and social advancement is dependent on physical improvement, and that on the sanitary improvement of dwellings'.[12]

Section Ten of the 1867 Exposition was important for design and architecture because of the way it shifted emphasis from the battle of the styles toward social and moral issues. Ultimately, this would be a main debating ground for both arts. Every French exposition after 1867 had an equivalent section, albeit far smaller, raising the issue as to whether some of the pioneer architects and designers of the international modern movement were influenced by them.[13] In 1889 the Peabody Trust proudly displayed housing in Paris, and in 1900 the theme of 'the life of the worker' was almost as strong as it had been in 1867, although admittedly in the later event the emphasis was on the prosaic rather than the practical.

The non-Western contingent at the exhibitions probably had a bigger impact on design than anything else. For many of the colonies these were the only places their decorative and design arts could be seen in large quantities in the West; the impact this must have had on manufacturing trades has still not been the subject of thorough research. The arrival of non-Western countries as exhibitors of designed produce had the immediate effect of making the design of European nations look remarkably similar in the eyes of critics. When discussing Asian, Arabic or African design, commentators had little difficulty in comparing them to European design as though the latter were an amorphous whole, the individual nuances of the national styles apparently being less important than the numerous qualities they had in common.[14] Moreover, a significant number of writers found non-Western forms superior to the familiar overcrowded historicism dominating European produce:

The absence of fixed principles in ornamental design is most apparent in the exhibition, not among ourselves only, but throughout all European nations. Many other nations show better faith and better practice in design than those of Europe. Does the progress of civilization and the increased value put on knowledge and labour destroy principles of taste?[15]

In Paris in 1867, after perusal of the produce, a writer concluded:

> Art is thus not instinctive among Western nations. The objects that minister to the daily needs and conveniences of common life are for the most part wholly wanting – and it is a lamentable want – in every quality that can give pleasure to the eye. The entire household furniture, carpets, fittings, articles of daily use, complete clothing for young and old, . . . and yet not one object found which ministers in the smallest degree to that art instinct which is gratified by the commonest productions of Oriental workmanship . . . Among Oriental nations what may be called an instinct of art-feeling guides their work conspicuously in colour, and to a lesser degree in other sources of beauty. It is not so among the most civilised of Western nations – not so in France, anymore than elsewhere.[16]

Striking confessions by peoples considering themselves superior beings and the carriers of civilized ideas. The sad confusion European aesthetes experienced at the realisation of the superiority of non-Western design was resolved, however, without upsetting the sacrosanct imperial-racial order. Art, it will be noted from the last quotation, did not emerge from intelligence or the ability to make progress, it was an essence, a feeling, an instinct. Like the non-Europeans who made it, it was myster-ious, untamed, an unknown quantity. Theories that were developed during the romantic era could allow artefacts to be made well by other-wise 'under-evolved' peoples, because art was irrational and unquanti-fiable, defiant of control or direction.[17]

The discovery of Japanese art by the West occurred largely because of its constant presence in exhibitions from 1862 onwards. In that year it had a marked impact in London, in 1867 it took Paris by storm, likewise in 1876 in Philadelphia, in Paris again in 1878 and 1889 and in Chicago in 1893. By that time it had had a clear effect on all the arts and had become one of the most important sources for proto-modernist develop-ments across the board. Utter restraint in the use of decoration, an absence of illusory devices such as perspective, and an insistence upon the dignity of the simple, rather than complex, were the hallmarks of Japanese style. Architecture based on the frame rather than the wall, minimal interior decoration, open-plan and screen walling, unembell-ished form in furniture, flat colour and bold line in the print and screen, ran against virtually everything practiced in Europe at the time. It was seized upon by the impressionists, the aesthetic movement, by those involved with art nouveau, and it became fashionable enough to have shops specialising in it.[18] In America the best architects and designers made use of it after the Philadelphia Centennial, so that it came to be an important stylistic ingredient in 'stick' and 'shingle' domestic building.

After the Columbian exhibition, Frank Lloyd Wright began to experiment with open-plan and screen-wall systems similar to the one he had seen in the Japanese pavilion there.[19] His furniture for houses and offices, which was to become vital for the European modern movement, also revealed a Japanese rigour and simplicity. Japan gave the West a mature alternative to historicism and eclecticism, and a stylistic approach which could potentially be adapted to machine production without causing awkward aesthetic and philosophical problems. Unlike his Western counterpart, the Japanese craftsman appeared to have no difficulty in making content co-operate with the necessities of form.

Architecture revealed itself in two distinct ways at exhibitions, in the actual buildings on the site and in the architecture sections of the Fine Arts Pavilions. In the case of the former, the central committee in control of the site would commission individuals to design pavilions, stipulating the dimensions, materials and even the colour of the structures. In the case of the latter, a jury connected to the fine art section would select suitable exhibits comprising of plans, elevations and models. Often the two manifestations were so different from each other it was difficult to perceive of them as belonging to the same discipline, and indeed, those controlling the exhibits on display in the fine art pavilions often expressed the view that they did not. Normally these sections were dominated by official bodies of the profession, in the case of France this was the Ecole des Beaux Arts, in Britain the Royal Academy and the Royal Institute of British Architects, in America by whichever State Academy presiding over the region the Fair was in.[20] To a considerable extent the displays would simply tell the visitor what the official preferred styles in commercial, public and domestic building were and who were the best known producers of those styles. Occasionally topical oddities would appear but this was far less common than with other areas of the fine arts, architecture being far more conservative than these. By contrast the site architecture, even though it was often built by the same types of architect, was frequently more innovative. This was partly because the buildings were temporary and therefore less serious, partly because the crowds had to be entertained with more dramatic edifices than one would normally associate with a model of a town hall or a bank, and partly because people from outside of the architectural establishment had influence. In the first exhibitions these outsiders were invariably engineers or those with engineering connections. Engineers were responsible for many of the most spectacular conceptions ever to be built on exhibition sites, some of them having marked implications for architectural practice long after they were dismantled. Ironically, much of the site at an average exhibition might be designed and built by non-architects, while the architects themselves were represented inside by plaster and wood models.

Whilst new technologies often accounted for the appearance of the sites, especially in the earlier exhibitions, it would be a mistake to suggest engineering as an architectural phenomenon owed them a great deal in any inventive or innovatory sense. With notable exceptions most of the buildings erected at exhibitions during the period used technologies which had already been tested on bridges and railway sheds. Rather, it was the publicity exhibitions brought to the issue of engineering structures as livable spaces that was the source of their importance. The ability of iron and glass to shelter, to span enormous spaces, to admit light and to be assembled quickly by semi-skilled men suggested a new method of architecture was at hand. The sheer scale of many of the buildings rendered them famous and made the technologies responsible for their erection all the more exciting in the public eye. Indeed, the need to solve awkward architectural problems with temporary structures, in tandem with the desire to impress an ignorant public, led to the creation of some of the most dramatic buildings of the nineteenth century. The first and perhaps the greatest of these was the Crystal Palace.

The Crystal Palace was the great icon of exhibition architecture, setting the pace for all that followed. It has been seen as prophetic of the modern movement and as one of the most important architectural edifices of the nineteenth century. F.T Kihlstedt:

> The Crystal Palace, as a product of Victorian England, was one of the most influential buildings ever erected. Innovative in structure, completely new in its function, unusual in form and significant in the associations it embodied, it takes its place with a handful of other pre-eminent buildings such as the Pantheon, Hagia Sophia and Abbot Sugar's St. Denis. As with these earlier constructions, the extraordinary functional demands made on the Crystal Palace stimulated a design that refined and extended the structural practices of the time, resulting in an architecture novel in its form and aesthetic.[21]

The building for the Great Exhibition had to fulfill a number of tasks which even thirty years previous would have seemed preposterous. It had to enclose a space so big that several of the world's largest existing buildings could fit inside it, side by side. It had to cost, in terms of square feet, proportionately less than the cheapest building imaginable. It had to be erected in months, not years, and it had to be dismantled once the exhibition was over. To add a comic element to these extraordinary demands, it had to be built over four mature elm trees without harming them and leave the ground it stood upon in good order.[22] In some ways

the brief defined the building, in that it automatically excluded materials traditionally associated with public works, on grounds of expense
and speed. So when the design was opened to competition in 1850 it
surprised no-one when quite a few of the two hundred and forty-five
entrants suggested the use of iron and glass. None of them however in
the opinion of the Building Committee had a suitable solution and the
competition was declared void. The Building Committee itself then
attempted to design a building, producing a strange edifice in brick
topped by a glass dome which was wholly unsatisfactory by their own
standards. A potential crisis was only averted by the dramatic arrival on
the scene of Joseph Paxton, who produced a plan that was accepted after
much arguing and string-pulling on all sides.

More than simply the designer, Paxton's vision of the building led
him to be involved at every level of its construction and decoration.
Along with the Prince of Wales and Henry Cole, his name was to be long
remembered as one of the guiding spirits of the exhibition. In many
ways he was the epitome of the Victorian self-made man. Antony Bird,
in his monograph on the Crystal Palace, rightly observes that 'if Joseph
Paxton had not existed it would have been necessary for Samuel Smiles
to invent him'.[23] The son of a farmer born in 1803, he had made his way
as an horticulturalist until he was 'discovered' by the Duke of
Devonshire, who employed him at his estate at Chatsworth. As head
gardener Paxton remodelled the estate over several decades, acquiring a
reputation as a capable man in every area of garden design. It was his
building of hot-houses, notably the Great Stove (1836–1841) and the
house for a Victoria Regia Lily (1849) which inspired him in his design
for the Crystal Palace, the former of these having a wider span than any
railway station of the time.[24] Essentially, his exhibition building was to
be a gigantic greenhouse made from iron, glass and wood, and as such it
attracted much derision between its conception and its opening, from
lampoonists, cartoonists, and, predictably, art-critics. It was no less a
figure than John Ruskin who christened it the 'giant cucumber-frame'.

The key to Paxton's success however was not in the materials themselves, but in the ingenious modular base he developed, whereby stand-
ardised components of glass, iron and wood were used throughout. Thus
the two major contracting firms, the Chance brothers (glass) and Fox and
Henderson (ironwork) could quickly manufacture the parts at their
Birmingham foundries and despatch the building in millions of parts to
the Hyde Park site. Then supervised teams of men could bolt, weld and
slot the building together. The whole conception was a master-piece of
prefabrication; it instantaneously became a symbol of its age and an
awesome indication of the capabilities of industry. The plan was as
simple as possible; a long horizontal block was divided in the centre by a

tall vaulted transept, this serving as the grand entrance. It also created an internal space which effectively divided the building into distinct halves. A vast mezzanine added over a third to the total floor space. In every direction the iron ribs framed the vision and gave a perspectival effect which mimicked infinity, the sensation of light outstripping any architectural experience before it. Covering approximately nineteen acres and enclosing thirty-three million cubic feet, the building was the marvel of the exhibition, out-doing every object brought to reside under its transparent skin.

From 1851 to the turn of the century, the idea of the Crystal Palace recurred at virtually every major international exhibition in the form of giant structures produced by engineering technology. Iron and glass were used at Dublin and New York in 1853 and an impressive Palais de l'Industrie was built for the first Exposition Universelle in 1855. The organisers in New York went as far as to ask Paxton to provide a design for their building.[25] Unfortunately his plan proved unsuitable for the site and they were forced to open the commission to competition. The eventual winners, Messrs. Carstensen and Gildemeister, produced an unfortunate pastiche of the London prototype, using brick and wood in-fill to disguise the awkwardness of the building's profile.[26] The French building, although a self-conscious reply to the Crystal Palace even from the earliest planning stages, was a marked improvement on the one in New York. Unfortunately, it was compromised all along by the unhappy relationship between the architect contracted to design it, J. M. V. Viel (with help from Tony Desjardins) and the engineers brought in to supervise the structural aspects, Alexis Barrault and Georges Bridel. Viel designed a rectangular space forty-eight by one hundred and ninety-two metres, flanked by six adjoining pavilions. As part of his scheme for the interior he planned to put a masonry skin over the iron columns and supports, in order to mask the contemporary nature of the structure. Barrault and Bridel objected to this and forced him to make a modification to his original plans. Their reasons were strikingly in tune with the kind of thinking that would be common amongst progressive architects seventy years later:

> We do not want to try and create in metal a manner of construction that was invented for stone, and we don't wish to hide the material we are working with by use of devices in bad taste. In a word, we have almost everywhere exposed the cast iron and the nature of the material . . . thinking that the simpicity of the forms and the internal grandeur of the building is enough to give it a style suitable for its purpose.[27]

The tension between new technologies and old forms was already making itself very apparent. Viel, committed to an idea of public architecture which revealed itself through richness of material and evidence of craft skill, felt himself obliged to mask the impermanent nature of his structure. To him, stone was an indicator of status, the weight and opacity of the wall an emblem of the training he had received. Iron columns and glass walls by-passed the methodology and status of his profession, making it difficult for him to cope. This was exacerbated by his brief. The Palais de l'Industrie was not to be a temporary structure as the Crystal Palace had been, Napoleon III's government having decided it should remain for an indefinite period to function as an exhibition and events centre. Thus as a cultural edifice of some importance it had to carry the weight of national profile. The stone casings around the columns were an attempt to guarantee a certain standing for the building, a standing which naked iron seemed to lack. The Palais de l'Industrie, like numerous exposition buildings after it, was compromised between the functional reality of engineering science and the vision of France as the traditional harbinger of high culture. A time-honoured symbolism had clashed with an alternative means of construction. The Palais remained in place until 1900, when it was demolished to make way for the Grand and Petit Palais'.

Back in London in 1862 the South Kensington Exhibition was housed in a structure by a Captain Francis Fowke, who decided to use brick curtain walls and an iron and glass roof. His building was basically a long nave cut by two end transepts, with domes at the intersections. It boasted three open courts on the north end of the nave and over one and a half miles of upper gallery space. Despite its more traditional appearance than the Crystal Palace it was pilloried in the press and by the architectural fraternity:

> The building recently erected at Kensington has probably awakened more criticism than any structure of our time. Viewed from without, its general characteristic is that of simple ugliness; and it is only when considered in connection with the purpose for which it was designed, does it in any sense come up to our idea of a Great Exhibition.[28]

The intention of the organisers was that the building should remain intact after the show and possibly be reused for succeeding exhibitions. Noting this, most assessments of it looked forward to a healthier future, 'the exterior of the building, . . . must be viewed as a skeleton to be clothed and decorated after the exhibition closes.'[29] Even an official publication like the 'Illustrated Catalogue of the Industrial Department' could not raise excessive enthusiasm, although it did provide excuses:

> The building can be viewed only as a utilitarian structure for the present. Although it thoroughly provides for the wants of the exhibition, much remains to be done to render it complete and perfect. Perhaps no building in the world, twenty-four and a half acres in extent, has ever been erected at so low a liability . . . (after the exhibition) we may venture to hope that

the Society will be proud of its property, and have the means, as well as the desire, to render it, both inside and outside, a complete building, worthy of being the home of industrial exhibitions.[30]

The building was clearly inferior in design to the Crystal Palace, though in itself this was not the reason for its popular failure. By 1862 gargantuan engineering structures were commonplace in railway stations and bridges, scale alone holding little interest for the general public. The miracles of science were less exciting than they had been; size was the only real feature of the 1862 building, this failing to compensate for its lack of creative adventure. In fact the age of experimental exhibition buildings was temporarily over in Britain only a decade after it had begun; it would be into the new century before a spark of life would return to British sites. By that time the Crystal Palace remained, standing on a new site in Sydenham, a great architectural achievement in a welter of mediocrity.

In the second half of the nineteenth century the initiative swung heavily to France, where a line of successes highlighted the leading position French engineers had taken. The building for the 1867 Exposition was a brilliant conception, the main themes of the show being integrated into the total plan:

> The Paris Exhibition building, which throughout is of a single storey only in height, is composed of a series of vast concentric ovals, the innermost of the series enclosing a central garden open to the air and encircled by an open colonnade. Each one of the oval compartments, as it is continued around the entire plan, contains one separate class or group of exhibits, as they are exhibited by all nations. A walk completely round any one oval compartment of the building, therefore, conducts the spectator from the representatives of one country to those of another; all of them, however, representing the same art or industry or product; . . . Again: lines drawn from the exterior of the building to the central garden, and cutting through the whole of the concentric ovals, form a second set of compartments, of which each one is assigned to the various works or productions of one and the same country. These compartments, having a plan somewhat resembling a wedge, necessarily vary considerably in extent, while they all preserve the same general form.[31]

A superb organizational conceit, the building made the Exposition the most logical of the whole tradition. Contemporary accounts also recognised the lightness and subtlety of the interior spaces, set off by the beautifully crafted ironwork profiled against the glass. As a purpose built exhibition building this had no rivals, the Crystal Palace included.

At the 1878 show a Machine Hall was built by a M. de Dion, although overall the trend was temporarily away from the established notion of iron and glass. The Palais de Trocadéro, a flamboyant piece of eclectic styling in brick and stone, was the new centre-piece, this surviving more or less intact until 1937 when it was finally removed to make room for the Palais de Chaillot.[32] 1889 saw the dramatic return of engineering to centre-stage with what became two of the most famous structures of the century, the Eiffel Tower and the Galerie des Machines. The Tower, designed by Gustav Eiffel, was to remain the highest man-made structure for forty years. Constructed from 15,000 wrought iron sections, it was an icon to the power of technology, a giant with unlimited strength and endless capabilities. Conceived of in 1885, partly as a spin-off from the work Eiffel had done on the Statue of Liberty,[33] the tower was not by any means universally welcomed as an addition to the Paris skyline. Eiffel in fact drew up a list of useful purposes it would serve if it were to remain intact after the Exposition, an extraordinary exercise in the light of the tower's splendidly functionless raison d'être. Included amongst these were strategical operations if Paris were under siege, meteorological observations, astromonical experimentation and general scientific use. Whilst all of these were performed through the tower's unexpectedly long life, its real use has remained as a beautiful climbing-frame for energetic tourists. It also made a personal fortune for Eiffel, who owned four-fifths of the shares in it and who continued to make a profit from entrance fees into the new century, when it finally became state property. It remains, the most popular tourist site in the world and the symbol of the city.

The Galerie des Machines was the last great engineering experiment to appear at an exhibition; it occupies a place of real importance in architectural history. It impressed laymen and experts alike with its combination of gargantuan scale and sinuous delicacy:

> If the Eiffel Tower was an unexpected surprise, a triumph of originality and of daring skill, the machinery hall was found to be only one degree less marvellous; and this because the progress of modern architecture and of the science of engineering had, from one decade to another, led us up to this superb realisation of the unexplored possibilities of both. Never before, in the opinion of engineers of all countries who have visited it, has a building, proportionately to its vast dimensions, been constructed with such a wondrous combination of solidity, lightness, and grace, the general effect being enhanced by the flood of light freely admitted to all parts of the palace.[34]

The building was designed by architect Dutert, with engineer Contamin calculating the sizes and stresses of the ironwork. The span of the arches across the central space was one hundred and fifteen metres, a distance achieved through use of a system employed by Oudry in his swinging bridge at Brest, and by several German engineers in railway stations. This allowed for the elimination of tie-rods or other intermediary supports. John Allwood: 'Cotamin . . . was to balance his gigantic roof, like an elephantine ballet dancer on points, on huge hinged supports in the concrete foundation raft. The roof was also pivoted on a gigantic pin at the apex of each arch, thus allowing the great structure to take up the necessary amount of structural movement within itself'.[35] The Galerie was awarded the prestigious Osiris prize, of one hundred thousand francs, twenty thousand going to Dutert, fifteen to Cotamin, three each to the five assistant architects and engineers, and fifty amongst the workforce who erected it.[36]

The 1900 Exposition revealed a confusion in the site architecture that was reflected in the state of practice in general. Only the remnants of the previous exposition, the Eiffel tower and the Galerie des Machines, appeared to have any confidence in themselves, much of the rest being an aimless and eclectic explosion of overblown and tired formulae. The Grand Palais, one of two permanent buildings erected, exemplified this confusion, embodying in its cumbersome body tensions going well beyond the limits of architecture. The internal structure of the building was a wrought iron frame and the roof was of iron and glass. This was encased in a massive masonry shell, giving the whole edifice a feeling of compromise: 'What can one say about the Grand Palais, a sort of railway station where masses of stone have been piled up to support what? – A high, thin roof of glass. A bizarre contrast of materials. It is as if a giant were flexing its muscles, stiffening his arms and making a tremendous effort to raise a simple head-dress of lace above his head.'[37] The unresolved tension between architect and engineer, between earlier and recent methodologies and between two quite distinct visions of the world had met in one building, giving rise to a formal disaster. There were pronounced symbolic tensions; the monumental hulk of masonry was evocative of an insecure France, unsure as to how to project its national profile, its rôle as the bringer of high culture and civilization. It stood for an architectural profession which still saw itself as an elite, divided from the world of utility and social purpose. More generally it stood for regressive forces in society who wished to benefit from the material advances capital and technology had brought, without accepting their consequences in other spheres. The iron and glass which the masonry shell surrounded was the symbol of progressive liberalism, of those who had invented and championed industry, empire and free trade, who had generated the wealth and power that held the world in balance. Adaptability, lightness, strength and aggressive advance from the traditional status quo were the hallmarks of this approach. In 1889 iron and glass had no real rivals. In 1900, as the march of capital faltered and the European nations increasingly undermined one another, forces that had previously been unstoppable began to fail, and older power mechanisms regained a hold. Regression seemed a sensible course; stone enveloped iron and glass, not to destroy it, but simply to slow and disguise it. The Galerie des Machines had embodied industry and empire, the Grand Palais represented in stone the confused slide to the First World War.

The stunning success of some of the European engineering structures had no real equivalents in America. Whilst iron and glass were used in the first American Fairs, usually in tandem with brick and wood, little in the way of novel or innovative architecture emerged. Following Carstensen and Gildemeister's inauspicuous start in New York in 1853, the organizers of the Philadelphia Centennial had much ground to make up on their European counterparts. Despite the enormous amount of building carried out on the Centennial grounds however, it was the landscaping of the site which proved its finest feature. Five large pavilions were built, these casting their shadows over the dozens of State, national and private pavilions surrounding them. The Main Building (1880 by 464 feet), the Machinery Hall (1402 by 360 feet), the Agricultural Hall (540 by 820 feet) and the Horticultural Hall (383 by 193 feet) were all iron frame buildings with glass roofing, brick and wood screen walls. The Memorial Hall was to be a permanent museum after the Fair closed and so was built mainly in granite. None of these was of real interest though, being unsure expressions of a culture still lacking an independent architectural voice in public building.[38] The only work to cause a stir for its innovative qualities was the New Jersey State Pavilion. This was a clever exercise in timber beam construction, making use of a balloon frame, which allowed for variation in both the interior and exterior space. Vincent Scully has recognised the pavilion as one of the earliest examples of an architectural form he christened the 'stick style', the first truly indigenous American style in architecture.[39]

Seventeen years later at the Chicago Columbian Exposition, the condition of American architecture was very different. In 1885 William Le Baron Jenney had built in Chicago what was later to be acknowledged as the first sky-scraper, the Home Insurance building. Best defined as tall buildings, hung on steel frames, with modern amenities like elevators, central heating and incandescent lighting, sky-scraper office blocks were to be the back-bone of the Chicago School, a progressive movement which altered the course of architecture between 1880 and 1914. The School also transformed the shape of the house and can rightly be thought of as an important ingredient in the rise of international modernism in Europe.[40] Thus in 1893, the organisers of the Columbian had a great deal of acclaimed expertise to tap for the construction of their site. Daniel Burnham, a leading light in the Chicago school, was made chairman of the executive committee in charge of the architecture, and other figures of note were involved. It might well have been expected that the Fair would combine engineering and architectural design much in the way the Chicago School had in the city's commercial buildings. Somewhat surprisingly however, this did not occur. A classical format was chosen for the plan and for almost all the major buildings, in apparent contradiction to the recognised architectural situation of Chicago. Looking at the Fair in a wider cultural context though, the choice was more understandable. The ideological climate had dictated the style of the show, classicism satisfying the symbolic requirements of the new republic far better than the decorative functionalism the new generation was famous for.[41] Only Louis Sullivan's Transportation Building showed a little of the spirit that had been the inspiration behind some of the most beautiful buildings in the nineteenth century. The greatest in the school, he objected to classicism as a suitable vehicle, claiming 'the damage wrought by the World's Fair will last for half a century from its date, if not longer'.[42] Frank Lloyd-Wright also saw the classicism of the Columbian as harmfully regressive, believing 1893 to be a 'fateful year in the culture of these United States. They are about to go pseudo-classic in Architecture.'[43] The very city which might have presented the ultimate combination of engineering and architecture at an exhibition had determined not to do so, for reasons that had little to do with either discipline. It would be forty years before Americans chose to represent themselves with modern forms in a Fair, leaving us simply to wonder at what the Chicago Columbian might have been.

Engineering faded as an architectural device at exhibitions between 1890 and 1930, stone and plaster facings being seen to be preferable to express the spirit of the age with. As noted with the Grand Palais, the shift back to historicism, eclecticism and escapism in Europe indicated faltering confidence in the forces which had created the power and wealth the West enjoyed. In tandem with the growth of imperial propaganda, as opposed to imperial celebration, the verbose, overblown melodrama of twentieth century sites revealed a gaggle of shouting nations, who grew louder by the year, yet who were far less sure of what they were shouting about. The difference between the dynamic simplicity of the Crystal Palace, and the pompous acres of plaster and stone at Wembley seventy-three years later, was the difference between a nation in the ascendant and one in decline.

The only real rôle engineering openly had on sites through this later period was in the entertainment areas, where spectacular structures were erected for the express purpose of pleasure. Indeed, symbolic significance accepted, pleasure was the central principle behind the building of the Eiffel tower; it can be seen as the first in an impressive line of engineering feats specifically designed to send shivers of excitement up the spines of expectant visitors. In 1893 the Chicagoans built the first, now legendary, Ferris Wheel. Two giant wheels, two hundred and sixty feet in diameter, were clamped together, holding on their perimeters carriages which could hold sixty people each. Over two thousand people at a time could be hoisted into the air, on an axle claiming to be the largest single piece of steel ever forged. Chicago also had a moving pavement capable of carrying thousands around the site by electronic power. In 1900 at Paris these were copied, the 'trottoir roulant' there having three lanes at varying speeds to accomodate visitors with different needs. An electronically powered overhead railway also featured here and a gigantic 'Dome of Discovery', a spherical structure containing under its curved facade a plantetarium. Sites came increasingly to resemble fairgrounds, although it would be inaccurate to suggest that this is what they became, as an established code of sobriety always prevented excess. Nonetheless, the part engineering had come to play was bizarrely different from the one it had between 1851 and 1889. In 1908 at the Franco–British Exhibition, a massive continous steel framework was devised and constructed by the Commissioner-General, Imre Kiralfy, to function as the structural support system for the whole site. Once this was in place, everything was covered by architect-designed fibrous-plaster facades, completely disguising what lay underneath. The only pieces of openly exposed engineering prowess were the Flip-flap, a giant pincer-like device which swung visitors across the grounds at great height, and the Stadium, built to stage the fourth modern Olympiad. Thus the public functions on the site were allocated; the plaster facings stood for culture and seriousness, the steel for recreation and frivolity. Whichever way it was viewed, the physical and visual make-up of the exhibition revealed a culture that had gotten its value systems perversely inverted. The spartan simplicity of the stadium, subsequently known as the White City, was commented on at the time by architectural observers who, whilst they recognised value in the integration of structure into the total design, still found difficulty in seeing engineering as a real ally to architecture: 'It boasts no architectural features, the steel is still gaunt and unclothed; but there are few who will deny that it runs some of our architectural conceptions very close. It is vast, splendid, monumental . . . It is the great achievement of the Franco–British Exhibition, and of the engineering profession.'[44]

The bias against engineering in architectural circles was a result not only of general, ideological discomfort with a new order, but also of a fear that the profession itself was under threat. Methods of training, modes of practice, traditional skills, approaches and forms were all potential victims of iron and glass. Nevertheless, the acceptance of engineering principles by the architectural profession and by influential elements within the lay public was vital before architecture could advance into the new century in any meaningful way. The needs of a mobile mass-population demanded a maleable architecture to cope with endless variables, and architects capable of satisfying diverse social needs. Whilst it may well be argued we are still waiting for the architectural profession to understand its rôle in our society, it is quite clear in retrospect that the exhibitions did help to promote and naturalise new ideas in building, smoothing the path for progressive builders from the end of the nineteenth century.

As suggested earlier, the history of design can be seen as one of recurring tension between historical eclecticism and those ideologies which sought to replace it. Between 1851 and 1939 most exhibitions harboured at least one historical style, and from 1876 there was usually an opposition to it somewhere on the site. Thus at Paris in 1889, classicism and neobaroque dominated the site architecture, the decorative and design arts, yet the rationalism of followers of Viollet-le-Duc was conspicuous amongst architectural exhibits; the Gallerie des Machines proudly offered a new vision of building, and Emile Gallé was already formulating his version of art nouveau in glass and furniture. In Chicago in 1893, the new approach to decoration and technology forged by the Chicago School fought an isolated but lively battle against the dominant classicism. In the 1900 Paris show, art nouveau had arrived in real force even though the generally preferred styles were still neobaroque and neorococo; in 1925, the same struggle continued, if anything more violently than ever before. Opponents of historicism, whatever their theoretical position might collectively have been, were invariably in the minority but invariably present also. Up to and including the First World War, illustrated catalogues of exhibitions held throughout Europe and America reveal remarkable similarities in the way design was presented and understood. Historicism was the norm, designers feeding mainly off revival forms emanating from classical, baroque, rococo, gothic and vernacular styles, the first three being by far the most durable. Into the post-War era, despite the more eclectic use of sources, it remained firmly the preferred approach of the core of the design profession. Few exhibitions managed to exclude historical styles even when an exhibition brief was sent to manufacturers actively discouraging them, as with Paris in 1925, 1937 and New York in 1939. Indeed, the ability of historicism to survive the attacks of generations of designers, critics and historians can be witnessed by a visit to any departmental store at the present time, where classical, baroque and rococo details remain in furnishings, defiant and popular as ever. 'Modernism' has always been only a small part of the story of design, but it has been the one told most often. Undoubtedly this is because of the more engaging theoretical and formal position taken up by progressives, as well as their remarkable ability to publicise themselves and hence win a place in history.

The first and in the author's opinion the most important anti-historicist movement to gain an international audience via the exhibition medium was Art Nouveau, a style, attitude and methodology which effected visual art-forms in most nations between 1895 and 1925. Art nouveau practitioners were the first to self-consciously pursue the Wagnerian notion of 'gesamtkunstwerk', or total work of art, whereby a complete environment, unified in its aesthetic and symbolic content, could surround and infiltrate the viewer. Every aspect of the made environment was subject to art nouveau styling; buildings, fittings, furniture, wallpaper, paintings, sculpture, graphic illustration, carpets and street furniture. Historicism was replaced by an organic, sinew-like decoration derived from nature. Curving, whip-lash line infiltrated the fabric of the building and fittings, becoming part of the structure, in what was usually an exercise in frame, as opposed to wall, construction. The most impressive collections of art nouveau to be brought together in exhibitions were those in Paris (1900), Turin (1902) and London (1908).

The Paris show had the largest gathering of art nouveau artists ever to assemble on one site. The movement, having different names and stylistic tendencies from nation to nation, appeared mainly in the Decorative Arts Palace, inside the national pavilions, and in various structures built by private groups. Amongst the French, furniture, glass, ceramic and metal by De Feure, Gaillard, Guimard, Gallé, Charpentier, Majorelle, Grasset, Lalique, Carriès and Lachenal were spread through the Pavilion de la Union Centrale des Arts Decoratifs, the Pavilion Bing and those built by the stores Le Printemps, Le Louvre and Le Bon Marché. Amongst foreign exhibitors some of the greatest exponents were present, including Riemerschmidt, Mucha, Obrist, Olbrich, and Hoffmann. The last two designed fully fitted interiors. The internal exhibiting spaces in the Union Centrale and Bing pavilions were also set up as furnished rooms, making available an array of complete environments to the visitor. Perhaps the only serious omissions in the representation were the Glasgow school, especially the work of C. R. MacIntosh, and the work of Victor Horta, the architect-designer from Brussels who could easily have claimed to have invented the style.

The site boasted one or two examples of art nouveau architecture, in particular the Pavillon Bleu, a restaurant adjacent to the Pont d'Iena.

Essentially a space-frame with glass and wood in-fill, its beauty was in its curving departure from the linear grid of the structure. The building hung in tension between engineering and nature, holding the appearance both of a cube and a pod. Samuel Bing's pavilion was decoratively flamboyant but architecturally banal. The only real pieces of art nouveau to achieve excellence on an architectural scale apart from the Pavillon Bleu were the station entrances designed by Hector Guimard for the new Métropolitain underground railway. Opened to co-incide with the Exposition, they remain today as taut and sensuous as ever, amongst the best pieces of urban decoration ever designed.[45]

Critical reception given to art nouveau at the exposition tended to concentrate on its claims to being an appropriate modern style, and the wisdom of its insistence on rejecting the past: 'We appreciate the very legitimate wish to put the furniture arts, as with all the others, into intimate accord with our habits, our tastes and our thoughts. But it is advisable not to make modernism a simple mania and reject systematically all that was made by our fathers, unique because they made it.'[46] The same writer, as professor of aesthetics and art history at the Ecole des Beaux Arts, was also worried by the movement's foreign origins and the doubtful implications for French art:

> The style, very composite, is a mixture of gothic and Japanese, of rustic and super-refined, which came from England having passed through Belgium . . . It was already modified and muted; one could not see, in spite of everything, that it responded to our needs, to our social temperament . . . Simple and complicated at the same time, it contains, contradictorily, light open-work and a structure of a strange weight, an unfortunate rigidity, bad proportion and a pretence of convenience which is in reality inconvenience. I'd ignore all this if in the future, by a series of transformations, it would achieve a French appearance.[47]

For the French, the desire to remain in the artistic ascendent made the break with the successes of the past a difficult one to make, especially for those working in the established academies.

At Turin in 1902 the new style was in evidence everywhere, appearing by that time to have become an established and legitimate mode of practice. A large number of the designers who were in Paris showed there, with the welcome addition of the Glasgow school, the international reputation of which was already well in excess of its domestic one. Ironically for MacIntosh and his colleagues, the Turin show proved far more successful than the Glasgow International of the previous year, where they had not featured with any force. Turin is probably best remembered though for its architecture rather than any designer exhibiting indoors. The Central Rotunda and the Pavilion of the Decorative Arts, both by Raimondo D'Aronco, were spectacular examples of the style on a grand scale. Covered in stylised figurines and plant-forms, the rotunda appears as though ready to explode, with only thin strips of wrought iron, like vines, holding it from bursting forth.[48]

The largest single collection of art nouveau objects ever to be in a British exhibition appeared in 1908 at the Franco–British. Here entrepreneur André Delieux organised a group display of designers and craftspeople from all over France, with particular emphasis on the school of Nancy. Five hundred individuals and firms exhibited in the Collectivité Delieux, including the best practitioners of the day. Guimard, Bigaux, Taxile-Doat, Gaillard, Sauvage, Franz Jourdain and Selmersheim were members of a seventeen-strong jury headed by Delieux himself. Such a selection panel guaranteed the dominance of new ideas, much to the discomfort of a British art press deeply entrenched in a regressive support of what they considered indigenous national styles.[49] Most members of the jury were heavily represented in the pavilion which, following the pattern established in Paris, was a series of domestic interiors. Each one was fitted and decorated with the produce of many firms but with a single firm controlling the overall flavour of each. Rooms by Sauvage, Lambert, Galleray, Dufrène, Bigaux and Croix-Marie were picked out as particularly satisfactory, whilst dozens of craftspeople, their names now shrouded in obscurity, received favourable mentions. The Collectivité was seen by its supporters as a challenge to the accepted norm of historicism. Gabriel Mourey:

> Modernity in respect of architecture, decorative art, and applied art is sadly hard to find at Shepherd's Bush. The general aspect of the Franco–British Exhibition produces a deceptive feeling of things one has seen before, and is chiefly remarkable in this respect for an almost total absence of novelty. The explanation of this would take too long to discuss; the fact is incontestable . . . Possibly the time is not so far off as one might imagine when people will tire of living among these no doubt seductive but anachronistic styles . . . It is time that a great collective effort was set on foot amongst us, with daring, and above all, with method, so that the public should be made aware of the results of a movement which, despite the obstacles and shortcomings that have given many people an impression that so much good effort had come to naught, will not fail in the end to succeed.[50]

Delieux believed 'notre génie français était devenu sterile' and that the French tradition would die if it did not align itself with the new century. His modernism thus tinged with patriotism, he called for the renovation of the decorative arts, which he believed could be achieved through the acceptance of industry and the use of new techniques and materials. In an after dinner speech he asserted:

I believe, sirs, that it is a fault to think in too traditionalist a way that science and art have said their last word, and that for us it is best to copy the masterpieces of our predecessors. What! everything changes, all progresses, and you, in powerlessness, reduce your rôle to copyists! No sirs, this is against history, against the laws that rule the destiny of humanity.[51]

His idealism was not untypical of the movement as a whole. Art nouveau, whilst it maintained an exclusive craft-based mode of production in many areas, had shown itself willing to apply the forces responsible for the shape of the modern world to the art of the modern world. Historicism had to be dispensed with because it represented a previous phase of human evolution, the past, the unindustrialised world. Using social-Darwinian logic, art nouveau was presented as a result of more advanced, more civilized minds. In its theoretical obsession with progress, it had two distinct sides. It stood for democracy, the undermining of traditional hierarchies and the general advancement of creativity; it also matched perfectly the progressive liberalism that had given rise to the voracious expansion of industry, capital and empire. In this respect it harboured within its twining metallic tendrils a symbolism which could in our own age be perceived as contradictory. In Brussels for example, where it was used to superb formal ends, it stood simultaneously for socialism, capitalism and imperialism.[52] In Glasgow also, its stunningly free and lyrical application to urban architecture appears in retrospect to run against the otherwise grandiose grain of that most imperial of cities. In its symbolic pluralism the style reflected on the one hand the confused state of the fin de siécle world, and on the other the perenial multiplicity of the human condition. Nonetheless, in its social awareness, in its synthesis of material and form, of narrative and function and of means and ends, art nouveau left many of the modernisms which succeeded it far behind.

In 1925 after a period of unsureness which lingered well after the War, the exhibition tradition had its first real taste of full-blooded modernism, at the Paris Exposition des Arts Decoratifs et Industriels Modernes. Here the French guaranteed innovation in one form or another by demanding it in the exhibition brief:

The Exposition . . . is open to all manufacturers whose produce is artistic in character and shows clearly modern tendencies . . . That is to say that all copies or counterfeits of historical styles will be banned; that is to say also that any manufacturer is eligible since everyday objects are as capable of being beautiful as the most exclusive objects.
All industrialists, artists and artisans, in whatever material they specialize . . . in whatever form they use it, and for whatever purpose, can and should be modern.[53]

The result was an exhibition in which designers who had never previously wrestled with the problem of contemporaneity abruptly formulated styles for the new century and applied them to objects of all kinds. These shared certain common features, allowing them to be defined as a single style, later named Art Deco after the Exposition itself. Art Deco was to grow in scope, becoming the characteristic look of the later twenties and thirties. Accepting that the rudiments of it existed well before 1925, it would be reasonable to suggest this as a unique instance, where an exhibition gave birth to and then publicised a style.[54]

Despite its basic intentions, art deco was both eclectic and historicist, being little more than a peculiar amalgamation of many earlier styles. The essential ingredients were Aztec, ancient Egyptian, African (West and North), Oceanic, neoclassical, Louis Quatorze, Quinze and Seize, art nouveau, cubism and abstract art. Some items had three or four of these sources clinging simultaneously to their surfaces in unhappy rivalry. Many of the designers and architects had recently been involved with art nouveau, which had lingered on into the early twenties as the only real 'modern look'. By then however it was recognised as being tired. It was attacked in the official literature of the Exposition, presumably in the hope of dissuading designers from using it: 'Copier la nature . . . était une erreur aussi lourde que pasticher les formes du passé sans regarder à quoi elles appliquaient. Ce ne fut qu'une mode: la mode n'est pas le modernisme'.[55] Like all eclectic forms before it, art deco was to be a synthetic style, self-consciously avoiding one to one relations with nature.

The exotic and ancient inspiration behind art deco at first appears to contradict its struggle for modernity, as does its persistence with neoclassical and baroque profiles. The use of the last two came simply from a reluctance and inability to give them up. There were three basic reasons for the fashionability of the ancient and exotic: first, modern artists since Gauguin had made use of primitive and ancient art. They had been a vital ingredient in avant-garde movements up to and including 1925. Thus, in order to modernise their own practice, designers followed what they believed were the methods of the acknowledged progressives in the fine arts. Second, these sources were popular because of their distance from everyday experience; their 'otherness' made them new and unexpected. The fact that they were not part of the European historical tradition enabled their look to be translated into something appearing to have no precedent. Finally, the ability of all these forms to be abstracted and subjected to geometry made them suitable for furniture, architecture and product-casings. They could be adapted easily to mass-production processes. It would be far from easy to style an art nouveau radio, with its insistence on sinewy, asymetrical line, far easier to box it into a smoothed-off, ziggerat art deco format.

In the first instance, French art deco was dominated by fashionable and exclusive craft firms. Designers like Ruhlmann, Pierre Legrain, Edgar Brandt, Jean Dunand, the Jallot Brothers, Clement Rousseau, Sue and Mare, Eileen Gray and Rene Lalique had little to do with industry as such. The movement as presented at the Exposition can be seen as an attempt by the French to put their produce back into the forefront of the world market by bringing their traditional areas of strength up to date. What they came up with was basically a Louis XIV methodology hidden under a machine age veneer.[56] After this exclusive inauguration however, the style rapidly filtered down to everyday objects, from cutlery, ceramic and glass to fireplaces, radios and cinema facades.

Art deco, and many of the modernist 'isms' which have followed it down to the present time, was a symbolic solution to a problem that needed methodological answers. It was involved in the manipulation of appearances by adjusting the superficial elements in the object to suggest the contemporary world, and, by implication, the future. It attempted to carry the consumer away from the immediate world, hinting at a universe he or she had not yet experienced; more than anything else, it was about disguise. As such, it largely conformed to the idea of style put forward by R. N. Wornum at the Great Exhibition, failing to integrate the narratives it contained with the modes of production it used.

Elsewhere on the site there were small quantities of design and architecture which rejected the notion of style as a cosmetic additive. These were to be found in areas controlled by members of the pioneer modern movement often collectively labelled the International Style. For these propounders of modernism, the break with historical eclecticism was to be achieved by an absolute elimination of all extraneous symbolism. Decoration of any kind was thus dispensed with, the beauty of the building or object being arrived at through the creative and functional manipulation of the spaces. International style designers also saw their practice as being firmly in a moral context, as a means of transforming the lives of the population. There were two pavilions uncompromisingly within this category, the Pavillon de l'Esprit Nouveau by Le Corbusier and the pavilion of the U.S.S.R.. The former, largely ignored at the time, had all the features of the style ultimately to be seen by many as the absolute and inevitable architecture of our century. It was an icon of international modernism; white walls, flat roof, emphasis on fenestration, an internal space which was not so much an organisation of rooms as a partitioning of a single open area, and an absence of surface decoration. Planned as a module which could be stacked into flats or left as a small detached dwelling, it was a brilliant exercise in the use of prefabrication, in an attempt to show how mass-housing could be built well and cheaply.[57] The furniture and fittings were utterly utilitarian, being mostly 'ready-made' pieces intended for industry and offices, and the walls were decorated with paintings by Fernand Léger.[58] The pavilion was named after 'L'Esprit Nouveau', the modernist journal controlled by Le Corbusier and Amedée Ozenfant. The Russian pavilion appears to have been formally more interesting, though surviving photographs of it give little indication as to how it functioned as a building. It confronted the visitor in its main facade with a huge bank of windows, like a transparent billboard; to the side, a staircase covered by a criss-cross arrangement of iron beams led up to the principal entrance, tucked away inauspiciously. The only element containing a narrative was the emblem of the hammer and sickle hung above the stair-well. The pavilion was a severe denial of the rôle of the wall, an exercise in space and light as opposed to volume and mass.

These two pavilions were isolated incidents. The majority of the architecture on the site fitted into the art deco category and as such it opposed itself firmly to the proletarian moralism they espoused. Perhaps the extreme opposite of Le Corbusier's vision, in both a moral and a formal sense, was provided by the Ruhlmann Group, whose building, designed by Pierre Patout, was unambiguously called 'Pavilion of a Rich Collector'. This had all the features of the art deco style; the ziggerat stepping toward the summit, a suggestion of classicism in stripped pilasters and use of a frieze, decorative motifs taken from sub-cubist painting, sculptural elements that were strange, mannered abrieviations of Roman relief carving. There was also an insistence upon the use of the wall to create a volumetric (as opposed to spatial) feel to the building. The pavilion was an altogether odd combination of ancient, exotic and modern formal strategies, and as such it reflected perfectly the flavour of the objects inside it. Patout designed several more buildings on the site, including the Porte de la Concorde, one of the six monumental entrances. This comprised of an arrangement of eight giant free-standing square pillars with a sculpture of a nude woman in the centre. Despite the obscurity now surrounding his name, he was one of the best known and most favoured of French architects through to the Second World War. His 'deco-classicism' was still in evidence at the Paris Exposition of 1937, his style appearing to have some influence over the design of the Musée d'Art Moderne, which still stands across the Seine from the Eiffel tower. He also won the commission to build the French Pavilion at the New York World's Fair, a choice on the part of the organisers which would seem to indicate his version of modernism was for them preferable to Le Corbusier's.

Art deco styling was apparent in most of the official structures in 1925 but it was probably at its most flamboyant in the pavilions built by Parisian stores and fashion houses. The feeling of exclusivity and opulence was everywhere, this brand of modernism having decidedly not left traditions of French craftmanship behind in order to embrace the age of mass-production. Between the extremes of the Pavilion of a Rich Collector and the Pavilion L'Esprit Nouveau, however, there were some interesting works which later exerted influence, the most notable of these being the Tourist Pavilion by Robert Mallet-Stevens. The interslotting of vertical and horizontal planes was clearly in the knowledge of works produced by the De Stijl architects, and possibly Walter Gropius' Chicago Tribune Tower of 1922,[59] yet here the extreme austerity is softened, the pavilion quietly acknowledging earlier forms without sliding into the turgid eclecticism evident elsewhere on the site. It was a prototype for much exhibition architecture after it, notably at the Chicago Century of Progress (1933) and the Glasgow Empire (1938). At the latter, the Scottish Pavilion and the central Tower in particular seem to owe a lot to Mallet-Stevens.[60]

The Paris and New York exhibitions in 1937 and 1939 were totally committed to modernism.[61] However, they had very different ideas as to what modern architecture and design should be. The Paris show exuded the international style whilst New York was dominated by a symbolic modernism coming largely out of Art Deco and Streamform. Paris determined its position partly through pressure from intellectuals and the substantial number of unemployed French artists and designers, some of whom had representation on key committees.[62] The modernist lobby, although by no means totally victorious, managed to guarantee stylistic predominance over much of the site. New York appears to have been more random in that relatively few of the buildings were subjected to committee judgment, and few architectural theorists gained access to discussions on site planning. The only rigour the styles were subjected to came from the natural selection of commercial enterprise; streamform, art deco and futuropolis were the leading popular forms, so they were used to design the Fair. They also fitted neatly into the overall theme, 'Democracity', in so far as they appeared to be the ones the masses preferred. In a world of high capital, the styles, it seems, selected themselves. As with all consumable goods, the Fair had to be purchased by its public before it could be counted a success, and the look of the pavilions helped to sell it. More than anything it showed that design was essentially a part of the marketing world.

Commenting on the Paris show, Serge Chermayeff complained that the Eiffel tower was the best piece of architecture on the site. He openly attacked the Palais de Chaillot, the replacement for the Palais de Tro-cadéro, as being retrogressive. The classicism of the new Musée d'Art Moderne also displeased him: 'Both the new Trocadéro and the Museum of Modern Art – Vieux Pompiers renderings of Renaissance up to date – are worthy to stand with the Peace Palace at Geneva among the the most dismal architectural failures of any size.' [63] There were however plenty of buildings of a type a modernist like Chermayeff could approve of, in principle at least. Denmark, Holland, Spain, Poland, Sweden, Switzer-land, Czechoslovakia and Finland were all rigorously spatial and func-tional, Alvar Aalto's Finnish pavilion probably being the best work on the site. More than this, the Palais de l'Aeronautique, the Porte d'Aliamentation, the Pavillon de la Paix (excluding the tower) and the Pavilion by Le Corbusier devoted to C.I.A.M. (Congrès Internationale d'Architectes Moderne) all celebrated international, abstract moder-nism.[64] In its white facade and generous fenestration, even the British pavilion had the superficial trappings of the new order.[65]

The contrast with New York could hardly have been more dramatic. Pavilions by major American industries dominated the site; the accent was on the commercial, temporal aspect of design. As in Paris in 1925, a stipulation of the show was modernity: 'no imitations either of historic architecture or imitations of permanent materials were permitted, with one exception only, namely the sector devoted to the states'.[66] The organisers claimed to have a vision of design that went beyond the commercial function, 'the true poets of the twentieth century are the designers, the architects and the engineers who glimpse some inner vision, create some beautiful figment of the imagination, and then translate it into valid actuality for the world to enjoy'.[67] The new generation of American industrial designers dominated the site in a confident affirmation of the strength of indigenous American styles. Raymond Loewy, Norman Bel Geddes, Walter Dorwin Teague and Henry Dreyfuss were all present in force, Dreyfuss producing the design for the massive interior of the Perisphere. 'Streamform', the style they made famous, was everywhere. Its main ingredient was the tear-drop form, whereby an object, regardless of its function, was smoothed down into an aerodynamic shape resemblant of an aeroplane.[68] Con-temporaneity was thus represented through the appearance of speed much in the way of the Italian Futurists, although the Americans answered to very different social, intellectual and economic forces. Streamform was emblematic of the pace at which modern society moved. In theoretical terms, it was part of the same ideology as art deco; not historicist but certainly eclectic, it was a stylistic additive, a narrative to tell the consumer what the aspirations of the object were. Once art deco became a style for mass-production it joined with streamform in celebrating the marketing virtues of expendability and mass-consumerism.

The difference between the Paris 1937 and New York 1939 shows lay not in good or bad taste – both had quantitities of each – or in functionability of plans and buildings, but in the socio-political situations they were created in. Those in Paris who espoused the international style had an in-built belief that design and architecture were social arts and were capable of helping in the drive toward Utopia. Architecture, it was argued, had a past, a present and a future which revealed the existence of a stylistic dialectic, one which would ultimately transform architecture completely and society with it. For them, the idea of style in the absence of morality was meaningless, for style symbolized the well-being of society, not the taste of individuals. It was not a superficial additive. In New York, no such dialectic was recognised as existing, the stylistic unity of the site came largely out of economic factors. A style was popularised through advertising, it was then demanded by the population and would remain in demand by them until such time as it became commercially redundant. The Corporations of America needed no dialectic, no Utopia.

The tragedy of modern design and architecture was epitomised by these two exhibitions. As versions of modernism they had both failed to provide an architectural environment fit for people to live in, and would continue to fail because both, in the vastness of their material and intellectual conceptions, had managed to lose sight of the actual problems of human, urban existence. Alienation, the state whereby one ceases to recognise oneself in the products and objects in the made-environment, and ultimately whereby one ceases to recognise oneself *in oneself*, was ignored as an issue and left unresolved through the century. Cities planned by the few for the many, in the absence of the needs of particular communities, and ignorant of local memories, were bound to alienate. Likewise the anonymity of corporate design, constructed from corporate decisions, could only exclude and in turn alienate. The one approach failed to recognise individual consciousness, the other generated a false one. The elimination of trade skills and the embracing of assembly-line modes of production – accepted unquestioningly by both approaches – meant that on the ground level, design and architecture were foreign intruders. The 'honest' exposure of structure, or 'stylish' addition of futuristic and historicist features, could have little effect on practices which had failed at a fundamental level. Indeed, by the 1950's, the superficial features of both approaches were readily used by builders across the socio-political spectrum, as it was obviously recognisable by then that all forms of modernism had come to mean the same thing. Exacerbating the decline, prefabrication and mass-production, instead of developing from the undoubted benefit of quantity, had come to stand for shoddiness and emotional poverty. Cheapness of materials, anonymity of design, lack of trade skills at appropriate levels, and the utter dominance of economic not human factors, have seen architecture continue to spiral downwards. The failing of international modernism was not in its vision of design and architecture as social arts, indeed, this was its glory, but in its methodologies. Its vision of the architect as an artist aside from society, not as an orchestrator of available ideas and skills from within society, rendered many of its solutions inappropriate and alien. The insistence upon non-objective abstraction and on the elimination of narratives shut it off from language, reducing drastically the ability of the viewer to gain access and interpret its spaces, surfaces and facades. By the time the Paris show opened in 1937, the modern movement had still failed to produce works as meaningful and resolved as gothic revival or art nouveau forerunners, as a cursory glimpse at exhibition sites from 1851 to 1900 demonstrates. One can only muse that if the lessons of some of the earlier exhibitions had been heeded, those of 1937 and 1939 might have been the confirmation of a century of realised, not missed opportunities.

Notes

1 Quoted from *The Crystal Palace and the Great Exhibition*, in *Art and Industry*, Open University A100 course material by Aaron Scharf, Open University Press 1971.
2 R. H. Soden Smith, *Dwellings for the Poor*, taken from *Reports on the Paris Universal Exhibition 1867*, Volume 3, London 1867.
3 R. N. Wornum, *The Exhibition as a Lesson in Taste*, taken from *The Crystal Palace Exhibition, Art Journal Issue*, London 1851. Facsimile reprint, New York 1970, DOVER Publications.
4 Ibid.
5 *The International Exhibition of 1862: The Illustrated Catalogue of the Industrial Department*, 2 Volumes, London 1862.
6 There are various useful references to this. Recommended is Eric de Maré *London 1851: The Year of the Great Exhibition* London 1972, The Folio Society. As with other aspects of the Great Exhibition, the rôle of the Prince is confusing because of the way he has been mythologised by historians. Obviously he was politically significant in the exhibition as a whole (see Chapter Two) but his honorary position often made him figure-head to enterprises he knew little about. As Honorary President of the Society for Improving the Condition of the Labouring Classes, his name would be attached to the Model House whether he played a real part in it or not.
7 The publication *The Plumber and Decorator and Journal of Heating, Ventilating, Gas and Sanitary Engineering* for example ran lengthy articles on the White City Exhibitions and took part in conferences there.
8 Soden-Smith, see note 2.
9 Ibid.
10 Ibid.
11 Edwin Chadwick, *Dwellings Characterised by Cheapness Combined with Conditions Necessary for Health and Comfort.* from *Reports on the Paris Universal Exhibition 1867* London 1867.
12 Ibid.

13 It would seem inconceivable that exhibitions after 1889 did not play a rôle in the rise of moral consciousness in architectural theory in France and the Netherlands.

14 The imperial implications of the grouping of European produce are also evident, even though it was being criticised. It was of obvious importance to most critics to stress the different character of non-Western art, even if it was to acknowledge its superiority.

15 William Dyce, quoted from *The Great Exhibition and the Crystal Palace*, see note 1.

16 Soden-Smith, see note 2.

17 The relationship between romanticism and orientalism would tend to support this position throughout the visual arts.

18 Samuel Bing's shop *L'Art Nouveau* is perhaps the best known example. Of course, there were trends of Japonaiserie and Chinoiserie that chose to use the complex figuration of those countries as an additive to the weighty historicist decoration already available. Japan had more than one style, and more than one effect on the West.

19 This is a controversial point, Wright himself refuting claims that Japan influenced him, years later in his diaries. Sadly, little of what he said can be taken at face value; for example, in his obsession with his own genius, he tended to disown his *Shingle* and *Stick* forerunners, an ommission which is quite preposterous.

20 Occasionally the situation was more confusing in America, as the first architectural academy was only founded in 1865 (Massachusetts) and the second in 1869 (Illinois). Prior to this, the handful of formally trained architects had been taught in Paris. In New York in 1853 the organisers initially asked Joseph Paxton to design their building, in Philadelphia in 1876 relatively few of the American structures were architect built.

21 Folke T. Kihlstedt, *The Crystal Palace*, Scientific American, 1982.

22 The famous *Elms Affair* was provoked by the infamous Colonel Sibthorp and various *Times* journalists. It was claimed the park would suffer unacceptably if the trees were felled. Paxton built the Palace over them. This left the nuisance of the sparrows in the trees soiling exhibits. The Duke of Wellington apparently suggested the solution to this latter problem, sparrow-hawks. Also, see Chapter 2.

23 Antony Bird, *Paxton's Palace*, London 1976, Cassell and Company.

24 G.F. Chadwick, *The Works of Sir Joseph Paxton*, London, 1961, Architectural Press. Also Bird and Kihlstedt, see notes 21 and 23.

25 Ibid, and *Frank Leslie's Illustrated Historical Register of the Centennial Exposition 1876*, facsimlie copy available, New York 1974, Paddington Press.

26 Ibid.

27 Quoted from Caroline Mathieu, *Le Palais de l'Industrie: à Propos de Deux Dessins de Max Berthelin*, Revue du Louvre, Part 5–6, Volume 31, Pages 373–80, 1982.

28 *The Penny Guide to the International Exhibition 1862*, London 1862.

29 *Prospects of the International Exhibition 1862*, Cornhill Magazine July 1861.

30 *The Illustrated Catalogue of the Industrial Department*, Volume Two, London 1862.

31 Reverend Charles Boutell, *The Illustrated Catalogue of the Universal Exhibition, Published with the Art Journal*, London 1867.

32 See Chapter 5.

33 See Charles Mercer, *Statue of Liberty*, New York 1979, G. P. Putnams.

34 *Reports of the United States Commissioners to the Universal Exposition of 1889 at Paris*, Volume 3 (of five), Washington 1891.

35 John Allwood, *The Great Exhibitions*, London 1977, Studio Vista.

36 See American Reports, note 36, for further details.

37 Quoted from Philippe Julian, *The Triumph of Art Nouveau: The Paris Exhibition of 1900*, London 1974, Phaidon.

38 For images and discussion of the Centennial architecture see J. S. Ingram, *The Centennial Exhibition, described and Illustrated*, Philadelphia 1876; R.C. Post, *1876: A Centennial Exhibition*, Washington 1976, Smithsonian Institution.

39 Vincent Scully, *The Shingle Style and the Stick Style: Architectural Theory and Design from Downing to the Origins of Wright*, New Haven 1955, Yale University Press.

40 See M. L. Peisch, *The Chicago School of Architecture – Early Followers of Sullivan and Wright.*; Carl Condit, *The Chicago School of Architecture* Chicago University Press 1964; H.R. Hitchcock, *The Pelican History of Art: Architecture, Nineteenth and Twentieth Centuries*, London, 1978.

41 See Chapter 5.

42 See Condit, note 40.

43 F.L. Wright, *Autobiography*

44 R.W. Carden, The Franco–British Exhibition, Part 1, Architectural Review Volume 24, 1908.

45 For a complete list of the remaining stations, and all of Guimard's other works in Paris, see Gillian Naylor, *Hector Guimard*, London 1978, Academy Editions.

46 Louis de Fourcaud, *Le Bois*, in *L'Art à l'Exposition Universelle de 1900*, Paris 1900, Libraire de l'Art Ancien et Moderne.

47 Ibid.

48 See Maurice Rheims, *The Age of Art Nouveau*, London, 1966, Thames and Hudson, and Frank Russell (Ed.) *Art Nouveau Architecture*, London 1979, Academy Editions.

49 See Paul Greenhalgh, *Art, Politics and Society at the Franco–British Exhibiton of 1908*, Art History December 1985.

50 Gabriel Mourey, *The Collectivite André Delieux*, in F. G. Dumas, *The Franco–British Exhibition Illustrated Review*, London 1909, Chatto and Windus.

51 *Collectivite André Delieux – Exposition Franco–Britannique 1908*, Paris 1908.

52 See Maurice Culot on Belgian art nouveau in Frank Russell, see note 48.

53 Quoted from Tim Benton, Charlotte Benton, Aaron Scharf, *Design 1920's*, from *History of Architecture and Design 1890–1939*, Open University course material, Open University Press 1975. This remains the best analysis of modernism in architecture.

54 Art deco was already evident in American architecture, and was present in quantities at the London (Wembley) Exhibition of 1924.

55 *Encyclopaedie des Arts Decoratifs et Industriels Modernes au XX Siècle* Paris 1925, twelve Volumes.

56 For further discussion on these lines see P. Garner, *The Birth of Art Deco: Paris Exhibition of 1925.*, Country Life, December 1975, Volume 158, Part 4095.

57 It does seem akin to the Model House for the Working Classes built by Henry Roberts for the Great Exhibition. The concept was used by Dolfus at Mulhouse, possibly providing a continental link to Le Corbusier's L'Esprit Nouveau pavilion. I do not know at this time what knowledge Le Corbusier had of these nineteenth century developments

58 See John Golding and Christopher Green, *Léger and Purist Paris*, London, 1970 Exhibition catalogue, Tate Gallery, and Fernand Léger, *Fonctions de la Peinture*, Paris 1965, ditions Gonthier.

59 Gropius' building was not built, but the drawings for it were widely known at the time.

60 Both these exhibitions are in need of further work by architectural historians. The modernism employed at Glasgow is particularly intriguing.

61 However, nationalism ultimately dominated, see Chapter 5.

62 See Patrick Weiser, *L'Exposition Internationale, L'etat et les Beaux Arts*, in *Paris 1937–1957* Paris 1981, Exhibition catalogue, Centre Georges Pompidou.

63 Serge Chermayeff, in a special edition of the Architectural Review, 1937.

64 Ibid.

65 Designed by Oliver Hill. Ibid.

66 *New York World's Fair 1939: Official Guide Book* New York 1939, Exposition Publications.

67 Ibid.

68 See Penny Sparke, *An Introduction to Design and Culture in the Twentieth Century*, London 1986, Allen and Unwin.

CHAPTER SEVEN

Women: exhibiting and exhibited

International exhibitions were one of the first and most effective cultural arenas in which women expressed their misgivings with established patriarchy. They provided one of the few places where women could exert influence, due mainly to the fact that they comprised fifty percent of the audience. Their inevitable inclusion as consumers meant they had a certain power of veto which afforded them consideration. Moreover, because of their claims to encyclopædic coverage of world culture, exhibitions could not easily exclude women in the way other institutions continually did. As feminist activity grew in scope toward the end of the nineteenth century the exhibitions increasingly became a focus of interest as centres of possible activity for women.

The main contribution of women to exhibitions was in the form of specially erected pavilions for the display of women's art, industry and work. The first and one of the most impressive was the Woman's Pavilion at the Philadelphia Centennial of 1876. After this there was a Women's Section at the New Orleans Exposition in 1886 and, somewhat surprisingly, a Pavilion of Women's Industries at the Glasgow International in 1888. These were strange, rather idiosyncratic affairs however, the real follow-up to Philadelphia coming in 1893 at the Chicago Columbian. This exhibition firmly established the idea of the women's building or section in the minds of future organizers, setting a precedent which led to the acceptance of it as a necessary part of events all over the world.

So far evidence has not emerged to show exactly where the pressure came from to allocate women a rôle in the Philadelphia Centennial. Certainly there was no precedent within the European exhibition tradition and little indication of enlightenment in major American cultural institutions during the period. It can only be assumed there was lobbying from women's groups and that this proved successful in gaining recognition from the Centennial Board. Such an assumption is made all the more plausible by abundant evidence of increasing vocality of American women across the political-cultural spectrum. Whatever the cause, in 1873 the Centennial Board appointed thirteen women from Philadelphia to form a Women's Centennial Executive Committee, with a Mrs. E. D. Gillespie as president. The Women's Committee was to advance the representation and activity of women at the Centennial and to generally lobby and support the efforts of the Board. It was decided early in 1874 that there would also be a women's section in the Main Building. Mrs. Gillespie proved to be an admirable campaigner for the whole exhibition, organizing fund-raising events, speaking at rallies and gathering signatures for various petitions to Congress. Despite this, in June 1875 the Board renegued on its promise to provide a space for women in the Main Building, advising the Women's Committee that the only way they would be able to have separate representation would be in their own building, paid for by themselves. Within months, led passionately by Mrs. Gillespie, the committee had raised $30,000 and had reserved a space on the site for the first ever Women's Building.

Due to the shortage of time, a design for the one acre building was commissioned from H. J. Schwarzmann, architect-in-chief to the site. Mrs. Gillespie later regretted the employment of a man in what was the key artistic rôle:

> Weary and longing for rest, we never thought of employing a woman architect! and thus made our first great mistake . . . I left home, promising to return early in September, when the plans would be ready for inspection. I had not been gone many days before I heard the praises sung of a woman architect in Boston, and I wished I could annul the contract with Mr. Schwarzmann. To this hour I feel pained, because I fear we hindered this legitimate branch of women's work instead of helping it.[1]

Inside the building everything was by women. All disciplines within the arts, sciences and humanities were represented, with particular emphasis on those activities generally acknowledged to be within the women's sphere. Thus an overriding accent was on domestic produce and on crafts such as lace-making and embroidery. This tended to breed commentary which was an uncomfortable mixture of admiration and condescension:

> (The building) was a very neat and tasteful edifice, in the form of a Maltese cross 208 by 208 feet. It was emphatically what its name implied – a woman's pavilion – originated and paid for by the women of America, and devoted to the exclusive exhibition of the products of womens art, skill and industry . . . To the ladies, the Women's Pavilion was one of the chief points of attraction, while the ruder sex could not but admire the many beautiful and artistic specimens of women's handiwork with which the place was adorned. Fine needlework, laces as light as gossamer and as delicate in design as any ever spun by Arachne herself . . . paper and wax flowers, and wax fruits that were works of art . . . productions of women's skill and genius were displayed on every side, to the glory of womanhood

and the delight of feminine eyes. All sorts of curious little boots and slippers, and caps and baby dresses, and frills and tucks, and plaits and flounces, were there without number.[2]

Whilst the immense skills of various textile artists were recognised, reportage tended to concentrate on the plentiful ephemera in the pavilion. For example, there were a pair of mittens knitted by a woman one hundred years old, flowers made from fish-scales, a head of 'Sleeping Iolanthe' sculpted in butter, shells with painted marine views, imitation tiger-skin, wax roses and a whistle made from a pigs tail. In actuality the total collection was far weightier than this list suggests. One section concentrated on women inventors, containing seventy-four models of patented inventions by women. Notable were Martha Coston's Pyrotechnic Night-Signal (at that time being used by the Federal Government), a sewing machine to be operated entirely by hand by G. L. Townscend, a model house made from interlocking bricks by Mary Nolan, electric therapy equipment by Dr. Elizabeth French and a life-preserving mattress for steam-boats by Hannah Mountain. Most other inventions were involved with domestic technology, such as a blanket-washer, a mangle, a travelling bag, an iron, a dress-elevator, a food-heater, a bedstead, a bureau and a window fastener.[3] The building had working machinery operated by women engineers, the main power source coming from a six horse-power steam engine tended by Canadian Emma Allison. A section on education demonstrated the Froebel System using sixteen children from a local orphanage,[4] another on clothing raised the controversial issue of dress reform and proposed alternatives to the murderous girdle demanded by current convention. In the decorative arts section two institutions stood out as pioneers, the Lowell and Cincinnati Schools of Design. The former excelled in textiles, the latter in furniture. Particularly interesting were examples of wood-carving by F. M. Boats, Agnes Pitman and a Miss Johnson.[5] There was little in the way of significant painting or sculpture as the practitioners in these fields, few as they were, had opted to show in the Fine Art Pavilions. There Emily Sartain, Anna Lea, Cornelia Fassett and Mary Anna Hallock won medals. Writers were given a high profile, celebrating the fact that some of America's most popular novelists were women. Indeed, the first American book to sell a million copies was Susan Bogart Warner's 'Wide, wide world', a statistic proudly flaunted in the literature section. On the whole the sciences were less well represented than the arts and crafts, even though there were probably more successful women in the sciences than in any other sphere at that time. The exception was medicine, which had a sizable area devoted to it.

The response the Women's Building received was mixed. The

majority of indigenous comment was patronisingly pleasant; by contrast, some European writers found the assertiveness which brought the building into existence disturbing, and correspondingly focused upon the women themselves rather than their work. American women were, according to Henryk Sienkiewicz, 'despotic . . . aggressive . . . superficial . . . lacking the qualities of mind and heart';[6] Catharina Migerka of Vienna admired American women but feared they were 'domineering wives and poor home-makers'.[7] Swiss reporter Eduard Guyer was worried by social and political implications of the building:

> Some individuals want to extend women's rights to unnatural and insane extremes . . . (An) important question, in my opinion, is this: in what way has the exhibition in the Women's pavilion proved that American family life . . . is based upon right, natural and moral principles? Is it perhaps impoverished by ambitions for emancipation which go too far? The wife who dispels from the husband's brow outside influences and money worries, and who keeps him receptive to everything noble and good – the mother whose economy, order and loving child care lay the foundation for solid development of character and spirit – of these most beautiful and noble feminine professions there was little to see in the Women's Pavilion.[8]

Blind to the obvious emphasis upon the domestic sphere, he was obsessed with the building as a manifestation of female assertiveness. Conventional and unaggressive as it was, the Women's Building was far too radical for Guyer and for others like him.

The response from contemporary activists was ambivalent. Some features of the pavilion could easily be seen as progressive and feminist. For example, the building housed the fourth annual conference of the 'Association for the Advancement of Women', chaired by noted astronomer Maria Mitchell. This was concerned with the advancement of professional women, making it topical and controversial. In 1876 twenty percent of the total American workforce were women, giving them a direct economic significance rarely acknowledged. The conference, and many of the exhibits in the Women's Building, made the American public physically aware of the rôle women fulfilled in the industrial world. This emphasis must have satisfied feminists. Recognition of women's work however was only one issue they were concerned with at that time; another was suffrage and in this area the pavilion was far less distinguished. Any suffragettes involved in the exhibition were arrogantly compromised by the naming of November 7th. – polling day – as 'Women's Day'. J. S. Ingram explained the reasoning behind the choice: 'November 7th. had been set apart as Women's Day at the exhibition, and the thought was happily conceived in the choice; for while the men were doing their duty at the polls the women would have the day all to themselves'.[9] The divisive use of polling day served to reinforce views of suffragette groups who refused to take part in the exhibition, that no good could come of participation in male-controlled, institutionalised events. On July 4th., 'Women's Building Day', leading suffragettes Elizabeth Stanton, Susan Antony and M. J. Gage organised demonstrations to show the extent of their opposition to the whole enterprise. The Women's Building therefore displeased elements both for and against in the debate over women's rights.

Seventeen years later at the Chicago Columbian, the organizers of the Women's Building were in a more radical mood. The Board of Lady Managers established grander aims than their forerunners in Philadelphia, seeing their building as a focus of international attention. Bertha Palmer, president of the Board, identified global aims at the onset; the building was planned to 'clear away any misconceptions as to the value of inventions and industries of women . . . (and to) present a complete picture of the condition of women in every country of the world . . . particularly of those women who are breadwinners'.[10] One of the ways this aim was achieved was through a genuinely international selection of exhibits; another was the location at the centre of the building of a library of seven thousand volumes on the culture, lifestyle and working conditions of women all over the world. Twenty-five nations and twenty languages were represented by authoresses practising from as early as 1587.[11]

Substantial displays came from virtually all of the European contingent, the contributions of Belgium, Britain, France, Italy, Russia and Scandinavia receiving critical acclaim. In contrast to the Philadelphia Centennial the painting and sculpture sections were large, equalling in size the decorative and craft arts, although textile related crafts probably still constituted the single largest category. Indeed, this area of female practice most certainly enjoyed its best showing ever, with a range including Italian and Belgian Renaissance lace, Irish and Welsh weaving, American patchwork, Mexican embroidery and Sioux and Navajo blanket-work. The art-status of the various types of needlework was undoubtedly raised by the exhibition, the general vision of it as domesticated, lowly 'women's work' being shattered by the global and chronological presentation of it. Similarly, the presence of women ceramicists, metal-workers, furniture-makers, engravers and industrial designers undermined established notions of gender in relation to all art-forms. Female practices previously hidden were now visible.

The interior decor of the building, rather than being completed piecemeal, was unified by the appointment of an interior designer to oversee the total work. This was Alice Rideout of San Francisco.[12] The successive series of open and covered spaces were co-ordinated by her into cohesive themes, the decoration largely consisting of murals and sculptures. The fact that enough professional painters and sculptresses could be found at short notice was a testament to the ground American women had gained in the visual arts. In this area American feminism had overtaken almost all of the European nations. Perhaps the masterpiece of the decorative ensemble was a mural entitled 'Modern Woman', in the north tympanum of the main court, by Mary Cassatt.[13] Forty years later at the Chicago 'Century of Progress' exposition on the same site, the official catalogue acknowledged Mary Cassatt as 'the only American woman singled out by the French as ranking with Manet and Degas'[14]; in fact she was the only American of either sex to rank such status amongst the impressionists. Sadly, her mural is now lost.

The Board of Lady Managers did more than gather the produce and organise it, they also constructed a theoretical position to justify and promote their position. This made aggressive use of historical evidence as to the rôle women had played in the creation of the modern world:

> It will be shown that women, among all the primitive peoples, were originators of most of the industrial arts, and that it was not until these became lucrative that they were appropriated by men, and women pushed aside. While man, the protector, was engaged in fighting or the chase, woman constructed the rude semblance of a home. She dressed and cooked the game, and later ground the grain between the stones, and prepared it for bread. She cured and dressed the skins of animals, and fashioned them awkwardly into garments. Impelled by the necessity for its use, she invented the needle, and twisted the fibres of plants into threads. She invented the shuttle . . . She was the first potter . . . She originated basket-making . . . She learned to ornament these articles of primitive construction.[15]

An ethnological display was set up in the building to illustrate the idea of woman as originator of human industry. The significance of such assertions lies not in whether they represented the truth or not – indeed a very dubious gender rôle allocation was embedded in them – but in the determination to see women as absolute equals if not superiors in the construction of Western civilization. Those involved in the Women's Building wanted to prove their equality beyond any doubt to detractors still insisting upon the genetic and spiritual inferiority of women. In this regard the building was an effective weapon in the struggle toward parity.

To further demonstrate the standing of women there were retrospective exhibitions showing the achievement of womankind since the Renaissance. Status was also won for the pavilion through the involvement of titled women from all over the world. Included in honorary positions on various committees were, for example, the Duchess de

Veragua, Countess di Brazza, Baroness Burdett-Coutts, Lady Aberdeen, Princess Shahovsky and the wife of President Diaz. The glamour and power of these dignitaries dissipated the atmosphere of domesticity normally accompanying displays for and about women; apart from this they guaranteed the funding of the pavilion.

Bertha Palmer did not make the fundamental error Mrs. Gillespie had made in Philadelphia; it was decided from the onset that a woman architect would design the building. The commission was opened to competition, to women only, with a brief limiting the scope of the design to fit in with surrounding buildings. The Board required:

> A simple light-colored classic type of building . . . The extreme dimensions not exceeding 200 by 400 feet; exterior to be of some simple and definite style, classic lines preferred; the general effect of the color to be in light tints. First storey eighteen feet high; the second storey twenty-five feet high . . . the plans should follow the outline desired leaving all detail to the ingenuity of the competing architect.[16]

The first prize of $1000 went to Sophia Hayden, a twenty-one year old graduate of Massachusetts Institute of Technology, the second of $500 to Lois Home and the third of $250 to Laura Hayes. Hayden's building was based on Italian Renaissance models. The frontal facade had a double-arcade with a central portico, the emphasis of the whole being toward the use of the arch as a repetitive unit. The novel feature of the structure was a roof garden, this proving to be a popular spot for socialising and relaxation. In relation to many others on the site the building was small, giving rise to awkward formal problems. Hayden herself recognised the difficulty of using classicism in close proximity to other classical structures of greater size and opulence, and so she determined not to compete in terms of scale, but to concentrate on the detailing of her building: 'Details are modelled after classic and Italian Renaissance types, and on account of the relatively small size and scale of the building, are more delicate and refined than those of the other main structures of the fair.'[17] Size necessitated a reduction in the scale of detail and a heightening of profile. Critics unable or unwilling to see the building in a disinterested light believed this revealed the gender of its maker. In praise or vilification, most felt impelled to comment upon its apparent womanliness; Henry Van Brunt,

> It is eminently proper that the exposition of woman's work should be housed in a building in which a certain delicacy and elegance of general treatment, a smaller limit of dimension, a finer scale of detail, a certain quality of sentiment, which might be designated in no derogatory sense as graceful timidity or gentleness, combined however, with evident technical knowledge, at once differentiate it from its colossal neighbours, and reveals the sex of its author.[18]

Others were less generous. The journal 'American Architect and Building News' for example had been opposed to the principle of an exclusively female competition in the first place, and determined to attack the completed structure mercilessly. The foci of its attention, naturally enough, were women in general and Sophia Hayden in particular, rather than the building itself:

> As a woman's work it goes of course; fortunately it was conceived in a proper vein and does not make a discordant note; it is simply weak and commonplace . . . (the building) is neither worse nor better than might be achieved by either a boy or a girl who had two or three years in an architectural school . . . (The roof garden) is a hen coop for petticoated hens, old and young . . . [19]

Under severe pressure from the architectural world to produce something of note, and over-worked throughout what was her first major commission, Sophia Hayden suffered a nervous breakdown before the building was completed. It was finished and opened in her absence. The strain she had been subjected to by being put into competition with leading practitioners working elsewhere on the site proved too much, as indeed it would have for any twenty-one year old graduate. Nevertheless, the 'American Architect and Building News' felt a duty to comment even further:

> It seems a question not yet answered how successfully a woman with her physical limitations can enter and engage in . . . a profession which is a very wearing one. If the building of which the women seem so proud is to mark the physical ruin of the architect, it will be a much more telling argument against the wisdom of women entering this especial profession than anything else could be.[20]

Sophia Hayden never saw another building to completion.

More than sixty associations were represented in the Women's Building, many of them having space to campaign for their causes from the administrative offices. Prominent amongst these was the National Council for Women, formed in 1888 after an international women's assembly in Washington. Interestingly enough, Susan Antony and Elizabeth Stanton, suffragettes who had demonstrated against the Women's Pavilion in Philadelphia, were present in Chicago as leading figures in the Council. This reveals two things: the growing influence feminists were enjoying in establishment circles, and the more radical nature of the Women's Building at the Columbian. The National Council held a conference on issues of interest to activist women. By far the most contentious of these related to dress reform, a subject which had increasingly attracted attention from the early 1870's. Although the Board of Lady Managers showed little direct commitment in this area, several of the more vocal organisations specifically concerned with it were given exhibiting space in the building, for example the 'Physical Culture and Correct Dress Society' of Chicago. Dress reform had taken an urgent turn, with publications by leading women doctors confirming that the tight girdle, demanded socially for many decades, was harmful to health and could even lead to premature death. Apart from this, long flowing skirts impaired the ability to walk, sit and generally manoeuvre. In short, the clothing women were forced to wear by convention harmed their physical, practical and professional well-being. The conference held at the Columbian thus attracted attention for more than one reason. Many women were worried by the health implications of current garb; fashionable magazines and department stores looked with interest at the alternative costumes recommended; reactionary newspapers and journals were keen to sneer at the new clothing.

Over two hundred thousand women attended the conference, ambitiously entitled the 'Worlds Congress of Representative Women'.[21] Three hundred and thirty speakers gave papers on topics revolving around suffrage and work, but the dress reform section was the real crowd-puller. Here fiery doctors spoke of girdles as a health risk, often wearing alternative costumes to speak in. Outfits on show included the 'American', the 'Gymnasium' and, most controversial of all, the 'Syrian'. The Chicago Tribune, following the conference closely for the basest of motives, could think of only one thing in favour of the 'Syrian': 'it is so irredeemably and appallingly ugly that no woman with proper regard for her duty towards man will yield to it'.[22] In fact it was far less exotic than its name, its major features being the elimination of the tight girdle, underlying bloomers and a hem-line two inches above the ground. Within twenty years such clothing would be common-place, leaving behind the cruellest aspects of Victorian establishment prudery.

It would be a mistake to regard the Women's Building as a theoretically faultless presentation of women from a feminist viewpoint, as it obviously was not. The acceptance of reactionary values as to women's rôle within the family, acknowledgement of her apparent physiological and psychological limitations, and the specific labelling of certain practices as 'feminine', all reduced the intellectual credibility of the exhibits. Nevertheless, as a manifestation of the extent and importance of women's work and as propaganda for claims to suffrage, it was a powerful symbol. Sadly, in these latter regards it was to stand out markedly from virtually all of the Women's Buildings succeeding it.

The Columbian made the Women's Building into an established feature of exhibitions; after 1893 it was usual even at modest events to find a section or building dedicated to women's produce. It was far less usual however to find the socio-political debate that had accompanied the Columbian, women's sections being rapidly appropriated by anti-suffrage forces to construct a vision of womanhood exclusive of the vote. This was the case in the Cotton States Exposition in Atlanta in 1895, in Buffalo in 1901, St. Louis in 1904 and San Francisco in 1915. Non-political women's organisations, especially those connected with the church, transformed Women's Buildings from arenas for the discussion of rights to comfortable bazaars, where the unequal status quo was accepted and even lauded. The trend continued in America even after the vote was won, being particularly evident in Fairs in the 1930's. The Women's Section at the Golden Gate Exposition (San Francisco 1939) for example was controlled by a Women's Board comprising mainly of officials from the Girl Scouts of America and the Women's Almanac. The rôle of the Board was to be a macrocosm of the housewife, taking on those tasks at the Exposition which equated to female jobs in the domestic setting. The Official Guide acknowledged this function:

> Women have played an important rôle in the planning and subsequent activities of the exposition. Appointed to act in an advisory capacity to the exposition's Board of Managers and to the California Commission representing the State, the Women's Board has been instrumental in establishing many of the feminine features of the Fair . . . Assuming a hospitality rôle typical of the California hostess, the Women's Board has directed the beautification of San Francisco, its suburbs and the State in preparation for the Fair.[23]

The American housewife was also a feature of the New York World's Fair in the same year. Here industrial design was firmly harnessed to the cause of domestic appliances, the housewife being the centre of technological attention. In one tableau-vivant, 'Mrs. Modern' easily outstripped 'Mrs. Drudge' in a dish washing race with the help of her new washing-machine. Additionally, New York presented the other side of this vision of womanhood, woman as sex object. A significant proportion of the entertainments at the Fair were of voyeuristic intention, including 'Amazons in No-mans Land', 'Congress of World Beauties', 'Arctic Girl's Tomb of Ice' and 'Living Magazine Covers'. A long distance indeed from the struggle for dress reform.

Europe followed the American pattern at some distance, the most important Woman's Buildings being erected in the early part of the twentieth century. By far the most considered and impressive of these was the 'Palace of Women's Work' at the Franco–British Exhibition (London 1908). Staged at a time when the suffragettes were violently active, the exhibition organisers decided to recognise the new consciousness of women by giving them their own committee and building. The Liberal government in control of Britain at that time was heavily involved and probably encouraged the Commissioner-General of the site to include a Women's Building. The flavour was not to be one of antagonism or protest but of appeasement, much in the way the Liberals had dealt with women's pleas for the vote, never quite rejecting them, but never quite accepting them either. This Women's Building was planned to neutralise in a non-violent way female forces who were beginning to make life distinctly uncomfortable both inside and outside of Parliament. The issue of votes for women was one of several Liberal leader Asquith faced in 1908 on the eve of the opening of the exhibition, and a major contributor to the constitutional crisis he would have to face from 1910. To give women the vote would have meant changing the shape of the world the Liberals had become accustomed to living in, yet to keep it from them would be to deny the most central of Liberal principles, the right to individual freedom. Such dilemmas would soon tear Liberalism apart. The Franco–British Exhibition was perhaps the last cultural manifestation of Liberal Britain, an odd mixture of values, a patchwork quilt of moral contradictions and social crises.[24]

An anonymous writer in the Times of May 29th. 1908 noted an intended theme of the Franco–British as being women's work and achievement: 'Women's interests, or, perhaps under the stress of modern circumstances it is safer to say subjects which are supposed to be of paramount interest to women, play a prominent part in the Franco–British Exhibition'.[25] The 'Palace of Women's Work' was to be the focus of these interests and consequently it was persistently in the public eye. In its formation it was a female microcosm of the total exhibition, having some of the most important women of 1908 on its committee. The president was Lady Jersey, vice-presidents the Duchess of Sutherland and Lady Haversham; out of some several dozen committee members only four were untitled. From its inception then the Palace was committed to an establishment position through the constitution of this prestigious selection panel. In fact the greater number of its members were wives or daughters of members of the exhibition Executive Committee.[26] In contrast to its American forerunners, the Palace had no genuinely feminist aspects to it. Rather, it voiced opposition to activists by presenting women as happy and willing participants in British life as they were, that was, domesticated and voteless.

The exhibits in the Palace set out to examine the contribution of women's work to British society through the ages. A section on the arts and crafts of women formed a substantial part of the display, including needlework, lace-making, embroidery, enamelling, book-binding, book illustration and illumination, and what was described as the latest art women had come to monopolise, photography. There was a section on pickling and preserve-making, but no specific sections for painting, sculpture or architecture, as the women in these practices had largely chosen to show their work in the Fine Art Palace. Likewise there was little to represent women's achievements in industry or science. This gave an overall impression that women had not entered into what were commonly considered as the major disciplines. Part of the Palace was filled with portraits and memorabilia of great women through the ages, including a fine painting of Elizabeth the First and the trap Florence Nightingale rode to the Front in. By far the most popular area was a mock hospital ward, where real nurses worked with mannequin patients. Incorporated into this area was a section on recent medical advances brought about by both sexes. In between the main sections objects of all kinds from the houses of some of the wealthiest women in the country filled the spaces. All manner of artworks and precious curios from the homes of the titled, made by men as well as women, created a dual feeling of opulence and confusion. Because of this in-fill and the absence of many of the major disciplines the whole experience tended to leave visitors unsure as to what exactly the theme of the Palace was, despite its title.

Ironically, sources by no means committed to female suffrage were often the most vocal in pointing to the dubious light women had been shown in. A reporter from the Times praised the needlework, 'Daughters of Arachne, they have furnished the world through the centuries with lovely triumphs of the needle', but felt the rest of the Palace was lacking: 'a visit to this section leaves the impression, always a sad one, of a great opportunity missed, at least in part. (The Palace) bewilders the visitor and does not represent in the slightest degree the real place that women hold in the art of today'.[27] D. H. Marillier, critic, was equally disappointed and particularly hard on the organiser's tendency to mix together different types of produce:

> I do not see the real woman worker represented in any way ... Palace of Women's Work, nay, it is rather the housing of women's filling up of time ... This case shelters sample bottles of a patent paste for falling hair, the latest instantaneous remedy; metal repousse combs; blouse trimmings; belts and buckles; and nearby the pictures are hung behind jars of jam and tomato pulp and gooseberry jelly. Should you, to show the world what women can do, hail with praise a jar of jam ... amateur, thats the note of this place.[28]

Marillier resented what he rightly perceived as dilettantism on the part of the organisers, who even displayed their own hobbies and pastimes alongside exhibits of importance. Women were continually presented as light-weight, lacking a serious or intellectual dimension and, importantly, as servants of men and protectors of children. The displays were arranged mainly by daugthers of committee members in the absence of a trained exhibition designer. The aristocratic amateurism of the selection committee, without the experience of any of the skills on show, was bound to lead to an exhibition to warm the hearts of those opposed to women's suffrage. Significantly, the central artistic issue, the design of the building itself, was not part of the responsibility of the Women's Committee but was under the remit of the Central Committee. The chosen architect was a man, Maurice Lucet. In its celebration of the status-quo and its presentation of women as beings who could not or would not undertake work in numerous fields of human activity, the Palace of Women's Work stood against those fighting for equality.

More telling than the mock examples of work in the Women's Palace was the actual work undertaken by women on the site of the Franco–British Exhibition. Large numbers of working class women were employed throughout the season as cleaners, ticket-venders and booth operators, usually in preference to men. Within weeks of the opening, pay and conditions of service became an issue, the Commissioner-General Imre Kiralfy being accused of exploitation. The Women's Industrial Council (W.I.C.), a recently formed organisation based in London, took up the women's cause. In a letter sent by the W.I.C. to the Times it was stated that 'at present there is no legislative protection for these women against long and continuous hours at their posts, as there is for workers in factories, and rest rooms'.[29] Women were expected to work a twelve hour shift, normally eleven to eleven, with few breaks. There was only one rest room on the site for women workers, built not by the exhibition organisers but by the Y.W.C.A. . This facility served over one thousand women in one area of the grounds, other women being unable to walk the distance during break-times in order to reach it. The W.I.C. requested that Kiralfy build another rest room at the other end of the site; so far no record has emerged to show whether this was done or not. The reality of working class women's lives in 1908, with the prospect of endless twelve hour days and six day weeks as an accompaniment to the rôle of housewife and mother, was indeed a far cry from the pleasant fantasy of the Palace of Women's Work. As the working women of the site trudged past its grand facade each day, they must have wondered in their distress how such a building could ever represent the work they knew. Any who pondered long enough could only conclude that the organisers believed in two types of woman; one to whom they felt bound to build a palace, the other from whom they denied a single rest room.

The Palace of Women's Work was open to visitors on June 24th. 1908, when an 'International Woman's Suffrage Conference' convened in Amsterdam with delegates from sixteen countries. Some of these had been funded by their governments to attend and speak. The atmosphere of enlightenment and progress represented by this conference was in stark contrast to the befuddled stupidity of British Liberal policy with regard to women. Similarly it highlighted the anachronistic confusion of the Palace of Women's Work. With historical hindsight it can be seen as the last desperate attempt of a government to preserve an outlook and value system which was rapidly becoming redundant.[30]

The succeeding exhibitions on the White City site maintained the Palace of Women's Work as a feature, though its scope and importance was steadily reduced toward the First World War. At the Imperial International of 1909 the Palace was used not only for women's work but also for displays they could not fit in elsewhere. One bemused writer pointed out the eccentricity of this:

> Indeed, the biggest collection of craftwork is to be found in the Women's Palace – though . . . one is sometimes puzzled to find the connection between the exhibits and the title of the building in which they are collected. One is at a loss to understand why Mr. Howson Taylor's pottery should be shown in the Women's Palace – together with a few other exhibits that do not seem to have any special relation to women's work.[31]

Interest had faded still further by the Japan-British of 1910. Finally, the Palace barely merited a mention in the publicity of the Anglo-American in 1914. As far as the government and the organisers were concerned it seems, the war of appeasement had been won.

The two largest exhibitions to be held in Britain after the war, the British Empire at Wembley (London 1924) and the Empire Exhibition (Glasgow 1938) had women's sections, both of which took empire as a central theme. The Queen was patron to both, with titled women making up the majority of the respective committees. The Official Catalogue of the Wembley show made it clear why women had been included: 'It was felt, and rightly, by the organisers of the exhibition that the success of Wembley can best be won by securing the actual sympathy of the women of the empire'.[32] The Royal Colonial Institute, the Overseas League and the Victoria League, all leading imperial associations, worked in tandem with the women's committee to ensure the empire was properly represented.[33] Women were brought from the Dominions to work in the section and a Women's Imperial Conference was arranged to be held during the exhibition. This lasted six days, with India, New Zealand, the Union of South Africa, Australia, Canada and Newfoundland taking a day each. Emphasis throughout was on the positive rôle women played in the maintenance of order in the empire. Among its more practical functions, the section had a crèche with trained teachers and nurses to look after children whilst their mothers explored the site.

The Glasgow exhibition was less overtly imperialistic in aim and far more progressive. A strikingly modern 'Women of the Empire' pavilion was erected, giving the impression that considerably more care and expense had gone into this area than at Wembley. The first hall of the building contained an exhibition of craft work from the nations of the empire. The second had a display of goods for the home, where all produce was for sale, and the third had a joint exhibition of the work of the Royal Society of Painters in Water-colour, the Royal Institute of Painters in Water-colour and the Royal Scottish Society of Painters in Water-colour. Also here was the work of leading sculptresses Gertrude Knoblock, Hazel Armour, Phyliss Bone, Phoebe Stabler and Lady Kennet. The Women's Gas Council exhibited a model kitchen designed by Mrs. D'Arcy Braddell, the Scottish Women's Rural Institute created a country kitchen and a model canteen was constructed by the Industrial Welfare Society. Women's organisations from all over Britain and the empire were offered space, the National Council for Women presenting the pavilion with a decorative panel twenty-four feet long.[34] The atmosphere and spirit of the pavilion, although still concerned with empire, was altogether healthier with regard to women's independence and rights. This was partly due to women having had the vote for over a decade and partly because the Glasgow exhibitions tended to be conducted in a spirit of greater enlightenment than their London counterparts. However there was little to indicate the position women might have enjoyed in the world of work had they been afforded a real opportunity, nor was there any fundamental recognition of the unequal state of British society. Within two years of the close of the exhibition the Second World War would put millions of women into factories, offices and building sites in order to keep the economy alive, demonstrating fully that the link between womanhood and the domestic setting insisted upon at exhibitions was not in any sense an innate one.

French exhibitions from the end of the nineteenth century treated women in a subtley different way from events in America and Britain. Whilst following the same formulae in an organisational sense, underlying attitudes shifted the focus of French strategies. In 1900 there was a 'Palais de la Femme' based on the American pattern and similar structures were erected at the following two Parisian shows. In themselves however these were stilted and rather boring edifices in relation to the strident and politically manoeuvred equivalents in other countries. The French approach to women resided not especially here, but could be found everywhere on the site as part of the total ideological atmosphere.

The French appeared to be willing and happy to recognise their culture in broad terms as being feminine. This went beyond the identification of abstract values as being female, such as 'La France', 'La Liberté' and 'La Revolution', to the point where stylistic traits in French art and design were associated with the female. Whether it was they themselves who pushed this particular vision or whether it was constructed by foreign buyers of French produce, French goods by 1880 were commonly thought to be emblematic of womanhood. Moreover, this was not a woman invented from a combination of housewife, baroness and scout-mistress, as it might have been in Britain, but a luxuriant, mysterious and erotic individual, whose wildness was combined peculiarly with orthodox middle-class values. The symbol of the 1900 Exposition was such a woman, 'La Parisienne'. A fifteen foot high statue of 'La Parisienne' stood proudly before the world on top of the Porte Binet (the monumental entrance onto the Place de la Concorde), the goddess of decadent mass-consumerism. Described at the time by Georges D'Avenel as 'the representation of a female being with teasing features, half fairy princess and half street-walker' [35], and later by Rosalind Williams as 'an icon both sexy and remote, goddess and slut . . . she resembles the women who were portrayed on advertising posters all over Paris' [36], La Parisienne was the Jeanne d'Arc of the French liberal classes, the symbol of radical cultural development. As with most symbols of power since the industrial revolution, the forces behind her stemmed from an economic base. From 1850 onwards France had undisputedly been the leading producer of luxury goods in fields as varied as furniture, jewellry, perfume, clothing, objets d'art and food. By 1880 these were vital to the economy. A fundamental aspect of all of them was their pertinence to the woman rather than to the man; as creator of the domestic setting and as a 'decorative being' in herself, woman controlled the purchase of produce which beautified the body and the home. In this indirect way she controlled the French economy and influenced the national profile. It was understandable therefore that French manufacturers catered for her, lauded and patronised her until she came to embody French bourgeois culture.[37]

The rapid evolution of consumer society in France in the second half of the nineteenth century entailed the growth of the rôle of woman as mass-consumer in a more central way than anywhere else in the West. The department store was 'invented' as it were to cope with middle class women's need for comfort and entertainment whilst shopping. These citadels of consumption went on to influence the form and aims of the expositions. Michael Millar:

> The Parisian department store of the late nineteenth century stood as a monument to the bourgeois culture that built it, marvelled at it, found its image in it. In its inspiration it captured that culture's entrepreneurial drive to master and organise the material world to its advantage . . . The department store was, in short, a bourgeois celebration, an expression of

what its culture stood for and where it had come over the past hundred years.[38]

Quite apart from the influence Parisian stores had on exposition sites through pavilions built by establishments like Le Printemps, Le Louvre and Le Bon Marché, the ideology of the luxury store infiltrated the consciousness of site organisers. The exposition was in a very real sense a massive display unit, a shop window arranged and constructed in the way the stores themselves were. As with the stores, women were a principal target. Decorative and applied arts palaces, fashion and textile pavilions, thousands of private manufacturers stalls and restaurant facilities were arranged self-consciously to attract what was thought to be the feminine eye. Thus a substantial part of the site was made specifically to captivate those sections of the female population able to buy, giving rise to massive areas of artificially constructed femininity.

The objects on show were also affected by gender. Particular French styles were readily identified as being feminine, most notably Louis Quinze and Louis Seize furniture and revivals of it. Commenting later on this at the Franco–British Exhibition critic M. H. Spielmann found it hard to disguise his lack of sympathy: 'elegance and taste are the note of French work, and though some have called it effeminate, that is as much as to admit its charm'.[39] As early as 1884 Huysmans had shockingly decoded the message of Louis Quinze furniture in terms of female sexuality in his novel 'A Rebours':

> There were in his opinion only two ways of arranging a bedroom: you could either make it a place for sensual pleasure . . . or else you could fix it out as a place of solitude. In the first place the Louis Quinze style was the obvious choice for people of delicate sensibility . . . The eighteenth century is in fact the only age which has known how to envelope a woman in a wholly depraved atmosphere, shaping the furniture on the model of her charms, imitating her passionate contortions and spasmodic convulsions in wood and copper . . . In his Paris house he had had a bedroom decorated in just this style . . . furnished with a great white bed which provides that added titillation.[40]

Critic Peter Philp has gone as far as to identify the components of this furniture which gave it its apparent femininity: the cabriole leg, the oval and the floral motif.[41] Whether such extraordinary claims for personification carry any weight or not, one thing is certain. The sites of the Expositions Universelles of 1889 and 1900 were saturated with what was then considered female imagery, from the form of the produce on show to the environment created for the leisure of the visitors. This was a female symbolism intended not to liberate or enlighten, but to make women buy, to use their influence over the household to make their husbands spend. If this was liberation, it was won not by women demanding equality but was handed over by shrewd manufacturers. The actual position of women in the power structure of French society was left unaltered by the consumer boom. Perhaps the only real gain was in social terms, whereby women could visit expositions and department stores without male accomplices and find facilities there to cater for their every whim. Middle class women were, because of this, suddenly more visible.

Indeed, visibility was the single real benefit the exhibition tradition bestowed on women. After the heady days of the Women's Buildings at Philadelphia and Chicago there was little in the treatment of women on exhibition sites that could be said to be objectively or intentionally beneficial apart from this one thing. They were seen. They were recognised to be an element within society which could not be by-passed or forgotten. Much in the way propaganda was generated to support and justify empire and the class system, women, as an exploited race, were addressed and appeased. Propaganda campaigns to quieten and control working class and colonial subjects signified a growing consciousness amongst both those groups, in the same way that manipulation of womanhood indicated the developing awareness of women of their unacceptable position. Suffragette agitation off the site had produced a reaction on it; negative and divisive as this usually was, it implied the struggle for equality was no longer something to be blatantly ignored.

Although site organizers appeared willing to cater wholeheartedly for women buyers, and would even erect a pavilion for women to create their own world-view in, they were apparently less willing or unable to give women much room in the major sections of professional activity. It would be incorrect however to suggest these areas were exclusively male, as numbers of women did succeed in having their work seen. This can be best demonstrated by a statistical analysis of a specific area of skilled practice. The most prestigious displays at exhibitions were those devoted to the fine arts, the largest and most important fine art palaces being those at the Paris Expositions Universelles. Here the painting, sculpture, architecture, drawing and printing of all the Western nations was collected in vast quantities; some of it was by women. Taking the first five Expositions Universelles as a case-study sample, the percentage of women exhibitors amongst the eleven most prominent nations was as follows:[42]

	% Women artists	% Of the total work shown
1855	4.8	3.9
1867	3.0	2.9
1878	3.3	2.2
1889	4.0	3.8
1900	4.6	4.5

Thus on average for the second half of the nineteenth century, 3.5% of the work at the most important showing of the fine arts was by women. As low as the figure is, it indicates that numbers of women managed to receive some form of training and attained a level of nationally recognised competence. 602 women in fact from the eleven most prominent nations showed a total of 1004 works in these five exhibitions. This was out of a staggering grand total of 12,215 artists and 24,774 works.[43] Surprisingly, the percentage of women artists at the 1855 exposition was the highest throughout the century, undermining any idea that the progression toward equality was a linear one. More surprisingly still, the lowest percentage of women artists came in 1867 when several of the key organizers were committed Saint-Simonians. The whole period shows a rough consistency in the West, whereby there was little real overall change in the fortunes of women practitioners in the visual arts. By far the worst area was architecture, the expositions having virtually no representation here at all from women. Painting consistently had more women involved in it than any other discipline, especially watercolour, an area where individual women occasionally showed as many as ten works.

There was considerable variance within nations, some having far higher percentages of women exhibitors than others. The following list gives a breakdown of representation within nations. The first figure shows the percentage of women, the second the percentage of work they exhibited in the national contingent at the expositions [44]:

	1855	1867	1878	1889	1900
France	5.9/ 6.8	3.6/ 8.4	4.5/ 2.3	6.1/ 4.5	7.2/ 5.0
Britain	2.0/ 1.0	2.7/ 1.6	3.8/ 2.5	2.8/ 4.5	4.1/ 3.6
America	0	1.8/ 2.1	1.2/ .9	6.7/ 6.4	20.3/24.5
Germany	1.1/ .6	0	—	4.1/ 1.9	0
Holland	3.9/ 2.2	7.2/ 5.0	4.4/ 1.1	11.3/10.0	12.3/11.8
Belgium	2.1/ .8	—	0	—	7.6/ 4.9
Italy	—	0	0	0	1.4/ 2.6
Austria	1.3/ .4	0	—	4.2/ 4.5	.4/ .3
Sweden	8.3/18.2	13.9/11.0	20.3/16.7	26.8/19.7	11.5/ 9.9
Norway	6.3/ 4.5	11.1/ 6.3	3.9/ 2.9	14.0/17.5	19.4/14.5
Swit/lnd	13.0/ 5.4	10.2/10.2	5.7/ 3.7	1.3/ 1.8	—

This is possibly unfair to nations such as France and Britain, who showed more work than other nations and consequently more women in real terms than anyone else. The following list shows actual numbers of women artists, followed by numbers of works they exhibited:

	1855	1867	1878	1889	1900
France	71/162	17/ 44	33/ 47	74/125	109/168
Britain	8/ 8	8/ 9	13/ 19	11/ 25	8/ 10
America	0	1/ 2	1/ 1	24/ 37	46/ 65
Germany	2/ 2	0	—	2/ 2	0
Holland	3/ 3	7/ 10	4/ 5	16/ 29	16/ 19
Belgium	3/ 4	—	0	—	8/ 8
Italy	—	0	0	0	2/ 6
Austria	1/ 1	0	—	3/ 8	1/ 1
Sweden	2/ 8	5/ 7	13/ 17	26/ 45	9/ 17
Norway	1/ 1	3/ 3	2/ 2	11/ 25	12/ 21
Swit/lnd.	6/ 6	11/ 21	8/ 8	1/ 3	—

At the top end of the scale, France showed considerably more women artists than any other nation. This however was due to the vast amount of work exhibited. In 1855 for example 1041 French artists presented 2726 works, putting the 71 women presenting 162 works into proper perspective. The case is the same with Britain, who showed more women than most others simply because their contingent was substantially larger than any other apart from France. Percentage-wise, both nations showed less women than several other nations. By far the highest exhibitor of women artists as a proportion of the national contingent was Sweden. Through the five expositions, Sweden revealed an ongoing willingness to give space to women, which went beyond co-incidence, outstripping other countries in every exposition except the last. Sweden was followed by Norway and Holland, where levels of women exhibitors occasionally reached a pitch suggesting a policy had been formulated to reduce gender prejudice. The only other nation to show signs of enlightenment was America, who exhibited very few women until 1889, when there was a marked increase, followed by a dramatic increase in 1900. In 1900 American women represented a quarter of the total national contingent. In itself this was a remarkable achievement, the statistic being brought down from even dizzier heights by the fact that there was only one female exhibitor in the architecture section; taken in isolation, the painting and sculpture areas were the highest numerical levels women ever achieved in a fine art section of a major exhibition.

At the nadir languished Italy and Germany. Out of the four expositions the Italians participated in they could only bring themselves to allow two women to show six works, an appalling indictment of the situation of women in that country. The Germans showed two more artists but two less works than the Italians, revealing fully the chauvinistic grip male authorities had over the various German academies. There appears to be no discernible shift in the position of women artists after the two nations underwent unification. To complete the plight of

German-speaking women artists, Austria followed the pattern closely, choosing only ten works by five women over the fifty year period. Put together, the statistics indicate a clear correlation between the strength of women's movements in the different countries and the size of their representation in the arts. Scandinavia, Holland and America emerged in the second half of the nineteenth century as the most progressive nations with regard to women's rights, Italy, Austria and Southern Germany were amongst the least advanced.[45] The independent struggle of women to better their position did have its effect on the visual arts then, winning representation for women in one of the most male dominated spheres of human endeavour. Where the struggle for equality was weakest, representation in the arts was lowest. As low and disheartening as the overall figures are for the participation of women in this area, solace can be taken in that occasionally, in some countries, some of the time, the voices were heard and listened to.

The majority of women showed one work in one exposition, only a small handful gaining a larger representation over several events. Amongst the French, Mme. Bibron, Madame Girbaud, Jenny Girbaud (daughter of Madame Girbaud), Marie Lallemont, Mme. Lehaut, Hermine Mutel, Mme. O'Connell, Juliette Bourge, Virginie Demont-Breton, Élodie La Villette, Clémence Roth, Mme. Jacquemart and Mme. Lemarie distinguished themselves by having at least four works. Rosa Bonheur had ten works on show in 1867 and Henrietta Browne had five, eight and six respectively in 1855, 1867 and 1878. British women were almost entirely restricted to single objects, the spectacular exception to this being Kate Greenaway, who had the biggest showing of any woman throughout the tradition with thirteen works in 1889.[46] The most consistent British women were Mrs. and Miss Alma-Tadema, wife and daughter of painter Sir Lawrence Alma-Tadema. Both showed single works in 1889 and 1900. Amongst the Americans, Sarah Dodson, Elizabeth Gardner, Cecilia Beaux, Laura Hills, Virginia Reynolds, Theodora Thayer and Maria Woodbury all had three or more works. The majority throughout were painters, many of them working with the miniature or in water-colour. The only exception to this pattern was Sweden, where a significant number of women were sculptresses. Mme. Ahlborn was the most prolific amongst these, showing seven works in 1855. No record has yet been traced to show whether women sold works from the expositions or won commissions as a result of them. Indeed, little biographical material exists to cast any light on them or their careers. Effectively, the process of exclusion the academies and selection juries left incomplete was taken to resolution by art historians in succeeding decades.

The ground women won with regard to representation in fine art exhibitions in the nineteenth century ought to have been the basis for a move toward absolute equality in the twentieth. It would be reasonable to assume that the century in which women finally won the vote would also be the one where they came in from the cultural cold. In fact this has not been the case, much of the twentieth century being little better than the nineteenth in terms of the presence of women artists in expositions, galleries and museums. If the French held an Exposition Universelle at this time, it would not be unreasonable to assume that the percentage of women participants in the Fine Arts Palace would be roughly the same as it was in 1900. It might even be lower. The proportion of women artists of all kinds in major contemporary art galleries and museums most certainly does not exceed five percent. Ironically, the last decade of the nineteenth century could easily be seen not as a tentative beginning in the drive toward cultural equality but as the golden age of the struggle, so bleak does the position of women within our cultural institutions remain.

Notes

1 Quoted from J. Maas, *The Glorious Enterprize: The Centennial Exhibition of 1876 and H. J.Schwarzmann, Architect-in-Chief*, New York 1976, American Life Foundation.
2 J. S. Ingram, *The Centennial Exposition, Described and Illustrated*, Philadelphia 1876, Hubbard Brothers.
3 The fullest description of these artefacts amongst primary sources can be found in Ingrams (note 2), this being one of the most useful documents on the exhibition. See also R. C. Post, *1876: A Centennial Exhibition*, 1976 Smithsonian Institution; Lois Craig and others, The Federal Presence – Architecture, Politics and Symbols in United States Government Building, 1978 M.I.T. Press.
4 It was here that the mother of F. L. Wright saw the Froebel system and introduced it to the future architect. In his autobiography, Wright believed the Froebel system had enhanced his early creativity.
5 Ingrams, note 2.
6 Quoted from Maas, note 1.
7 Ibid.
8 Ibid.
9 Ingrams, note 2.
10 Quoted from Craig, note 3.
11 The very earliest writings were by British women, at this time it is not clear who donated them.
12 Alice Rideout won the commission to design the interiors, in a competition similar to the one organised for the building.
13 The mural is illustrated in H. H. Bancroft, *The Book of the Fair, An Historical and Descriptive Presentation, Volume One*, Chicago 1893, reprint available in Bounty Books, New York.
14 *Book of the Fair, Official Guide 1933*, Chicago 1933, pub. Century of Progress Publications.
15 Quoted from Bancroft, note 13.
16 Quoted from an essay by Judith Paine in Susanna Torre (Ed.), *Women in American Architecture: A Historic and Contemporary Perspective*, 1977 Whitney Library of Design.
17 Quoted from Craig, note 3.

18 Quoted from Bancroft who does not identify the speaker. Judith Paine does however (note 16), giving a version of the quote which is slightly different from the one in Bancroft.

19 Taken from two sources, Paine (note 16) and Craig (note 3).

20 Ibid.

21 The best (only?) source for the conference is Jeanne Madeline Weimann, *Fashion and the Fair*, Chicago History, the Magazine of the Chicago Historical Society, Volume XII, Number 3, Fall 1983.

22 Ibid.

23 *Golden Gate Exposition, 1939, Official Guide Book*, San Francisco 1939.

24 One of the best sources for the crisis of Liberalism and the women's issue is George Dangerfield, *The Strange Death of Liberal England*, London 1935, reissued by Paladin 1972.

25 Style and general attitude indicate that it is the same anonymous writer for the Times quoted throughout this chapter.

26 This in itself of course did not mean the Palace of Women's Work was bound to proclaim a reactionary stance. In Chicago most of the Board of Lady Managers had husbands and fathers on committees elsewhere, including Bertha Palmer.

27 Times August 12th, 1908. See note 25.

28 D. H. Marillier in F. G. Dumas (Ed.), *The Franco–British Exhibition Illustrated Review 1908*, London 1908, Chatto and Windus.

29 The Times July 30th. 1908.

30 See Dangerfield, note 24.

31 Anonymous, *The Arts and Crafts at Shepherd's Bush*, Journal of the Royal Society of Arts, July 2nd., 1909.

32 *British Empire Exhibition 1924 Official Guide*, London 1924, Fleetway Press.

33 For a detailed analysis of the activities of these organisations see Chapter 5 and also J. M. MacKenzie, *Propaganda and Empire: The Manipulation of British Public Opinion 1880–1960* 1984 Manchester University Press.

34 *Empire Exhibition Official Guide*, Glasgow 1938, published by Empire Exhibition.

35 Quoted from Rosalind H. Williams, *Dream Worlds: Mass Consumption in late 19th. Century France.*, University of California Press.

36 Ibid.

37 See Chapter 5 for the visit of La Parisienne to London.

38 Michael B. Millar, *The Bon Marché: Bourgeois Culture and the Department Store 1869–1920.*, 1981 Princeton University Press. See also Russell Lewis *Everything Under One Roof: World's Fairs and Departmental Stores in Paris and Chicago.*, Chicago History Volume XII, Number 3, Fall 1983. In his exemplary article, Lewis carries the idea of the department store as an influence on the shape of exhibitions over to America. He reveals the mark made by the store ethos on the Chicago Columbian. The almost obsessive concern with the idea of woman as consumer was not carried to the same pitch however. The complex female symbology developed in France never attained the same level anywhere else.

39 M. H. Spielmann, *Souvenir of the Fine Art Section, Franco–British Exhibition, 1908* London 1909, Bembrose and Sons.

40 Quoted from the Penguin Edition, 1959.

41 Peter Philp, *Feminine Furniture*, Antique Dealer and Collectors Guide, July 1975.

42 The statistics come from the various Catalogues Officiels. The first five expositions have been chosen for this case-study for several reasons. They form a block of events following at regular intervals; the catalogues are in a consistent format, women being identified throughout by prefixes or full Christian names; the exhibits were in standardized Palaces of Fine Art, meaning the conditions of exhibiting remained the same throughout. The exposition of 1925 broke with this format, making data connected with it uneven; these were the exhibitions foreign nations took most care over and therefore provide the soundest guide to national policy on the visual arts.

43 I have chosen to list the eleven most prominent nations simply because no others took part in enough expositions to provide a pattern of attitudes. Excluded nations showed small amounts of work only, no one nation exhibited a number of women inconsistent with the pattern created by the presented statistics.

44 Germany exhibited as separate nations before unification, I have added the figures

from contributing states together. Italy exhibited as a unit throughout the period. The Papal States always exhibited a handful of work separately. Needless to say, no women were included there.

45 There does seem to be a link also between catholicism and female exclusion.

46 She was also the most heavily represented British artist in Paris – male or female – through the fifty year period. Her popularity on the continent at the turn of the century could have had something to do with this showing. Amongst others Picasso was an admirer of her work in his formative years, as can be evidenced in the graphic work produced at the turn of the century and certain pieces in the blue period.

CHAPTER EIGHT

The fine arts

The Fine Arts were an important ingredient in any international exhibition of calibre. They were the counter-poise to industry and the sciences, the non-functional aspect of human endeavour every nation had to be seen to participate in to avoid the charge of philistinism. The fine arts carried great honour for those nations thought to excel in them and they bestowed prestige on exhibitions that gave them especial attention. Fine Art Palaces bristled with traditional aspects of civilization; they reminded urban dwellers of their pre-industrial heritage and of value systems vaguerised by modern life. They also made culture into a hierarchical system, separating the high from the popular, the functional from the ethereal and the expensive from the cheap. In their absence, an exhibition became a trade fair.

This is not to say the fine arts were the most popular aspects of exhibitions, or even that those investing them with prestige took much notice of the contents of the art pavilions they worshipped. The fine art palace at the Paris Exposition Universelle of 1855, one of the first and greatest in the whole tradition, had 906,530 visitors as compared to 3,626,934 for the machine hall. These figures, showing fine art with a quarter of the popularity of machinery, did not improve as the century progressed, especially when popular entertainment came flooding onto sites. It would be quite wrong to conclude from the vast attendances at exhibitions that art was more popular in ages previous to our own. Once on the site, the crowds did not enter the fine art palaces with undue frequency. Art historians have tended to retrospectively inflate the significance of the fine arts at exhibitions, allowing them to dictate the historical flavour of events they had relatively little impact on in actuality. Vital as their presence was on the curriculum vitae of an exhibition, no-one seriously believed it was they who brought the crowds, attracted attention or generated the atmosphere; they did not. It was commonly understood that they brought status, not pleasure, to the exhibition site.[1]

At international exhibitions fine art normally implied painting in oil or water-colour, sculpture, architecture, drawing, engraving of metals and precious stones and print-making. Occasionally the last three would be excluded, depending upon space available or whether the authorities in the host nation considered them fine arts or crafts. There was no absolute standard for what was or was not considered fine art during the period. The French for example, rarely went beyond architecture, sculpture, oil and water-colour painting, whereas the British often used the widest of definitions. In 1874 at the South Kensington Exhibition for example, an extremely wide range of practices were counted as fine art in the pre-exhibition literature. Amongst these were painting of all kinds, including oil, water-colour, distemper, wax, enamel, on glass and porcelain; sculpture, including modelling, carving, chasing in marble, stone, wood, terra-cotta, metal, ivory, glass, precious stones; mosaïc; engraving; lithography; photography 'as a fine art and executed in the last twelve months'; architectural designs and drawings, photographs of recently completed buildings, restorations and models; tapestries, carpets, embroideries, shawls, lace 'shown not as manufactures but for the fine art of their design of form or colour'; designs of all kinds for decorative manufactures; reproductions, i.e. exact full size copies of ancient and mediæval pictures painted before 1556, reproductions of mosaics and enamels, copies in plaster and fictile ivory, electrotypes of ancient works of art.[2] The majority of the categories on this list would not be considered as fine art today. Fine art sections had consistent features throughout the period however, the most prominent being painting, which was invariably considered the quintessence of fine art practice. Painting pushed other disciplines to one side, occupying the central position as the most important visual art-form at international exhibitions. Even architecture assumed a less prestigious rôle than painting through the period, although along with the painters the architects were well in front of the other professions. For this reason painting must assume a primacy in this chapter.[3]

Fine art sections were usually divided into two, one half going to the host country, the other to foreign nations. Normally America would be the only non-European nation. The host country would send each participating nation an invitation to send work to the fine art palace and ask how much space it would need. Richard Redgrave, for example, acting for the British commissioners in 1855, requested twelve thousand square feet of wall space from the French Imperial Commission in charge of the Paris Exposition. He divided the space into 7,000 square feet for oil painting, 1,500 for water-colour, 2,100 for engravings and 1,400 for architectural drawings, all sculpture and models to fit into the floor-space this enclosed.[4] The request was accepted, making Britain into comfortably the next biggest exhibitor after France. Once all nations knew how much room they had, they selected work by jury much in the way Salons and Academy displays were chosen. Some nations gave up the majority of their space to a handful of favoured individuals, others restricted the amount of space per person and gathered a wide representation. The French liked to give vast areas to their leading masters, the British and Americans preferred to give a little to a lot.

In keeping with the principle of progress, organisers everywhere initially insisted on exhibitions of living artists, although rules were laid down to allow the work of the recently dead. By 1867 a standard procedure fixed a date artists had to be born after in order to qualify as exhibitors. This became problematic in the 1870s, however, when the number of international exhibitions increased. Some nations took part in so many that high quality contemporary work was often unavailable. Any work of merit by an acknowledged master tended to be commissioned or would speedily sell on the open market. Thus much of the best contemporary art was privately owned, and patrons began to tire of perpetually lending out their acquisitions to the state in order to have them appear in foreign venues. By 1874 the British admitted the problem openly, as arrangements for the South Kensington Exhibition of that year were slowed because of unavailability of work. Organisers declared 'the possessors of fine pictures are becoming tired of lending for exhibition those works of art which they purchased for the decoration of their own homes and the pleasure of themselves and friends'.[5] It was thus decided to dispense with the idea of works by recent masters only, and a retrospective show of old masters from national collections was presented. The organisers felt themselves to have struck an innovative note, 'The International quits the field which is full of rivals and enters on another which is almost entirely free'.[6] In like fashion in 1889 at the Paris Exposition it was decided to formalise the inclusion of old masters. Painting and sculpture were divided into Decennale and Centennale exhibitions, showing work of the last ten and hundred years respectively. This happened again at the Paris 1900 show, the Centennale there being a spectacular success. In Britain the most developed form retrospective displays reached was at the Franco–British Exhibition of 1908, where there were vast collections of British and French art from the Renaissance to the end of the eighteenth century. In America from the Chicago Columbian onwards, large numbers of European old masters were shipped over the Atlantic to fill art palaces at the World's Fairs. The fine arts were therefore one of the few areas on exhibition sites where an exploration of the past was openly sanctioned.

The French set the standard in the fine arts at exhibitions. Both in the massive fine arts palaces they built at the Expositions Universelles and in the quantities of work they sent to foreign exhibitions they were unapproached. The Paris expositions were far and away the most important art displays within the exhibition tradition and rank amongst the greatest exhibitions of fine art of any kind held anywhere. Priding themselves on being leaders in European fine art, unlimited time, expense and energy went into the maintenance of that position. Central to their effort were painting and sculpture, with the former taking pride of place. Acknowledged masters of paint virtually from the decline of mannerist Italy, they consolidated their lead through State patronage, the Ecole des Beaux Arts and the Salon. By 1855 they had no rivals; it was therefore logical that fine art should be a central element in the first Exposition Universelle, with painting at the core. Over five thousand works of art were gathered, half of them French, in the greatest Salon so far held.[7] The effort would remain as intense through to the last event in 1937.

In France the 1850's witnessed a strange time in the visual arts, one of transition from a static, pre-industrial world to an unstable modern one. Ostensibly the painting areas at the 1855 exposition were still locked in the duel between romanticism and classicism, a tussle by then tired and academicised. Delacroix, the grand master of romanticism, had a superb showing of thirty-five works, Ingres, the pillar of classicism, forty. Below these two however, the ideals and formalisms had become confused and mudded. Artists such as Gudin, Lehman, Chenavard, Antigna and Couture, all heavily represented, showed in their art that the political and ideological debates on freedom, individuality, rationalism and emotion had deteriorated into meaningless mannerisms. The pupils did their teachers no service. The real fight in 1855 in fact, regardless of appearances, was not between romanticism and classicism; a new force had arrived which ultimately would sweep them both away. Gustave Courbet, describing himself and his work as 'realist', had eleven controversial canvases in the Palais des Beaux Arts. His insistence on the depiction of reality in direct terms, by-passing the flamboyant exoticism of romanticism and the mannered rationalism of the classicists, announced a new idea as to what the rôle of art was. The technique was proto-impressionist, owing much to Goya and Rembrandt in application but little to the conventionalised rhetoric of the Beaux Arts. Politically committed, he depicted without idealisation or allegory the rural poor and the rawness of the landscape they lived in. Rejecting the raison d'être of most of the art of his day, he believed his work had a moral duty to develop a relationship with life and not solely with previous art. His stand against historicism, his worship of the

actuality of human experience and his insistence upon an alla-prima
approach to paint mark him out as the first modern.

Self-centred and constantly excited by imagined plots against him,
Courbet was incensed that his large master-pieces 'The Studio' (1855)
and 'The Burial at Ornans' (1849) were two of three paintings the jury did
not accept. They explained the decision as being taken due to lack of
space, both paintings being enormous and the total number of works to
be hung being vast. In itself this was quite reasonable. Courbet, furious
at this apparent rebuff, determined to find a way for his work to be
shown. He decided on a course of action described here in a letter to his
friend Bruyas, with rejection still at the front of his mind:

> I'm almost frantic. Terrible things have happened to me. They've refused
> my burial and my last picture as well as the portrait of Chamfleury. They
> declared to arrest at any cost the progress of my tendencies in art, which
> were disastrous to French art. Eleven of my works are taken. 'The Meet-
> ing' is taken with reluctance; they consider it too personal and too preten-
> tious. I'll open a separate show of twenty-seven of my pictures, new and
> old, with the explanation I'm taking advantage of the favour shown me by
> the government in accepting eleven paintings for their own show. To
> prepare an exhibition of pictures from my studio will cost me 10,000 or
> 12,000 francs. I've already leased the site for 2,000 for six months. The
> construction will cost me 6,000 or 8,000 francs. The strange thing is that
> the site is actually enclosed within the area of their show.[8]

Thus he made a personal contribution to the Exposition in the form of a
building housing some of his best works. In this action he set a precedent for the future, whereby elements within the avant-garde would
show their work and make their protest from privately funded pavilions.
Famous examples after Courbet were Manet in 1867, Samuel Bing and
August Rodin in 1900 and Le Corbusier in 1925.[9] Sadly for Courbet, the
twenty sous entrance fee and the vast collections of objects elsewhere
on the site served to keep attendance low in his pavilion. He made a
heavy loss, few taking the trouble to see the stunning collection of
paintings which were poised to change the shape of French art.

Courbet was not wholly isolated; Millet, Daubigny and Corot were in
the official exhibit, indicating that whilst the Beaux Arts controlled jury
was obviously against approaches too far from their own canon, there
was a degree of tolerance toward alternative practices. In 1867 the same
could be argued. A Beaux Arts dominated French display still included
Courbet, Corot, Daubigny, Millet, Troyon and Theodore Rousseau,
giving good representation both to realism and the Barbizon School. At
this exposition Manet rented space off the Avenue d'Alma, where he
showed fifty works. The rift between the avant-garde and the academy
began with realism but it would be a mistake to overplay struggles

between them at that point in time. Whilst the majority of artists were within the realm of staid academicism, the best represented exhibitors were not necessarily so but rather were a mixture of regressive and progressive. Amongst the stalwarts of the Beaux Arts were Meissonier (14 works), Gérôme (13), Bouguereau (10), Bonnat (5), Dupré (12), Flandrin (4) and Ziem (4), but these were more or less balanced by Courbet (4), Daubigny (8), Corot (7), Rousseau (8), Millet (10) and Troyon (5). Confusing the issue were the two oddities of the Beaux Arts, Moreau and Puvis de Chavannes, who showed two and one works respectively. If censorship had been a feature of the selection, the pruning out had been a very delicate one.

The situation had changed by the Exposition of 1878 however, when exclusions were rife. Only six years after the Commune, in which prominent artists were involved, the authorities were in no mood for compromise. Courbet, a supporter of the Commune, was represented by a single landscape, 'La Vague' (1870); Millet, universally recognised as a social commentator, was completely excluded. As both artists had died in the years immediately before the Exposition, the event could easily have been used to commemorate them, both being widely acknowledged as masters even in 1878. Emile Zola, writing in 'Le Messager de l'Europe' noted the treatment of Courbet and affirmed his real position in French art: 'Courbet revivra et fleurira de l'eternelle jeunesse du talent. On lui ouvrira les portes du Louvre, l'heure de son apothéose sonnera'.[10] The new generation of artists to follow the realist/naturalist line, the impressionists, were excluded as a group. Zola acknowledged this also, predicting of the movement that 'l'avenir leur appartiendra'.[11] Only Corot and Daubigny remained, their art and their personal lives presumably being politically neutral enough to allow admission. The 1878 exposition therefore marked a pronounced rift between Beaux Arts and avant-garde, as one moved left and the other smartly to the right. Apart from Corot, Daubigny and the single Courbet, the Beaux Arts ruled, with Meissonier, Henner, Gérôme, Régnault, Bouguereau and Bonnat leading the way. Awkwardly poised in the middle were artists who attempted to bridge the gulf between realism and academicism, led principally by Pelouse and Bastien-Lepage.

A controversy without political overtone surrounded a sculpture entitled 'The Bronze Age' (1877) by a young sculptor working in Brussels, August Rodin. The jury and elements within the press wondered whether parts of the statue had been cast from a real person, as opposed to being modelled by hand. The sculpture, of a single, anguished-looking man, did look remarkably realistic. Rodin was scandalised, as casting from life was widely considered a shameful practice amongst the art fraternity. Going as far as to produce the man the statue was modelled from, to show the differences, the artist caused a stir both for his petulance and for the remarkable modelling ability he clearly had. By the end of the following decade he was to be recognised as the best living French sculptor, by the end of the century the greatest in that medium France had ever produced. At the Exposition of 1900 he towered as one of the living grand masters of French art, the Monet of sculpture and the Michelangelo of France. In a pavilion he himself paid for he staged a one-man show which was an artistic high-light of the event.

In ideological terms by 1889 the avant-garde/academy rift was more or less complete. Impressionism had given rise to the experimentation later known as post-impressionism and the avant-garde had grown into a formidable force containing some of the best artists ever to practice in France. Operating with private picture dealers outside of the Beaux Arts or the Salon, between 1880 and 1914 they produced a body of work which outshone most other periods and can rightly be thought of as giving rise to a golden age in Western art, effectively a second Renaissance. Yet the expositions allowed them to slip by largely unnoticed. It is insufficient to allow this omission to be explained away as a prolonged lapse of taste. It was not so much the formal characteristics of impressionism that disturbed the jury – academicians Moreau and Puvis de Chavannes both had far more bizarre formal approaches – it was what impressionism represented in a larger sense which was a cause for concern. An art-form committed to the depiction of the banal, using devices such as photography and scientific colour theory, was bound to worry those who feared modernity, especially in the form of urban democracy. Impressionism was the art of the new, a vision of the world as an impermanent continuum, a corporeal flux. It challenged cherished notions of training, skill and the rôle of art practice and so had to be opposed. Camille Pissarro saw an irony in the staging of the 1889 Exposition to commemorate the Revolution. As a socialist and a leading member of the impressionist group he was exasperated by the use of reactionary art to celebrate the centenary of a revolutionary event. He voiced his disgust in a letter to Esther Isaacson:

> Business (it always comes down to that) disastrous, and this stupid universal exhibition. Far from helping us at this time it does the contrary, making our strained position even more difficult . . . you see the Eiffel Tower which is causing so much interest. The gushing fountains, the paintings, the dance of the Javanese girls, and what else? the machines and the frightful show of Pastellistes Français.[12]

A pavilion for the Pastellistes Français was set up more or less to represent progressive practice, a move which galled impressionist artists. Pissarro himself had two canvases in the main exhibition, naturalism there having been appropriated by Bastien-Lepage and his followers. Bastien-Lepage had nineteen canvases in the show.

If impressionism was undesirable in Beaux Arts circles, post-impressionism was inconceivable. Post-impressionist artists correspondingly had little but contempt for the Beaux Arts. Paul Gauguin, writing on the Decennale (art of the last ten years) half of the 1889 exhibition:

> We are stubborn in our search for art and when we enter the space given to the Beaux Art school, which the State, that is, all of us, pays for so dearly, we are nauseated rather than astonished. I really mean astonished, because for a long time we have known what to expect – poor quality for which low prices are little consolation. All these vain creatures wantonly display their daubings with an unspeakable off-handedness.[13]

The Centennale (art of the last hundred years) was more liberal, as historical sections tended to be: 'I was mistaken when I wrote that there was no more pictorial art at the Universal Exhibition. Now that the Centennale exhibition is open, I think differently . . . that exhibition is the triumph of the artists I mentioned as having been reproved and scorned: Corot, Millet, Daumier, and, above all, Manet'.[14] Not for the last time, the historical section was vastly superior to the contemporary.

The increasingly isolated position the Ecole des Beaux Arts had come to occupy as the harbinger of French cultural values prevented adaptation and development. The determination to institutionalise art and harness it to the national/imperial cause inevitably meant the exclusion of artists and ideas unsympathetic to that end. The Beaux Arts controlled French art in the public sector and had become in effect an establishment dictator, one which was less and less tolerant as the century progressed. In the closing decades of the nineteenth century leading academicians Bonnat and Bouguereau dominated juries of the Expositions Universelles and the panels selecting French works for foreign shows. Their overwhelming tendency was to choose art resembling their own, a mixture of myth, religion, allegory, sentimentality and paternal morality, executed with a polished yet vacuous approach to paint. Relying on the ability to draw objects and people with considerable accuracy, they lacked all ability to compose, to generate atmosphere or emotion with colour, or to create a convincing space in the paintings. It was little more than a competent, pompous escapism. They ascended to power after the Franco–Prussian War when the political climate was right and held on to their positions until they died early in the new century.

There was an irony in this whole situation. France was pouring vast sums into the arts in order to bolster its vision of itself as the leader of civilization, and indeed great art was being made in Paris through the period. Sadly, it was not the art the French government was investing in. Gauguin, so often the caustic but accurate commentator on the art of his time, summed up the position with a succinct bitterness in his comments on the 1889 exposition:

> ... the State increasingly protects mediocrity and professors who suit everyone have had to be invented ... Where are all the artistic glories on which France can pride itself? Among the Pleiades of unsung thinkers with royal instinct: Rousseau, Delacroix, Millet, Corot, Courbet, Manet – all of them scorned in their own day ... In 1889 as well, there is doubtless, like the artists we have just named, a whole Pleiades of independent artists whom the official painters have anxiously been keeping track of for fifteen years, and whom all the sensitive people, thirsting for pure art, true art, watch with interest. And this movement is in everything: in literature just as it is in painting. All of twentieth century art will derive from them. And you, gentlemen of the institute, you want to ignore them.[15]

The lack of significant contemporary art was one of the most lamentable aspects of the expositions universelles. The heaviest representation impressionism and post-impressionism received at an exposition came, mainly through default, in 1900. Here, the Decennale was selected by a jury headed by Bonnat; naturally no impressionism or post-impressionism surfaced. The Centennale however was under the control of the relatively progressive critic Roger Marx. His selection traced the struggle between romanticism and classicism, the rise of realism and naturalism and the subsequent development of impressionism and post-impressionism. This magnificent collection included at the latter end, Manet, Monet, Renoir, Pissarro, Sisley, Seurat, Gauguin and Cézanne. By showing them as a natural resultant of the best art of the immediate past, Marx introduced the avant-garde into the Exposition in an historical context outside the immediate control of the Beaux Arts. Modernism had crept in, as it were, when the academy was not looking. An interesting aspect of the Centennale was Marx's awareness of the artists he chose and his clear-headed ability to make an appropriate selection. In itself this suggests modernism was known about and looked at by those interested in art, a few of whom even had power in establishment circles.

French authorities accepted modernism only when it became clear it had triumphed and that much of it had been made in France. It was then harnessed to the national profile and presented at the Expositions Universelles. In the 1925 Paris show there was no specific area for the fine arts as the theme was the decorative arts, but quasi-modernist paintings littered the site. The main inspiration was cubism, manipulated into a bold decorative art through the use of bright colour and realist detailing.

The most influential artists were Robert and Sonia Delaunay and Fernand Léger. Excluding these three, the work was on the whole a superficial pastiche rather than full-blooded modernism. It was much the same at the last Exposition Universelle in 1937. With the Popular Front in power, fine artists were encouraged to address themselves to social issues. Artists unions and an association for unemployed artists were active on selection committees, which led to a committment to decorate the site with murals and sculpture. The employment of as many artists as possible appeared to be the paramount concern, this taking precedence over any plans for formal orchestration. As in 1925, Léger and the Delaunays appeared to be the major influence on a generation of young artists suffering from the effects of the depression. Sadly, the result was once again superficiality and pastiche. The problem in 1937 was not the embracing of modernism but the type of modernism used. The French contributions to the modern movement in this century have been fauvism, cubism and surrealism; there has been no strong school of non-objective abstraction. This however was the form the Exposition tended toward, the Delaunays being virtually the only French practitioners to experiment in this area with any international credibility. Still it seemed, the French struggled to make best use of their available artistic resources at the expositions. The whole world was prepared to see Paris as the supreme art centre, yet organisers and juries persistently failed to show off the art which earned that status.

After France, Britain was consistently the largest displayer of fine art in the exhibition tradition. Britain was comfortably the second largest exhibitor in the fine art palaces at all the Expositions Universelles except one, being exceeded in 1900 by Germany and Austria. In exhibitions elsewhere Britain was always heavily present, and as with the Expositions Universelles their contingent was usually second only to that of France. Perhaps it was fitting that the British trailed behind the French in this area, since it was they who first alerted Britain to the importance of fine art at exhibitions. Left to their own devices, it is doubtful whether the British would have developed fine art as an integral part of international exhibitions since for them industry and empire were far more potent indicators of national status. It was only when it became clear fine art displays were vital to an event's prestige that Britain wholeheartedly participated in them. At the Great Exhibition of 1851, before this was the case, there was very little painting, none of it in oil, and sculpture was scattered throughout the building, being gathered in numbers only in a modest Sculpture Court. There seemed to be a general integration of fine and decorative art, to the point where the two were almost indistinguishable. By French definitions as to what fine art constituted, the Great Exhibition had little. Five areas were designated 'Fine Art Courts', being reconstructions of ancient styles considered to be at the apex of art. These were the Egyptian, Greek, Roman, Alhambra and Nineveh, all designed by Owen Jones except the Greek, by Jones and Digby Wyatt and Nineveh, by a Mr. Ferguson. This had nothing to do with fine art as it was later understood at exhibitions.[16]

In 1862 at the South Kensington Exhibition the situation was very different, a vast fine art section being prepared along the lines of the 1855 Paris show. The object was 'to illustrate the progress and present condition of modern art',[17] each participating nation deciding 'the period of art which in its own case will best attain that end'.[18] The British selection committee allowed no work by artists who died before May 1st. 1762, making the section into a centenary celebration. Prominent in the British area were Hogarth, Reynolds, Morland, Wilson, Gainsborough, Turner, Constable, Leighton, Landseer, Wilkie and Egg. It was generally agreed by English commentators that only France rivalled the British showing, featuring in their contingent Delacroix, Ingres, Flandrin, Cabanel, Delaroche and Ziem. As with the Paris show, half the space went to the host but unlike that event no prizes were awarded. Each nation was given complete freedom in the hanging of its own area, resulting in the arrival of teams of artists and workmen from all over the world to arrange displays.

The four international events at South Kensington held between 1871 and 1874 confirmed the rôle of fine art established in 1862, although the insistence upon a very wide definition as to what constituted fine art reduced the overall impact. By far the most impressive fine art shows were in 1871 and 1874, the former being particularly interesting for the strikingly progressive French contingent. Beginning before the Franco–Prussian War started and finishing as the first engagements were underway, the exhibition caught a representation of French painting before the disaster precipitated a retreat from modernism on the part of the authorities. Present were Delacroix (6 works), Courbet (2), Corot (17), Daubigny (8), Rousseau (4), Troyon (4), and, amazingly, Monet (2) and Pissarro (2). Whilst the young impressionists were still some way from the spontaneity and colour of the later 1870's, the exhibition was nevertheless a triumph for French naturalism. Also present was Rosa Bonheur with four works and a young academician with a single piece, William Bouguereau.

Faced with the problem of reluctant patronage the organisers of the British sections in 1874 set the precedent of exhibiting the work of deceased artists. Signs of failing enthusiasm had in fact been evident at the 1873 event, critics finding few artists they could complement in the

British section. Common consensus confirmed J. Phillips R.A. as the best artist of 1873, a sorry reflection on the level of participation. In 1874 four artists featured in virtual retrospectives; Constable (d. 1837), Wilkie (d. 1841), Egg (d. 1863) and Roberts (d. 1864); a huge show of water-colours supported this, with works by Turner, Pugin and Cotman. Whilst the foreign half of the section was physically bigger than at the previous three events, the relatively low quality of work showed that the frequency of exhibitions at South Kensington was reducing foreign interest. From the point of view of the fine arts, it was as well that the 1874 exhibition was the last in the sequence as there would have been serious difficulty in gathering work for another.

The European fine arts featured only incidentally at the last series of exhibitions held at South Kensington between 1883 and 1886. These were specialist events on the themes of Fisheries, Health, Inventions and India and the Colonies respectively. Painting and sculpture were accomodated in the display areas where they could be found conceptually to fit. In 1883 for example there was an exhibition of seascapes and of art generally related to fish. In 1886 there was no need for this, as a superb collection of art from India and the colonies was brought to London. An interesting feature here were references to some of the work on show as being 'fine art'. At international exhibitions this label was normally reserved for the produce of Western nations, art from the various dominions and colonies being categorised as 'craft', 'decorative art' or even 'raw materials'. It was also usual to exclude non-Western art from Palaces of Fine Art and put it into facilities built for the colonies. In the absence of Western art at the Colonial and Indian Exhibition however, the painting and sculpture of India was referred to as fine art. This did in fact follow a pattern in specifically imperial exhibitions where there was no Western art on show. Indian and various other Asian countries were separated out and temporarily given a higher cultural status than other nations. African art for example was never given the prefix 'fine'. Fine art practice at international exhibitions thus had a hierarchical dimension based on race. In social Darwinian terms, the Europeans made fine art; by comparison with Europe India did not, but in the absence of Europe it was allowed to use the label; Africans did not make fine art, but were condemned in advance to be craftspeople only. The category implied then not only an elitism within the visual arts but one within peoples also.[19]

The four exhibitions held between 1883 and 1886 reveal a lack of enthusiasm for the fine arts often evident in Britain through the 1851–1939 period. The British saw fine art practice as being central to their international exhibitions only on an occasional basis. The South Kensington exhibition of 1862 was the nearest they came to the French (or any other) model in the nineteenth century. The exhibitions of 1871 to 1874, whilst they had substantial displays of painting, sculpture, architectural models and drawings, diffused the impact of these by defining numerous other activities as being part of the fine arts. Into the twentieth century, a bizarrely wide range of practices were often included in Palaces of Fine Art. At the 1924 Empire Exhibition, the Palace of Fine Art seemed to be genuinely confused as to its rôle, ultimately appearing as an arbitrary gathering of hand-made produce. Its single virtue was its inclusion of artists from the dominions and colonies, exhibited for the first time in London as 'fine artists', albeit in a section separate from the British contingent. In Glasgow in 1911 and 1938 the fine art palaces were restricted to the standard disciplines but the insistence upon the primacy of Scottish artists left both displays barely above the mediocre. Only a retrospective of the Glasgow School prevented the latter event from being a total failure. It would be fair to say then that despite the extent of their investment in fine art displays at international exhibitions, Britain had no stable definition as to what it constituted or any consistent policy toward it.

By far the best Fine Art Palace this century in Britain was built for the Franco–British Exhibition of 1908; it was the only one which saw fine art as containing practices of genuine importance. Divided equally between the two nations, the palace consisted of four exhibitions: British art from the Renaissance to the mid-nineteenth century, modern British art, French art from the Renaissance to the mid-nineteenth century and modern French art. This was the largest single collection of French art ever exhibited in Britain and must have provided British artists and public alike with a valuable insight into the French tradition. As a survey however the British historical section was generally thought to be superior, as it contained a wider range of acknowledged masterpieces than the French side, which lacked prime examples of certain artists work.

A central concern of the exhibition was the cultural relationship Britain and France were in. This inevitably led to comparisons between French and British art. It was not the first time in fact that the art of the two had been analysed in relation to each other at an international exhibition. Normally such exercises were riddled with facile chauvinism, but occasionally something of interest emerged. In Paris in 1878 for example, a writer for 'Scribbeners Monthly' attempted a serious comparison:

> The English have certainly a school of painting of their own, differing almost entirely from that of the French; much superior in sincerity and aim to the theatrical and pretty side of French art, but falling far short in deep and artistic feeling to their best work. They are generally much

behind the French in technical skill, execution and colour, while their drawing is almost always as good. The best French art is simple in its expression, the English is either too complicated and difficult to understand, or they do not interpret their subjects as well as the French. Their art appeals to the intellect, rather than to the emotions, and could generally be better expressed in literature than in painting; whereas Millet or Daubigny tells you something in a way that no words could convey as well.[20]

The writer recognised a superior French technical skill, which was indeed in evidence throughout the period under discussion. He also felt bound to comment on the anecdotal tendency of British artists in the wake of preRaphaelitism. His depiction, of the French as skilful but hedonistic and the British as sincere but without flair, was a common one. Amongst the French artists used in the study were Corot ('great imaginative painter'), Daubigny, Millet, Pelouse, Bastien-Lapage, Levy, Delaunay, Henner, Régnault, Bertrand and Bouguereau. The English he gave special attention to were Millais, Orchardson, Brett, Burne-Jones ('I do not attempt to understand Burne-Jones; although fascinating, he is certainly not a healthy or manly phase of art') and Alma-Tadema. This latter artist was put forward as the greatest in Europe.

The idea of national temperament as a guide to artistic style was common in comparisons between the French and British schools. A writer in the Daily Mail used this angle at the Franco–British:

> The differences are striking, and are no doubt based on national temperament. There is more genius among the French, more dazzling skill of brushwork, more bravura; while the English art as seen here is more delicate in its search for beauty, more pleasing. The French will dazzle you in an exhibition the English will delight you in your home, as companions of your daily life. There is but little joy of colour and little joy of life expressed by the French painters. They leave you bewildered and depressed, while you cannot but leave the British rooms in a serenely happy frame of mind.[21]

Riddled with bias as this person was, his discussion does not attempt to hide the fact of French technical superiority. He merely reduced what he saw as the painful truth by attempting to charge the French with emotional shallowness. Generally speaking, the most striking aspect of the comparison wherever and whenever it occurred was a recognition of the superiority of French skill. This in itself managed to please a wide sweep of the British ideological spectrum. Conservatives could but admire the stable consistency of the Ecole des Beaux Arts, progressives were in the debt of romanticism, realism, impressionism and post-impressionism. In sculpture, the French school was even more emphatically lauded, being seen as great not because of any one individual but because of the length and maintenance of the tradition.

Despite the level of admiration, a controversy arose to blight the opening weeks of the Franco–British. The French jury, headed inevitably by Leon Bonnat, decided to exhibit no post-impressionism and only small numbers of impressionist works. The decision was taken less because of Bonnat's intransigence and more through French anticipations of what the British would appreciate. By 1908 even Bonnat was partly reconciled to impressionism, whilst post-impressionism had been rendered less extreme by the sensational emergence of fauvism at the Salon d'Automne of 1905. The exhibition was reasonably thorough on realism, naturalism and the Barbizon School. Even so the Times of August 19th. 1908 noted that 'leading French critics' were angry at the exclusion of 'the modern school'. On this side of the Channel response to the omission was mixed. On the whole critics still found quite enough if not too much impressionism for their liking, one referring to 'the mistakes of clever men'[22] another to a 'room full of prismatic impressionism',[23] both in reference to early pieces by Monet, Pissarro, Renoir and Sisley. A minority of others were aware of the French exclusions and were furious about them, displaying a knowledge of and enthusiasm for the new movements. Sir Walter Armstrong, writing in the Guardian, complained that only the 'more academic' end of leading public collections had been brought from France, and that

> The freest and most modern spirits are represented but poorly . . . Impressionism is represented of course, but only by comparatively unimportant things – three or four bad Renoirs, one Manet, one good Monet and several poor ones, a Sisley or two – while nothing further down the slope of revolution has been admitted at all, not even a Cézanne.[24]

Referring to Bonnat as having a 'strong but disagreeable manner', Armstrong revealed by his frustration that some British critics had been hoping for a full display of the moderns. This would only finally happen in 1911 when Roger Fry organised his famous exhibition 'Post-impressionism' at the Grafton Gallery. It would be wrong however to assume the latter introduced artists and critics to anything they were not already aware of, rather he merely brought to London objects many had already viewed in Paris or in magazines.[25] Press reportage of the Franco–British Exhibition demonstrates that by 1908, whether for or against the new art, the majority certainly knew about it.

Some critics believed the influence of impressionism in Britain was not supportive of attempts to define and support the idea of a contemporary British national art. Two powerful personalities at the Franco–British and at many other international exhibitions were Sir Isidore Spielmann and his brother M. H. Spielmann. They attempted to generate nationalist ideas for a modern British art which circumvented continental influence. The artists they chose to accomplish this with were the PreRaphaelites, who, they proposed, showed genuine English characteristics in their style and moral approach. In the 'Official Souvenir of the Fine Art Section' M. H. Spielmann tells us that the PreRaphaelite Brotherhood

> was a protest pure and simple – a protest which, shortlived as it was as an organised movement, led to the revolution of feeling against the uninspired art of the day far beyond the borders of the circle and of the country with which it is identified. Certain tenets Ruskin preached, and the Brotherhood practiced, tenets which are still the inspiration of some phases of the impressionist school and which when Monet, Manet and their followers accepted them, were hailed as inventions, or at least as innovations.[26]

By portraying impressionism as an off-shoot of preRaphaelitism he hoped to raise the profile of current British practitioners, a surprising number of whom still owed allegiance to artists like Burne-Jones, Rossetti, Holman-Hunt and Waterhouse. As co-organiser of the British section, Sir Isidore ensured the nationalist vision of his illustrious family was heavily present. He and his brother however were swimming heavily against the tide in their promotion of preRaphaelitism, many of the most creditable British painters having long accepted impressionism. Angry at the selection of British modern art, some of them protested to the Times:

> We have received a protest couched in somewhat extravagant terms and signed by; Messrs. Strang, F. Howard, C. Shannon, C. H. Ricketts, A. Ludovics, A. John, W. Orpen, W. Nicholson, H. Wilson, H. Wain, and J. Pryde against the organisation of the British section of the Franco–British Exhibition, which they maintain is under the sway of amateurism and haphazard official interests. In particular they complain that the International Society of Sculptors, Painters and Engravers is not officially represented on the committee.[27]

As weak as progressive British art was at that time, the urge toward international modernism was strong, as was the recognition of the rôle of French artists. The Spielmanns were bound to stand against this. Organisers of British contributions to numerous exhibitions from 1880, for them the preRaphaelites were to fine art what the Arts and Crafts Movement was to design and architecture; that was, a recent, indigenous style with a moral dimension and a reverence for the past. Impressionism and post-impressionism, they believed, were none of these things.[28]

The British artists to appear most consistently in international exhibitions both in Britain and abroad were Sir Edward Burne-Jones (1823–1898), Sir John Everett Millais (1829–1896), William Powell Frith

(1819–1909) and Sir Lawrence Alma-Tadema (1836–1912). All were proclaimed at various times as best British artist (even though Alma-Tadema was Dutch and exhibited with Holland in the Paris show of 1867) and all four exerted enormous influence over their contemporaries. It would be fair to say also that Burne-Jones had influence on European symbolism between 1880 and 1906. Between them the four covered remarkable stylistic and conceptual ground; historicism, eclecticism, exoticism, symbolism and classicism were within their collective remit, shrouded in veils of sentiment, anecdote and repressed sexuality. As four pinnacles of British art perhaps they point to the real problem within British fine art sections; the genuine lack of quality art inside and outside establishment circles. After the decline of romanticism Britain failed to generate a body of work of genuine merit in either painting or sculpture. The real dearth came in the closing decade of the nineteenth century, W. R. Sickert being one of the few exceptions to the general trend. It is not insignificant that the British were the first to enshrine the idea of old masters at exhibitions, for at the end of the nineteenth century the retreat back to Hogarth, Turner and Constable was the only way to provide weight to displays. The French chose to exclude artists of quality on ideological grounds; the British had no such luxury of choice. The general mediocrity of their art through the period was highlighted by international exhibitions; the causes of this failing are outside the remit of this text, the evidence of it is not and is indisputable.[29]

America had different problems in the fine arts from those of Europe. These were both physical and ideological. There were few indigenous trained artists of real ability in 1855 when the first fine art section opened in Paris, and America had no identifiable independent tradition. The problem of availability was immediate, practical and denied the luxury of debate. The solution was unhappily found by exhibiting the work of twelve Beaux-Arts trained Americans resident in Paris. Of the forty-two works exhibited, none were made in America and many of them had never been on the American continent. Only G. P. A. Healy noted himself as having a second residence and studio (apart from Paris) in America, in Boston. With fourteen works he was the most heavily exhibited American artist, followed by W. P. Babcock with eight works. By the time of the second Paris Exposition in 1867 the National Academy of Design in New York had begun to train painters and sculptors, Massachusetts, Cornell and Illinois were training architects and the number of fine artists in all disciplines receiving training in Europe had increased dramatically. Despite the nearness of the Civil War, representation in the fine art palace was increased to fifty-three artists showing ninety-five works, outstripping many of the smaller European nations. At this Exposition the majority of artists lived in America, Winslow Homer being the only exhibitor whose name remains immediately familiar. In Paris in 1878 there was only a slight increase, to eighty artists showing 107 works, but in 1889 a dramatic expansion took place. Inspired probably by the foundation of the Pennsylvania Academy of Fine Arts in 1876 and of museums in Boston and New York, the number of American artists of all kinds had increased remarkably. 357 artists showed work, a number exceeded only by France and Britain and in the grand total of works (572) America was outstripped only by France. This quietened a little by 1900 to 226 artists and 265 works but by then America had confirmed itself as one of the largest producers of fine art in the West. In forty-five years she had moved, in bulk if not in quality, from nowhere to the front rank.

Once the French had set the precedent of having vast quantities of fine art in expositions, no event was respectable without it. It was therefore decided at the onset to have a large art section in the Philadelphia Centennial in 1876, to be placed in the Memorial Hall, the only permanent building erected on the site. When estimates were made after consultation with the European contingent, an annex had to be built on the back of the Memorial Hall to accomodate a substantial overspill. The person appointed to organise the art section was John Sartain, a director of the Pennsylvania Academy and a well known figure on the American scene.[30] Sartain organised three committees to oversee procedures and select work in America, and three further juries in Paris, Munich and Rome to choose work by Americans working in Europe. Ships from the fleet were dispatched to Italy, France and Britain to pick up the selected work. In total 1008 pieces by American artists were collected, a massive achievement on the part of Sartain and his team on consideration of the distances involved.

Most popular in the Memorial Hall was the British section. The 247 paintings sent from public and private collections were a fair reflection both of contemporary practice and older art. Observers reported long queues to see Frith's 'Marriage of H.R.H. the Prince of Wales', the most successful work at the Fair.[31] France sent 407 works, though these were generally agreed to be of low quality mainly by unknown artists. Still troubled by the aftermath of the war and the Commune, perhaps the greatest tribute was that France sent anything at all. Germany, Italy, Holland and Belgium all sent sizable representations, making the exhibition physically bigger than most of its European forerunners. Sadly, quality was low in most areas because of a reluctance on the part of patrons to send their possessions such distances. The American sections disappointed most critics and did indeed seem to indicate that whilst the necessary institutions were now established, they needed to mature before they could achieve the required level of academic proficiency. Grand exceptions to this unsureness were Winslow Homer, William Merritt Chase and Thomas Eakins. Had the latter been born in France or Britain, his reputation would have been far greater than it was, being one of the best handlers of paint anywhere in the world at that time.

The Chicago Columbian seventeen years later was larger and more impressive than the Centennial, with almost nine thousand works of art in its Fine Arts Building. The building itself, by Charles Atwood, was reconstructed in 1932 and is now the Chicago Museum of Natural History. By 1893 it was clear America could emulate Europe in the quantity and scale of its fine art practice. The question of identity remained. At the Columbian the use of classical architecture signalled the acceptance of Europe as the forebear; accompanying this was the belief that a conservative approach to design would bestow American culture with dignity. The exhibition did the same for painting and sculpture. A dry academicism was to be found everywhere in the American sections, with a correspondingly severe representation from Europe. A mold was created there which survived half a century; in the wake of the Columbian an academy system took a grip on training and exhibiting, barely slackening even after the Second World War. When modernism surfaced in painting and sculpture in America it did so largely in the private sector, as in France. Unlike France however, where versions of modernism were embraced offically in all the visual arts during the 1930's, America accepted modernism in the design arts without inaugurating a parallel move in painting and sculpture. The struggles of painters toward internationalism and modernism in America thus went uncharted by the World's Fairs. Interestingly, when the Museum of Modern Art New York opened in 1929, followed by the Museum of Non-objective art in 1931 in the same city, the art shown was, by policy, almost exclusively European. American authorities, through feelings of inferiority and possibly snobbishness, evidently decided indigenous artists were incapable of genuine artistic innovation. American painters and sculptors were condemned in advance by exhibition organisers and gallery supervisors to follow Europe.[32]

In the twentieth century the only stylistic variance from European trends at World's Fairs emerged not in the painting and sculpture of the fine art buildings but in the mural and sculpture decoration on many of the sites. Here, a grandiose form of regionalism developed which had no exact equivalent in Europe. Reaching its definitive form in Fairs on the West Coast, the idiom allowed artists to treat themes from popular myth and culture in a bold, gregarious manner. This public art was later to have an influence on 'regionalist' artists such as Thomas Hart Benton, Reginald Marsh and Grant Wood and hundreds of artists employed on the Federal Art Project in the mid 1930's.[33]

World's Fairs were obsessive about the display of European old masters. Fine art pavilions after 1900 came to resemble superbly assembled museums, paintings flooding over the Atlantic to make some of the exhibitions the finest ever staged anywhere. Judging from the majority of Fairs after the First World War, Cezanne was considered to be as far as one could go chronologically before the realm of the old masters was left for that of the new. In Chicago at the 'Century of Progress' exhibition (1933) there was what amounted to a Cezanne retrospective show, backed by large numbers of works by Manet, Monet and Renoir.[34] A stunning collection of art from the Renaissance onwards was gathered for the New York World's Fair six years later, this touring various American museums after the Fair until 1942. The definitive gathering of old masters came at the San Francisco Golden Gate Exposition in the same year, when the section organisers set themselves to gather not the largest but the highest calibre exhibition possible. The director of the Division of European Art, Walter Heil, boasted that 'the splendid co-operation of European authorities has enabled us to show a considerable number of masterworks of singular greatness and fame such as the American public has not until now been privileged to see'.[35] As well as European works from American collections, paintings and sculptures were borrowed from Italy, Holland, France and Britain. The list of exhibits was remarkable, including work by Fra Angelico, Andrea Del Sarto, Antonello da Messina, Bellini, Bernini, Botticelli, Boucher, Bronzino, Brueghel, Caravaggio, Cézanne, Constable, Courbet, Corot, David, Degas, Delacroix, Donatello, Van Dyck, El Greco, Gainsborough, Van Gogh, Goya, Hals, Hogarth, Holbein, Ingres, Lotto, Manet, Mantegna, Massaccio, Michelangelo, Millet, Monet, Parmigianino, Piero di Cosimo, Pissarro, Pollaiuolo, Poussin, Raphael, Rembrandt, Renoir, Rubens, Signorelli, Sisley, Steen, Tintoretto, Titian, Turner, Velasquez, Veronese and Zurbarin.[36] In its quality and breadth this exhibition was never surpassed in the whole tradition, a stunning array of the greatest painting Europe could muster. The interior of the gallery must have struck up a strange contrast with the futuristic structures and entertainment facilities on 'Treasure Island'.[37]

International exhibitions had an enormous impact on institutional aspects of the fine art world. Because of them, museums and galleries were built, temporary art exhibitions became commonplace and arts administrative bodies grew into huge organisations. There is far less evidence however to suggest Palaces of Fine Art at exhibitions influenced stylistic or theoretical trends in art practice itself. On the contrary, everything indicates the artists we now regard as important from the period 1851–1939 ignored the bulk of the work in fine art sections and on occasion openly fought against it. In their turn, the fine art sections often ignored them. There were exceptions. It is hard to imagine for example that the best British artists did not benefit from some of the art brought to Britain by the French, or that the Americans were not influenced, whether for good or bad, by European art at World's Fairs. Obviously the displays of old masters must have inspired all who went to see them. In relation to the vast quantities of art shipped from exhibition to exhibition however, the size of the influence upon artists themselves was surprisingly slight. The predominance of contemporary academic art effectively reduced the impact of the shows, room after room of anecdotal formalism presumably nullifying any inspiration which might have arisen from the odd gem. In retrospect then the fine art sections failed in one of their key rôles; to educate artists.

It would be a mistake however to condemn completely the exhibitions as artistic inspiration. There was one area where they clearly had a marked impact, namely the ethnographic displays in the imperial sections. The exhibitions played a part in introducing artists to new forms and peoples previously unavailable except through occasional museum exhibits. Particularly in French art, orientalism and primitivism were important factors in the evolution of some of the greatest practitioners, the expositions most certainly being a prime source.

The Paris expositions of 1878, 1889 and 1900 brought primitive art from Oceania and Africa to the attention of a European public more dramatically than any events before or after. The exhibits were obviously of importance to anthropologists and ethnologists, but at the latter two events for the first time artists began to take serious note. In 1889 in particular primitive art was studied as art and not as exotic trimming or curio. The first artist of stature to study and use Oceanic art was Paul Gauguin, whose interest took him on now legendary journeys to Tahiti in 1891 and 1899, where he died in 1903. After the Exposition of 1900 African art appeared to supersede Oceanic as the focus of attention. Members of the avant-garde collected pieces, Maurice de Vlaminck and André Derain, for example, having numerous West African sculptures. Interest stirred from 1878 led to the growth of private and public collections and shops dealing specifically in primitive artefacts. An ethnographic collection was kept open to the public on a constant basis at the Palais du Trocadéro after 1889.

The expositions were crucial for the formation of the theoretical position which allowed artists to push their own visual culture to one side to embrace another. The stance involved not only formal adaptations but engagement with what was thought to be the social significance of the art. Gauguin's use of Oceania did not involve a simple lifting of form, but an adoption of what he thought was the Oceanic lifestyle. He had read about Tahiti, he had been on a foray to Martinique in 1887, in 1889 however he saw primitive peoples in Paris and was able to make comparisons with Europe which proved critical for his art. Convinced by Jean Jacques Rousseau of the degeneracy of European urban life and the legitimacy of the idea of the 'noble savage', he found exactly what he needed to trigger his move to Tahiti on the Champs de Mars, living examples of people whose very mode of existence seemed to be an embodiment of art. Writing to Emile Bernard in 1890 he described his intentions:

> I am not going out there to look for a job or to offer you one. What I want to do there is found the Studio of the Tropics. With the money I'll have I can buy a native hut, like the ones you saw at the Universal Exposition. Made of wood and clay, thatched over . . . That costs next to nothing; I'll make it bigger by cutting wood and turn it into a comfortable residence. We'll have a cow, hens and fruit – the main expenses in our diet – and after a while we'll be living without any expenses at all, we'll be free . . . I'll go out there and live withdrawn from the so-called civilised world and frequent only the so-called savages . . . Out there, having a woman is compulsory, so to speak, which will give me a model every day . . .[38]

Shortly afterwards he left on his brave and idealistic quest. His astonishing naïvety with regard to Tahitan life would be dispelled within weeks of arriving there, reality proving far rougher than the tableau-vivant he had seen in Paris. Before deciding on Tahiti he had in fact attempted to go to Tonkin, also represented in Paris by a village. The Exposition it seems had allowed him to see the world outside Europe as a single dreamlike encampment, one place being just the same and desirable as as any other. His exotic formal and symbolic approach to painting, evolved through his primitivist philosophy, were to be massively influential on succeeding generations of young artists.[39]

At the 1900 Exposition Africa featured in the colonial pavilions and in the Palais du Trocadéro; in addition to this artists and craftspeople lived and worked in their villages on site. The art appealed to the young Fauves and Cubists for a variety of reasons. For them, as with Gauguin, it had appealing implications for their own lifestyles. Almost completely misinterpreting the sexual and social symbolism in the art as suggestive of total freedom, they felt themselves spiritually akin to peoples they knew nothing of. Much more than this, the directness and abstract quality of the sculpture offered viable alternatives to academic conventions; in the way they analysed African art the cubists were far more rigorous than Gauguin had been with Oceanic. They used it to help in the search for new stratagems in the creation of volume and space. When early modernism was finally formulated five years later, Africa was a vital ingredient. The Trocadéro, left to deteriorate after the Exposition but still containing fine examples of African and Oceanic sculpture, became a regular haunt of the avant-garde. Picasso later recalled with nostalgia: 'When I went along to the Trocadéro, there was no-one there, just an old custodian. It was very cold; there was no fire. Everything was verminous and moth-eaten; the walls were covered with turkey twill. It was there I found my defence. I thought it was wonderful. That's how it always happens'.[40] 'Les Demoiselles d'Avignon' (1907), thought by many to be the first cubist painting, and hence one of the most important works of art this century, contains two African masks in the top right-hand corner. André Salmon, writing in 1907, described the artist at work: 'Soon Picasso attacked the faces, whose noses were for the most part placed full-face, in the form of isosceles triangles. The apprentice sorcerer was still seeking answers to his questions among the enchantments of Oceania and Africa'.[41] Between 1906 and 1908 Picasso used African imagery more directly and uncompromisingly than any other Western artist before or after him. It was a major trigger to his creativity at that time.

For other artists Africa functioned more as an alternative than as a studied source. Georges Braque, for example, tended to admire all art-forms that did not stem from the Renaissance, treating them with a reverent but naïve equality. For him, the escape from Western conventions was the critical issue, not the use of any particular tradition:

> Scientific perspective is nothing but eye-fooling illusionism; it is simply a trick – a bad trick – which makes it impossible for an artist to convey a full expression of space . . . That's why I have such a liking for primitive art: for very early Greek art, Etruscan art, Negro art. None of this has been deformed by Renaissance science. Negro masks in particular opened up a new horizon for me.[42]

Guillaume Apollinaire reiterated this:

> Consequently the artistic handwriting of all kinds of styles – those of the hieratic Egyptians, the refined Greeks and the voluptuous Cambodians, the works of ancient Peruvians, the African statuettes proportioned accordingly to the passions which have inspired them – can interest the artist and help him develop his personality.[43]

Amongst almost all artists and writers during the period who expressed an interest, the idea was not to embrace African or Oceanic culture in any factual or complete way, but to escape from Western hegemony. This gave rise to what was in effect an eclecticism of subversion, whereby the most extraordinary of combinations were used to by-pass the known and the familiar. Also evident during the period was an obsession with anonymous art, a surprising feature in an age of unbridled individualism. African art was invariably linked with other non-Western and ancient sources, all of these being treated not as cultures producing objects made by individual human beings for specific purposes, but as mysterious, inert phenomena. African art, as with other forms of primitive and ancient art, was alien and impersonal enough to be used much in the way artists might have used nature, as a primary not a secondary source. There is no recorded discussion amongst artists or critics about the possibility of specific African practitioners, of old or recent African schools of thought or of sources and influences in African art. In other words, African artists were thought of as belonging to a different category of practitioner from themselves. Whilst the sexual symbolism in the art was happily interpreted in terms of the West, the Africans themselves were constantly kept at distance. They remained an anonymous 'other', a part of nature, a mysterious, blindly honest force, a fascinating inspiration which could not threaten the delicate egos of a generation of pathological individualists.[44]

Picasso's 'Les Demoiselles d'Avignon' offers a fascinating example of how Africa served as a source for a progressive artist, embodying as it did all the heroism and confusion of a culture in transition. Apart from African heads it contains ancient Iberian sculpture and mannerisms taken from Cézanne. The whole can be construed as an attack on traditional ideals of classical beauty, and hence a critique of the culture the artist belonged to. The painting was an extraordinary hybrid, an eclectic exercise plundering cultures other than its own in an attempt to extend the possibilities of visual expression. Unaware of the specific meanings of Iberian or African art, Picasso equalised them out by virtue of his ignorance. More than this the painting was an expression of a culture grown used to its imperial rôle, an appropriation of another people's world in the absence of understanding. As contradictory as the native villages nestled at the base of the Eiffel Tower in 1900, the African masks in the painting stare out of their Cézannesque matrix in tragedy and confusion. They were the symbols of an emasculated and broken race. Without the African mask there might well have been no cubism; without imperialism there would have been no African masks for the cubists to look at. Regardless of the grandeur of the painting, or the innocence of the artist, 'Les Demoiselles d'Avignon' was the expression of an imperial world haunted by complacency and guilt. In his striving toward freedom from the faceless conventionalism of his time, Picasso demonstrated the inescapability of society and ideology. In itself the painting remains blameless. Art objects are by their very nature plural entities, as are human beings, displaying with absolute simultaneity qualities that vie with and contradict each other. Like the Expositions Universelles which brought primitive art emphatically to the attention of the artists, the plurality of 'Les Demoiselles d'Avignon' is buried deep, residing in its formal make-up, its content, its social context and in the mind of the viewer. Whilst we are comfortably able to look at it without the reality of imperial destruction consuming us, the dark side cannot be isolated or extracted, but must remain an integral part of the piece. Imperialism should not undermine our interest in cubism, but the beauty of cubist forms should not allow us to forget their derivation and buried meanings. Art is never pure, it is always about more than one issue.

Orientalism in fine art, as opposed to primitivism, owed little in the first instance to displays of North African and Eastern art at exhibitions. Eugene Delacroix used North African and Near Eastern imagery in his work long before imperial conquests became a feature of the French national exhibitions. He painted his famous 'Women of Algiers' for example in 1834, within four years of the capture of the city. Likewise Ingres' recurring theme of the 'Odalisque' (exotic nude) predated the exhibitions. The appearance of Algerian and Morroccan arts and crafts at exhibitions from the national event of 1849 onwards did however help stabilise the use of exotic trimmings in paintings and sculptures, establishing the Odalisque and the Hareem as standard themes. Even at the Ecole des Beaux Arts, orientalism filtered into common usage by 1890, allowing artists to vary themes without leaving the basic stylistic tenets of classicism. The expositions of 1878, 1889 and 1900 took thousands of examples of Eastern and North African art to Paris, showing them in as authentic an environment as was possible in a north European city. There can be no doubt that hundreds of minor artists found sources there. Occasionally better known masters made use of them also; Gustav Moreau, one of the Beaux arts more outlandish professors, was famous for his combination of orientalism and symbolism. His student Henri Matisse initially acquired his own love of the exotic from his work and teachings, before having his enthusiasm directly stirred at the Paris Exposition of 1900, where he encountered North African culture directly for the first time. The Algerian, Moroccan, Tunisian pavilions and the Rue de Caire with their arabesques, their sensuousness and their distance from everyday life made an impression which would later inform some of Matisse's greatest art. His 'Odalisques' at the height of the Nice period carried the oriental tradition in French art to the end of the 1920's.[45]

Ultimately artists received as much from the the exhibitions as they gave back. Without the imperial sections of the Expositions Universelles, the avant-garde in Paris from 1889 would have been deprived of one of their most precious sources and the progress of the modern movement would have been retarded. Having said this, without the fine arts, as elite and rarified as they were prone to be, the exhibitions would have lacked one of the conceptual elements which keep them perenially interesting. It would be a mistake to over-estimate the actual impact of fine art at the exhibitions; equally it would be wrong to imagine a satisfactory event without them.

Notes

1 In most available texts, the fine arts have not been satisfactorily integrated into the activity on the exhibition site as a whole. Reprint catalogues of exhibitions are invariably of fine art sections only, most secondary sources remain firmly with fine art issues, occasionally advancing into design. On the other hand, anthropolgists, sociologists and historians of popular culture have failed to recognise the wide-ranging cultural and political implications of fine art sections. The exhibitions are more subject to the short-comings of specialization within the humanities than most other cultural manifestations.

2 *London International Exhibition 1874: Official Guide, Illustrated.* London 1874, pub. J. M. Johnson and Sons.

3 For site architecture see Chapter Six.

4 *Reports on the Paris Universal Exhibition*, London 1856 H.M.S.O.

5 Official Guide, see note 2.

6 Ibid.

7 All statistics are taken from the Official Catalogues of exhibitions unless otherwise stated. In Paris in 1867 3295 works were shown by 1823 artists; in 1878 4457 were shown by 2233; in 1889 5952 were shown by 2913 and in 1900 5968 were shown by 3146.

8 Quoted from Jack Lindsay, *Gustave Courbet, His Life and Art*, London 1977, Jupiter Press. *The Meeting* referred to in the quote is of course *Bonjour, Monsieur Courbet*.

9 For discussion of Bing and Le Corbusier's pavilions, see Chapter Six.

10 Quoted from Rodolphe Walter, *L'Exposition Universelle de 1878, ou Amours et Haines de Emile Zola*, L'Oeil November–December 1978. See also Pierre Kjellberg, *Le Bon Goût il y a Cent Ans*, Connaissance des Arts, Volume 321, November 1978.

11 Ibid.

12 Quoted from R. Thompson, *Camille Pissarro, Turpitudes Sociale and the Universal Exhibition of 1889*, Arts Magazine, Volume 56, Part 8, April 1982.

13 Quoted from Daniel Guérin (Ed), *Writings of a Savage: Paul Gauguin*, New York 1978 Viking Press. Original edition French addition Gallimard 1974.

14 Ibid.

15 Ibid.

16 One could view the reluctance to separate the decorative and craft arts out from fine art as a result of the campaigns of the Gothic revivalists, who wished to destroy the elitism of fine art on moral grounds. In this instance however, the mingling of disciplines is more due to confusion as to what they individually stood for. As the tradition progressed, lack of committment caused the mix.

17 *The International Exhibitional 1862: Illustrated Catalogue of the Industrial Department*, two volumes, London 1862.

18 Ibid.

19 The only exception to the pattern in major exhibitions was the Paris Exposition Universelle of 1867, where nations were obliged to show their colonies in the same space as the rest of the fine art exhibit.

20 Anonymous, *Art and the Paris Exhibition*, Scribbener's Monthly, December 1878.

21 Anonymous, Daily Mail May 26th. 1908.
22 Times August 19th. 1908.
23 Ibid.
24 Sir Walter Armstrong, *Art at the Exhibition*, Guardian June 3rd. 1908.
25 The Roger Fry exhibition has been made into a legend and hence attributed rôles it never had at the time. British knowledge of the European modern movement is still in need of adequate research during the 1880–1914 period.
26 M. H. Spielmann, *Souvenir of the Fine Arts Section Franco–British Exhibition 1908*, London 1909, Bembrose and Son.
27 Times May 16th. 1908
28 See Paul Greenhalgh, *Art, Politics and Society at the Franco–British Exhibition of 1908*, Art History, December 1985. Also Chapter 5.
29 The failure to produce an effective modernism haunts the other visual arts also. The rôle of training and exhibiting institutions is obviously at issue here, as with the French case.
30 See John Maas, *The Glorious Enterprise: The Centennial Exhibition of 1876 and H. J. Schwarzmann, Architect-in-Chief.*, New York 1976 American Life Foundation.
31 Ibid.
32 The rôle of Alfred H. Barr Jnr., the founding director of M.O.M.A. New York was crucial for the exclusion of indigenous artists. Barr was not reconciled to the idea of an American modernism until after the Second World War, when he simultaneously began to promote Abstract Expressionism and Pop.
33 See for example the mural work at the San Francisco Fair 1939, *The Art of Treasure Island*, by Eugene Neuhaus, San Francisco 1939, has good examples.
34 At this event Picasso and Matisse were also shown, marking it out as more in favour of modernism than virtually all of its American contemporaries.
35 *The Masterworks of Five Centuries: Official Catalogue Department of Fine Arts, Division of European Art, Golden Gate Centennial 1939*, San Francisco 1939.
36 This is only a small selection of the better known names.
37 This was the official nick-name of the exhibition.
38 Quoted from Guérin, note 13.
39 Particularly on the Nabis and on the Fauves, for different reasons in each case. See John Rewald, *Post-impressionism: From Van Gogh to Gauguin*. New York 1978.
40 Quoted from Dore Ashton (Ed.) *Picasso on Art: A Selection of Views.*, London 1972 Thames and Hudson. In this particular quote Picasso goes on to say one always needed theoretical justification for ones work and that for him, African art was exactly this.
41 Quoted from Marilyn McCully (Ed.) *A Picasso Anthology: Documents, Criticism, Reminiscences*, London 1981 Arts Council.
42 Quoted from John Richardson, *Georges Braque: An American Tribute*, New York.
43 Quoted from Edward Fry, *Cubism*, London 1966 Thames and Hudson.
44 The irony was of course that the Africans indeed were a different category of artist from Western practitioners, the very term 'artist' perhaps being inappropriate to express the complex social rôle their work fulfilled. The cubists were mostly ignorant of this.
45 Matisse, as with Delacroix before him, visited North Africa several times before the First World War.

Postscript

In Sydenham, South London, on a piece of scrub-land to one side of a modern sports complex, a few pieces of broken statuary languish. Two giant Sphinxes framing a flight of stone steps, a heavy balustrade, a twisted and fragmented standing figure of a Greek Nymph, a charred and blackened Arab still on his podium. These are the physical remains of the Great Exhibition of 1851, the only pieces of the Crystal Palace left after the fire of 1936. On a hot summer's day one could be forgiven for believing this was a quiet spot in North Africa, or even on the edges of Rome, so powerful is the ghostly atmosphere of past events, the enigma of ruin. These are indeed the remaining fragments of an empire, the surviving embellishment of an event that lauded the mightiest nation on earth. The physical evidence is meagre, but the building it struggles to represent had more voice, more popular power and wider significance during its short life than many cathedrals that have stood for five hundred years. Likewise the now vanished exhibition buildings of America and France. In the way they saturated the heads of all who attended them with irrational pride and false hope, in their confirming of racial and class division and their obsession with power and progress, the exhibitions stamped their mark on the age. Set against this, every one of them was an absolute highlight for millions of people suffering the drudgery and alienation of working life in industrial society. The exhibitions were one of the few creations of the nineteenth century aimed at the masses with something other than work in mind, in the direct sense at least. Few who attended regretted the experience. The exhibitions carried fringe cultural benefits for their audience and for posterity; for this at least we can be grateful. Had they not happened, some other medium would have served to present the economic and imperial message of Western governments.

Ultimately, though, the international exhibitions leave one with a sense of dismay which their positive aspects cannot dispel. There are two sources for this; first, the feeling of desolation that such magnificent conceptions could be designed with such negative aims in mind;

second, that these dreamlike cities could not have exercised a greater influence on those responsible for creating the banal urban environment we are now forced to inhabit. The negative ideology the exhibitions espoused is still with us; sadly, the beauty of the façades has gone forever.

Bibliography

The exhibitions themselves provided three types of published document of use to historians: Official Catalogues, Official or Approved Guides and Official Reports. Often also the minutes of preliminary meetings emerged in published form. Invariably all these documents were published in or around the year of the exhibition, in either the host or capital city. To save space the bibliography will only list those which are in some way unusual, i.e. those containing useful information on other exhibitions, or articles not normal to official literature, or those which have subsequently been reprinted and are once again readily available. Guides, commentaries, special editions of journals, souvenirs and other material produced unofficially for the exhibitions are included here; newspapers are not: see the relevant notes for references. Some chapters deal with topics for which there are vast literatures not specifically related to exhibitions; this bibliography lists only those items the author considers to have direct bearing on exhibitions. See the notes for guidance to other topics. For other useful bibliographies see Benedict, Coulson and MacKenzie below.

Allwood, John – *The Great Exhibitions*, London 1977, Studio Vista.
Amsterdam International Exhibition 1883 – *Catalogue of the Dutch Sections*, Amsterdam 1883.
Anscombe and Gere – *Arts and Crafts in Britain and America*, London 1978, Academy Editions.
Answers (Weekly Magazine) – *Do Exhibitions Pay?*, Anon, May 23rd. London 1908.
Antwerp 1930 – *Exposition Internationale Coloniale, Maritime et d'Art Flamand Anvers 1930, Rapport Général*, Antwerp 1931.
Architectural Review – 'Iron Pioneers', Anon, July 1961.
Arwas, Victor – *Berthon and Grasset*, London 1978, Academy Editions.
Arwas, Victor – *Art Deco*, London 1980, Academy Editions.
Bancroft, H. H. – *The Book of the Fair: An Historical and Descriptive Presentation of the . . . Columbian Exposition at Chicago in 1893*, Chicago 1893. Facsimile available, Bounty Books, New York.
Banham, M. and Hillier (Eds.) – *A Tonic to the Nation: The Festival of Britain 1951*, London 1966, Thames and Hudson.
Banham, R. – *Theory and Design in the First Machine Age*, London 1967, Architectural Press.
Beaumier, A. – *Notice sur le Maroc*, Paris 1867, Mogador.
Bellaigue, G. de, – 'Queen Victoria Buys French in 1855', *Antique Collector*, April 1975.
Benedict, Burton – *The Anthropology of World's Fairs: San Francisco's Panama Pacific International Exposition of 1915*, California 1983, Scolar Press.
Bennett, Mercer and Woollacott (Eds.) – *Popular Culture and Social Relations*, Open University Press 1986.
Benson A. C. and Esher, Viscount – *The Letters of Queen Victoria: A Selection from Her Majesty's Correspondence Between the Years 1837 and 1861*, (3 Volumes), London 1908, John Murray.
Best, Geoffrey – *Mid-Victorian Britain 1851–70*, London 1979, Fontana.
Bing, Samuel – *Artistic America, Tiffany Glass and Art Nouveau* (introduction Kock, R.), M. I. T. Press 1970.

BIBLIOGRAPHY

Bird, Antony – *Paxton's Palace*, London 1976, Cassell.

Birdwood, G. L. C. – *Handbook to the British Indian Section, Paris Exhibition 1878*, London 1878.

Bordes, M. J. – *Christian Hester and the Cult of Japan*, Record of the Art Museum, Volume 34, Part 2, 1975, Princeton University Press.

Boyer, C. – *Dreaming the Rational City: The Myth of American City Planning*, M. I. T. Press 1983.

Briggs, Asa – 'A Cavalcade of Tastes', *Architectural Review*, April 1977.

Briggs, Asa – *Victorian People*, London 1955, Penguin.

Brockman, H. A. N. – *The British Architect in Industry 1841–1940*, London, Allen and Unwin.

Butler, J. T. – '1876: A Centennial Exhibition (National Collection of Fine Arts, Washington D. C.)', *Connoisseur*, Volume 193, December 1976.

Calcutta Exhibition – *Indian Art Manufactures 1882*, compiled by J. Brown, Calcutta 1882.

Carden, R. W. – 'The Franco–British Exhibition, Parts 1 and 2', *Archiectural Review*, Volume 24, 1908.

Cawelti, John – *America on Display: The World's Fairs of 1876, 1893 and 1933*, New York.

Chadwick, G. F. – *The Works of Sir Joseph Paxton, 1803–1865*, London 1965, Architectural Press.

Chicago 1893 – *World's Columbian Exhibition Chicago*, Chicago 1893.

Chicago 1893 – 'How Chicago Happened', *Architectural Review*, Volume 162, October 1977.

Chicago 1893 – 'Canadian Showcase, Chicago 1893', (Thomas and Thomas), *Racar*, Volume 5, Part 2, 1978–9.

Chicago 1893 – *Snapshots by an Artist: The World's Fair Through a Camera*, Chicago 1893.

Chicago 1893 – *The Royal Commission for the Chicago Exhibition: Catalogue of the British Section*, London 1893, Clowes and Son.

Chicago 1933 – *The Book of the Fair 1933*, Chicago 1933, Published by A Century of Progress.

Chicago 1933 – *A Century of Progress International Exposition*, Chicago 1933, Cuneo Press.

Cipolla, C. M. (Ed.) – *Fontana Economic History of Europe*, Volumes on *The Emergence of Industrial Societies 1, The Emergence of Industrial Societies 2* and *The Industrial Revolution*, London 1973.

Cobban, Alfred – *A History of Modern France* (3 Volumes), London 1965, Penguin.

Cockburn, Sir J. – 'The Franco–British Exhibition', *Journal of the Royal Society of Arts*, Volume 56, 1907.

Commager, Leuchtenburg and Morison – *A Concise History of the United States of America*, Oxford University Press 1977.

Comte, Jules – *L'Art à l'Exposition Universelle de 1900*, Paris 1900.

Conway, Hazel – 'Industrialization, Leisure and Morality', Paper to the Design Historians Association Conference, published 1981.

Coombes, A. E. S. – 'For God and For England: Contributions to an Image of Africa in the First Decade of the Twentieth Century', *Art History*, Volume 8, December 1985.

Coulson, A. J. – *A Bibliography of Design in Britain*, London 1979, Design Council.

Craig, L. – *The Federal Presence: Architecture, Politics and Symbols in the United States Government Building*, M. I. T. Press 1978.

Dangerfield, George – *The Strange Death of Liberal England*, London 1970 (originally 1935), Paladin.

Davey, Peter – *Arts and Crafts Architecture: The Search for Earthly Paradise*, London 1980, Architectural Press.

Davies, A. C. – 'The First Irish Industrial Exhibition: Cork 1852', *Irish Economic and Social History*, Volume 2, 1975.

Delieux, André – *Exposition Franco–Britannique 1908*, Paris 1908.

Dore, C. – 'Un Ensemblier à l'avant garde des années 20: Francis Jourdain', *Connaissance des Arts*, December 1975.

Droz, Jacques, *Europe Between Revolutions*, London 1967, Fontana.

Dublin 1853 – *Great Industrial Exhibition Dublin 1853*, Dublin 1853.

Dumas, F. G. – *The Franco–British Exhibition Illustrated Review*, London 1908, Bembrose and Sons.

Dupays, Paul – *Vie Prestigieuse des Expositions Historique*, Paris 1939, Henry Didier.

Edwards, Stuart – *The Paris Commune 1871*, London, 1977, Quadrangle.

Egbert, D. D. – *The Beaux Arts Tradition in French Architecture, Illustrated by the Grands Prix de Rome*, Princeton University Press 1980.

Esquiros, Alphonse – 'L'Angleterre et la Vie Anglaise', *Revue des Deux Mondes*, July 1862.

Farr, Denis – *English Art 1870–1940*, Oxford History of English Art, Oxford 1978.

Fastnedge, Ralph – *English Furniture Styles 1500–1830*, London 1955, Penguin.

Festival of Empire – *Guide to the Indian Section*, London 1911, Bembrose and Son.

Forbes-Royal, J – *Papers Referring to the Proposed Contributions from India for the Industrial Exhibition of 1851*, London 1849.

Fourdrignier, Eduard – *Antiquités des Gaules: Exposition Historique du Palais du Trocadéro*, Paris 1878.

Francis, D. R. – *The Universal Exposition of 1904* (2 Volumes), St. Louis 1913.

Gamble, Andrew – *Britain in Decline*, London 1981, Macmillan.

Garner, Philippe – 'The Birth of Art Deco: Paris Exhibition of 1925', *Country Life*, December 1975.

Geddes, Patrick – 'The Closing Exhibition: Paris 1900', *Prologue*, Volume 68, November 1900.

Gee, Malcolm – 'Dealers, Critics and Collectors of Modern Painting. Aspects of the Parisian Art Market Between 1910 and 1930', Courtauld Institute PhD. thesis 1977.

German, G – *Gothic Revival in Europe and Britain. Sources, Influences and Ideas*, London 1972, Lund Humphries and the Architectural Association.

Gibbs-Smith, C. H. – *The Great Exhibition of 1851*, London 1981, H.M.S.O.

Giedion, S. – *Space, Time and Architecture*, Harvard University Press 1963.

Giedion, S. – *Mechanization Takes Command*, Oxford University Press 1948.

Gloag, John – *Victorian Taste*, London 1961, Adam and Black.

Gloag, John – *The English Tradition in Design*, London 1947, King Peregrine.

Gloag, John (Introduction) – *The Crystal Palace Exhibition Illustrated Catalogue London 1851: Art Journal Special Issue*, New York 1970, Dover reprint.

Greenhalgh, Paul – 'Art, Politics and Society at the Franco–British Exhibition of 1908', *Art History*, December 1985.

Grenville, J. A. S. – *Europe Reshaped*, London 1976, Fontana.

Hamdani, Amar – *La Vérité sur l'Expédition d'Alger*, 1985 Éditions Balland.

Hamerton, P. G. – *Modern Frenchmen*, London 1878.

Harvie, Martin and Scharf (Eds.) – *Industrialization and Culture*, London 1981, Macmillan.

Hatton, R. G. – *A Text-book of Elementary Design*, London 1895.

Hauser, Arnold – *A Social History of Art* (2 Volumes), London 1951, Routledge and Kegan Paul.

Heskett, John – *Industrial Design*, London, 1980, Thames and Hudson.

Hicks, J. H. – 'The United States Centennial Exhibition of 1876', PhD. Thesis University of Georgia, 1972.

Hilton, S – *Here Today and Gone Tomorrow: The Story of World's Fairs and Expositions*, Philadelphia 1978, Westminster Press.

Hilton, Timothy – *The PreRaphaelites*, London 1976, Thames and Hudson.

Hitchcock, H. R. – *Architecture 19th. and 20th. Centuries*, London 1977, Pelican.

Hobsbawm, E. J. – *The Age of Capital*, London 1977, Abacus.

Hobsbawm, E. J. – *Industry and Empire*, London 1968, Pelican.

Hobson, J. A. – *The Psychology of Jingoism*, London 1901, Grant Richards.

Holt, E. G. – *The Art of All Nations: The Emerging Role of Exhibitions and Critics 1850–73*, New York 1981, Anchor Press.

Holt, E. J. – *The Triumph of Art for the Public: The Emerging Role of Exhibitions and Critics up to 1850*, New York 1981, Anchor Press.

Horne, D. – *The Great Museum: The Representation of History*, London 1984, Pluto.

Horsfield-Nixon – *The Franco–British Exhibition of Science, Arts and Industries*, Journal of the Royal Institute of British Architects, Volume 15, Part 3, 1908.

Howat, J. K. – *The Shaping of Art and Architecture in 19th Century America*, New York

1973, Metropolitan Museum of Art.

Hulme, F. E. – *The Birth and Development of Ornament*, London 1894.

Imperial International 1909 – 'The Imperial International Exhibition 1909', *Journal for the Royal Society of Arts*.

Imperial International 1909 – 'The Arts at Shepherds Bush', *Journal for the Royal Society of Arts July 1909*.

Ingram, J. S. – *The Centennial Exposition, Described and Illustrated . . .*, Philadelphia 1876, Hubbard Brothers.

Isay, Raymond – *Panorama des Expositions Universelles*, Paris 1937, Gallimard.

Jacobson, T. C. (Ed.) – 'Chicago History – Special Issue on the Columbian Fair 1893', *Chicago History Journal*, Volume 12, No. 3, Fall 1983.

Japan–British Exhibition – *Modern Japanese Fine Arts Illustrated Catalogue* and *Old Japanese Fine Arts Catalogue*, both London 1910.

Japan–British Exhibition – *Department of the Imperial Army of Japan*, London 1910.

Jencks, Charles – *Modern Movements in Architecture*, London 1973, Penguin.

Jenkyns, R. – *The Victorians and Ancient Greece*, Oxford 1980.

Jennings, Humphrey, *Pandæmonium: The Coming of the Machine as Seen by Contemporary Observers*, London 1985, André Deutsch.

Julian, Philippe – *The Triumph of Art Nouveau: Paris Exhibition 1900* London 1974, Phaidon.

Keiger, J. F. V. – *France and the Origins of the First World War*, Macmillan 1983.

Kiralfy, I. – *Venice, Bride of the Sea. Great Historical and Romantic Spectacle*, Olympia 1891–2, London 1891.

Kiralfy, I. – *Nero, or the Destruction of Rome*, London 1889.

Kitson-Clark, G. – *The Making of Victorian England*, London 1977, University Paperbacks.

Kjellberg, P. – 'Le Bon Goût Il y a Cent Ans', *Connaissance des Arts*, Volume 321, November 1978.

Knight and Sabey – *The Lion Roars at Wembley: The British Empire Exhibition at Wembley*, London 1984.

Kusamitsu, Toshio – 'Great Exhibitions before 1851', *History Workshop Journal*, Number 9, Spring 1980.

Lavedan, Pierre – *French Architecture*, Scolar Press 1979.

Lee, Elizabeth – *The Humour of France*, London 1893.

Leslie, F. – *Frank Leslie's Illustrated Historical Register of the Centennial Exposition 1876*, Philadelphia 1876. Reprint available New York 1974, Paddington Press.

Lesnikowski, W. G. – *Rationalism and Romanticism in Architecture*, New York 1982, McGraw-Hill.

London 1851 – 'The Industrial Exhibition of 1851', *Westminster and Foreign Quarterly Review*, April 1850.

London 1851 – *Voices from the Workshop: Poems on the Exhibition of 1851*, London 1851.

London 1851 – *Catalogue to the Turkish Section*, London 1851.

London 1851 – *Indian Archipelago: Articles Collected for the Exhibition*, London 1851.

London 1851 – 'The Proposed Exhibition of 1851', *Blackwood's Magazine*, September 1850.

London 1851 – 'Official Catalogue of the Great Exhibition', *Edinburgh Review*, Volume 94, No. 192, October 1851.

London 1851 – *Love and Loyalty*, London 1851.

London 1851 – *The East Indian Productions . . . forwarded to the Exhibition of the Works of Art and Industry to be Held in London in 1851*, London 1851.

London 1851 – *The Fine Art Courts in the Crystal Palace*, London 1851.

London 1862 – *The Illustrated Catalogue of the Industrial Department*, (2 Volumes), London 1862.

London 1862 – *An Account of the Buildings Designed by Francis Fowke*, London 1862.

London 1862 – 'Educational Advantages of the International Exhibition', *Sixpenny Magazine*, August 1862.

London 1862 – *Penny Guide*, London 1862.

London 1862 – *Compendium Catalogue*, London 1862.

London 1862 – *Handy Book to the International Exhibition*, London 1862.

London 1862 – *Great Britain in Fairyland*, London 1862.

London 1862 – *The World's Palace, Old and New: An Ode*, London 1862.

London 1862 – 'International Exhibition of 1861', *Journal of the Society for the Encouragement of Arts, Manufactures and Commerce*, 1861.

London 1862 – 'Prospects of the International Exhibition in 1862', *Cornhill Magazine*, July 1861.

London 1862 – *The International Exhibition of 1862*, London 1962, Victoria and Albert Museum Publications.

London 1862 – *Threepenny Guide to the Pictures*, London 1862.

London 1871 – *Catalogue of the Industrial Sections*, (3 Volumes), London 1871.

London 1874 – *Illustrated Guide*, London 1874, Johnson and Sons.

Low, D. A. – *Lion Rampant*, London 1973, Cass.

Luckhurst, K – *The Story of Exhibitions*, London 1951, Studio Publications.

Maass, J. – *The Glorious Enterprise: The Centennial Exhibition of 1876 and H. J. Schwarzmann, Architect-in-Chief*, New York 1977.

MacKenzie, John M. – *Propaganda and Empire: The Manipulation of British Public Opinion 1880–1960*, Manchester University Press 1985.

Magraw, Roger – *France 1815–1914: The Bourgeois Century*, London 1983, Fontana.

Mandell, R. D. – *Paris 1900: The Great World's Fair*, University of Toronto 1967.

Maré, Eric de – *London 1851, The Year of the Great Exhibition*, London 1972, The Folio Society.

Mathias, Peter – *The First Industrial Nation: An Economic History of Britain 1700–1914*, London 1976, Methuen.

Mathieu, C. – 'Le Palais de l'Industrie: A Propos de Deux Dessins de Max Berthelin', *Revue du Louvre*, Volume 31, Part 5–6, 1982.

McCabe, J. D. – *The Illustrated History of the Centennial Exhibition Held in Commemoration of the One Hundredth Anniversary of American Independence*, Philadelphia 1876, Reprint Philadelphia 1975.

Michel, Leon – *L'Exposition Internationale de Liège 1930*, Brussels 1929.

Middleton, Robert – *The Beaux Arts and French Architecture*, London 1982, Thames and Hudson.

Miller, M. B. – *The Bon Marché: Bourgeois Culture and the Department Store 1869–1920*, Princeton University Press 1981.

Miner, H. C. – 'The United States Government Building at the Centennial Exhibition 1874–77', *Prologue*, Volume 4, Part 4, 1972.

Monroe-Winslow, C. (Ed.) – *The Panama-California International Exposition (San Diego)*, San Francisco 1916, Paul Elder.

Mosser, M. – 'Garnier et l'Opera: Une Symphonie Architecturale', *Plaisir de France*, Volume 41, Part 426, 1975.

Mumford, Lewis – *The Roots of Contemporary American Architecture*, New York 1972, Dover.

Naylor, Gillian – 'Modernism, Threadbare or Heroic?', *Architectural Review*, August 1977.

Neuberg, Hans – *Conceptions of International Exhibitions*, ABC, Zurich 1976.

Neuhaus, E. – *The Art of the Exposition: Panama Pacific 1915*, San Francisco 1915.

New York 1939 – *Magna Carta Hall: British Pavilion New York World's Fair 1939* (J. C. Fitzpatrick), New York 1939.

New York 1939 – *American Express Guide*, New York 1939.

New York 1939 – *Masterpieces from the New York and San Francisco World's Fairs*, Cleveland 1940.

New York 1939 – *Guide Book of the New York World's Fair*, New York 1939.

Norfolk, Duke of – 'The Japan–British Exhibition', *The Plumber and Decorator Journal*, May 1910.

Paris 1855 – *Reports on the Paris Universal Exhibition* (3 Volumes), London 1856.

Paris 1867 – *Guide de l'Exposant et du Visiteur*, Paris 1867, Hachette.

Paris 1867 – *Exposition Universelle de Paris* (Soliman Al-Haraïri), Paris 1867.

Paris 1867 – *Report on the Paris Exhibition* (3 Volumes), London 1868.

Paris 1867 – *Le Moniteur de l'Exposition*, Paris 1865.

Paris 1867 – *Tunis: Traduction Litterale du Travail*, Paris 1867.

Paris 1867 – 'An Early Peep at the Show', *Blackwood's Magazine*.

Paris 1867 – *Exposition Universelle de 1867: Illustrée Publication Internationale*, Paris 1867.

Paris 1867 – 'Nicholas at the Exhibition', *Broadway Magazine* (London).

Paris 1867 – *Brief Catalogue of the Fine Art Section*, London 1867.

Paris 1867 – *Art Journal Illustrated Guide, Paris Exhibition 1867*, London 1867.

Paris 1878 – *Exposition Historique: Palais du Trocadéro*, Paris 1878.

Paris 1878 – *Exposition 1878: Palais du Trocadéro*, Paris 1878.

Paris 1878 – *Le Palais du Trocadéro: Le Coteau de Chaillot, Le Nouveau Palais*, Paris 1878, Morel.

Paris 1878 – *L'Exposition de Paris: Journal Hebdomadaire*, Paris 1878.

Paris 1878 – *Chefs d'Oeuvre de l'Exposition 1878*, Paris 1878.

Paris 1878 – *L'Album de l'Exposition de 1878*, Paris 1878.

Paris 1878 – 'Art at the Exhibition', *Scribbener's Monthly*, August 1878.

Paris 1878 – *Vues Interieures et Exterieures*, Paris 1878.

Paris 1889 – *Le Moniteur de l'Exposition*, Paris 1889.

Paris 1889 – *Exposition Universelle de 1889, Frise Interieure du Dome*, Paris 1889.

Paris 1889 – *American Reports of the Universal Exposition Paris 1889* (5 Volumes), Washington 1890.

Paris 1889 – 'Paris and its Exhibition', *Pall Mall Gazette Extra*, No. 49, Friday July 26th 1889.

Paris 1900 – *Album Photographique de Exposition 1900*, Paris 1900, A. Taride.

Paris 1900 – *L'Art à l'Exposition Universelle de 1900*, volume produced by the Revue de l'Art Ancient et Moderne, Paris 1900.

Paris 1900 – 'L'Exposition du Siècle', *Le Monde Moderne*, Paris 1900.

Paris 1900 – *Petit Journal Supplément*, Paris 1900.

Paris 1900 – *Dangle's Guide to Paris and the Exhibition*, London 1900.

Paris 1900 – *La Décoration et l'Ameublement à l'Exposition de 1900* Paris 1900.

Paris 1900 – *Royal Commission Paris International Exhibition: The Royal Pavilion*, London 1900, Hudson and Kearns.

Paris 1925 – *Lectures pour Tous*, (special edition of a popular journal of that name), Pari,s May 1925.

Paris 1925 – *Encyclopédie des Arts Decoratifs et Industriels Modernes au XXeme Siècle* (12 Volumes), Paris 1925. Exact facsimile reprints available, New York 1977, Garland. See also Reff, Theodore.

Paris 1925 – *Reports on the Present Position and Tendencies of the Industrial Arts, as Indicated at the International Exhibition of Modern Decorative and Industrial Arts, Paris 1925*, London 1925, Department of Overseas Trade.

Paris 1931 – *The International Colonial Exhibition Guide*, Paris 1931 (in English).

Paris 1931 – *Promenade à Travers L'Exposition Coloniale Internationale*, Paris 1931, Paris 1931.

Paris 1937 – *Exposition Internationale Arts et Techniques Paris: Guide*, Paris 1937.

Paris 1937 – 'Paris: Wagons Lits/Cook', (tourist literature), Paris 1937.

Paris 1937 – *Portugal: Exposition Internationale Paris 1937*, Paris 1937.

Paris 1937 – *Architectural Review Special Issue*, London 1937.

Paris 1937 – *Paris 1937–1957*, Exhibition Catalogue, Centre Georges Pompidou, Paris 1981.

Pevsner, Nicholas – *Ruskin and Viollet-le-Duc: Englishness and Frenchness in the Appreciation of Gothic Architecture*, London 1969, Thames and Hudson.

Pevsner, Nicholas – *The Englishness of English Art*, London 1964, Peregrine.

Pevsner, Nicholas – *A History of Building Types*, London, Thames and Hudson.

Pevsner and Richards, *The Anti-Rationalists*, London 1973, Architectural Press.

Pinkney, D. H. – *Napoleon III and the Rebuilding of Paris*, Princeton University Press 1958.

Porter, B – *The Lion's Share: A Short History of British Imperialism 1850–1970*, London 1975, Longman.

Post, R. – *1876: A Centennial Exhibition*, Washington 1976, Smithsonian Institution.

Reff, Theodore (Ed.) – *Complete reprints of all Fine Art Catalogues for the Paris Expositions Universelles of 1855, 1867, 1878, 1889 and 1900, including the Centennale and Decennale sections*. Garland Publications, New York 1981.

Reid-Badger – *The Great American Fair: The World's Columbian Exposition and*

American Culture, Chicago 1979, Nelson Hall.

Rendall, J. – *The Origins of Modern Feminism: Women in Britain, France and the United States of America 1870–1860*, Macmillan 1985.

Rewald, J. – *The History of Impressionism*, New York 1980, Secker and Warburg.

Rewald, J. – *Post-Impressionism: From Van Gogh to Gauguin*, New York 1978, Secker and Warburg.

Richards, J. M. – 'Black and White: An Introductory Study of a National Design Idiom', *Architectural Review*, 1937.

Richards, J. M. – 'The Problem of a National Projection: What is the Function of a National Pavilion? Where Does Britain Stand?', *Architectural Review*, 1937.

Robichon, F. – 'France, du Symbole au Bazaar', *Magazine des Beaux Arts*, June 1983.

Robin, Charles – *Histoire Illustrée de l'Exposition Universelle, par Categories d'industries, avec Notes sur les Exposants*, Paris 1855.

Roth, L. M. – *A Concise History of American Architecture*, New York 1980.

Rousselet, Louis – *L'Exposition Universelle de 1900*, Paris 1900, Hachette.

Rudorff, R. – *Belle Epoque: Paris in the 1890's*, London 1972, Hamish Hamilton.

Russell, F. (Ed.) – *Art Nouveau Architecture*, London 1979, Academy Editions.

Rydell, R. W. – *All the World's a Fair: America's International Expositions*, PhD. thesis, University of California, Los Angeles 1980.

Sala, G. A. – *Notes and Sketches on the Paris Exhibition*, London 1868.

San Francisco 1939 – *The Art of Treasure Island*, San Francisco 1939.

San Francisco 1939 – *Master Works of Five Centuries*, San Francisco 1939.

San Francisco 1939 – *Souvenir View Book of San Francisco*, San Francisco 1939, Wobbers Inc.

San Francisco 1939 – *Golden Gate Exposition Guide-book*, San Francisco 1939.

Scharf, A. – 'The Crystal Palace and the Great Exhibition', from *Art and Industry*, Open University Press 1971.

Schneider, W. H. – *An Empire for the Masses: The French Popular Image of Africa 1870–1900*, London 1985, Greenwood Press.

Service, A. (Ed.) – *Edwardian Architecture: A Handbook to Building in Britain 1890–1914*, London 1977, Thames and Hudson.

Sheon, A. – 'Lucien Rollin: Architect Decorateur of the 1930's', *Arts Magazine*, 1982.

Silverman, D. L. – 'The 1889 Exhibition: The Crisis of Bourgeois Individualism', *Oppositions*, 1986.

Spielmann, M. H. – *Souvenir of the Fine Art Section Franco–British Exhibition 1908*, London 1908, Bembrose and Son.

St. Louis 1904 – *Louisiana Purchase Exposition Commission 1906, Committee on Industrial Expositions* (2 Volumes), Washington 1906.

Summerson, Sir John – *The London Building World of the 1860's*, London 1973, Thames and Hudson.

Taylor, P. M. – *The Projection of Britain: British Overseas Publicity and Propaganda 1919–1939*, Cambridge University Press.

Texas 1936 – *Souvenir Guide Texas Centennial 1936*, Texas 1936.

Thomson, R. – 'Camille Pissarro, Turpitudes Sociale and the Exposition Universelle of 1889', *Arts Magazine*, Volume 56, Part 8, April 1982.

Torre, S. – *Women in American Architecture: A Historic and Contemporary Perpective*, New York 1977, Whitney Library of Design.

Trapp, F. – 'The London International Exhibition of Art and Industry 1874', *Connoisseur*, Volume 187, December 1974.

Walter, Rudolphe – 'L'Exposition de 1878: ou Amours et Haines de Emile Zola', *L'Oeil*, Nov–Dec 1978.

Warnod, Jeanne – 'La Ruche et Montparnasse', *L'Oeil*, Jan–Feb 1979.

Watkin, D. – *Architecture and Morality*, Oxford 1977, Clarendon Press.

Weber, E. – *Peasants into Frenchmen: The Modernization of Rural France, 1870–1914*, London 1976, Chatto and Windus.

Weisberg, G. P. – 'Aspects of Japonisme', *Bulletin of the Cleveland Museum of Art*, Volume 62, Part 4, April 1975.

Wilhelm – 'Life in Paris Under the Second Empire and Third Republic', *Apollo*, Volume 106, Part 190, December 1977.

Williams, Raymond – *The Long Revolution*, London 1961, Penguin.

BIBLIOGRAPHY

Williams, Rosalind – *Dream Worlds: Mass Consumption in Late 19th Century France*, University of California Press.

Wines, J. – *Quelle Exposition Universelle?*, Connaissance des Arts, July/August 1983.

Wolff, Janet – The Social Production of Art, Macmillan Press 1981.

Woodham, J – 'Design and Empire: British Design in the 1920's', *Art History*, Volume 3, No. 2, June 1980.

Zeldin, Theodore – *France 1848–1945* (5 Volumes: *Taste and Corruption; Politics and Anger; Ambition and Love; Anxiety and Hypocrisy; Intellect and Pride*), Oxford Paperbacks 1979–81.

INDEX